THE SCARLETT LETTERS

The Scarlett

MY SECRET YEAR OF MEN IN AN L.A. DUNGEON

Letters

JENNY NORDBAK

ST. MARTIN'S PRESS ⚏ NEW YORK

THE SCARLETT LETTERS. Copyright 2017 by Jenny Nordbak.
All rights reserved. Printed in the United States of America. For information,
address St. Martin's Press, 175 Fifth Avenue, New York, N.Y. 10010.

www.stmartins.com

Designed by Anna Gorovoy

The Library of Congress Cataloging-in-Publication Data is
available upon request.

ISBN 978-1-250-09113-0 (hardcover)
ISBN 978-1-250-09115-4 (ebook)

Our books may be purchased in bulk for promotional, educational, or
business use. Please contact your local bookseller or the Macmillan Corporate
and Premium Sales Department at 1-800-221-7945, extension 5442, or
by e-mail at MacmillanSpecialMarkets@macmillan.com.

First Edition: April 2017

10 9 8 7 6 5 4 3 2 1

For my match

AUTHOR'S NOTE

This is a true story, though some names and details have been changed.

THE SCARLETT LETTERS

1. MARK

I was having a typical Monday. My foot worship client had been late, which meant I was now running a few minutes behind for an appointment with a new client. Sometimes new clients gave the desk Mistress an idea of what kind of session they're looking for, but with this one I was walking in blind. He could want me to be anything from an Amazonian warrior to a schoolteacher. I should probably have been more stressed rushing to the dressing room to touch up before meeting him, but it's just so hard to work up an appropriate level of stress after getting paid to have a foot massage while being treated like a goddess for an hour. Every woman should have a foot slave.

When I got to the dressing room, I checked my makeup and dug through a pile of costumes in my work bag to find my vibrating phone. My roommate, Amelia, was calling, but I didn't have time to answer her before this session. Without any clues about his particular fetish, I played it safe and changed into my go-to power suit—sky-high platform heels, a black leather dress, and a corset that cinched my waist into an impossibly tiny twenty-one inches. This was the outfit that made me feel most in my element. In it, I became a bitch with whom you do not fuck, ready for war.

I tucked my cell phone into the bottom of my corset, took a

moment to mentally switch back from Jenny to Mistress Scarlett, and strode confidently down the hallway into the waiting room.

"You must be Mark," I said to the uncomfortable-looking man sitting in a chair in the corner.

Mark was a young, good-looking guy. He had the lean build of a cyclist, beautiful gray eyes, and delicate hands, which were nervously fiddling with a magazine.

I sensed that instead of pulling the imperious ice queen routine with this one, I needed to reassure him. Smiling warmly, I looked him in the eye and extended my hand.

"I'm Scarlett. I'm so pleased to meet you."

We sat down across from each other in the interview room adjacent to the lobby. It was in this room that scenes were negotiated and long-buried fantasies were finally laid on the table. It was a complex social situation. I had to be confessor, therapist, and temptress while in the space of a few minutes negotiating a business transaction, anticipating what boundaries needed to be established ahead of time, and reading the subtext of a client's fetishes. A client may say that he wants a scene in which a nun punishes him, but does he want an angry nun, a playful nun, a naughty nun, a scary nun, or an aloof nun? Is she attracted to him, repulsed by him, or indifferent (as nuns of course should be)? Is she humiliating, teasing, or pleasing him? Should there be verbal interaction? Is there a plot or background to the scene or is it just the sensory experience that is alluring? This is before even establishing what implements he wants to be punished with. How hard? Stingy or thuddy pain? Does he have any relevant medical conditions that should limit us? Guessing incorrectly at any one of these and a number of other answers could result in a completely wrong scene and an unhappy client.

I once ended up with a sobbing puppy-play client because I failed to ascertain that he was supposed to always be a well-behaved dog and I, a happy dog trainer. He had envisioned a scene in which he pranced around and made me a proud owner after winning the dog show championships. It was extremely important to him that he please me and be seen as a good dog. I misunderstood in the interview and flagged the word *trainer* as an indicator that he was still being trained, and thus would need to be corrected for the occasional imagined error. The instant "Bad dog!" left my lips, I knew I had made some kind of horrible mistake. He reacted the same way a frightened puppy would—he peed his pants and dissolved into a shivering, whimpering heap. It's all about nuances.

But of course, it would be terribly unattractive and intimidating to simply rattle off this list of questions that in many cases the client has never answered openly before, so all of the information must be gathered under the guise of an intriguing and arousing conversation.

Mark was incredibly nervous during his interview. I had to carefully coax information out of him while reassuring him.

He immediately admitted, "Sorry, I've never done this before. I'm not really sure what to do."

"No need to apologize. That's what I'm here for. Why don't you start by giving me an idea of what you're into and then I'm sure we can come up with a session that will work for both of us?"

His was one of the less bizarre, easier to understand fetishes, yet he was deeply insecure about it. He described to me that as a child he was beaten up by a girl on the playground who squeezed his head between her thighs, and then ignored his muffled pleas for help and humiliated tears. I smiled, remembering doing similar things, though not quite as extreme, to boys on the playground. I wondered how many fetishes I had unwittingly sparked along the way. Is Rick Taylor out there somewhere begging his every sex partner to sit on his chest so he can't move his arms while pouring sand on his head?

Mark was evidently held between that girl's thighs for so long that he genuinely thought he was going to die. His fetish bolsters a theory of mine that, quite often, these strange sexual fixations are triggered at a young age by an intense emotional experience. Before sex enters our minds, those experiences are the most pronounced and thrilling that we have encountered. Suddenly, we hit puberty and experience a new kind of emotional intensity. It seems that some people who have felt something as powerful as what Mark did fuse the two together so that they view the first intense experience as a sexual experience. The specificity of most of these fetishes speaks to how deeply embedded the memories become. For almost all of them, there are particular phrases, actions, or visual elements that are required to fulfill the fantasy. For some people, this is the only way they can achieve sexual release.

There were two scenarios that Mark wanted to experiment with, splitting our hour session in half. Both had the same result with a slightly different beginning. He wanted to end with his usual playground role-play that had aroused him since childhood. Before we did that, though, he wanted to try a more adult scenario to see whether it could still play out the same way. I guess it was kind of like me trying to masturbate with my left hand. It should work in theory, but it's just a little off, which might be enough to prevent it from happening.

Instead of starting with us both role-playing as children, he wanted us to pretend to be adult neighbors. In this fantasy, I had been obnoxiously playing my music too loud, night after night. Even though deep down he was a pansy, on this night he had decided to sac up and say something. He was going to march over to my house like a man and make me turn it down. And I was going to summarily destroy his manhood. I was to verbally abuse him, throw him around, trap him between my thighs, and pretend to call one of my girlfriends to chat. I would nonchalantly chatter away on the phone, ignoring his terror and suffering, while acting as though I had all the time in the world to talk. Sounded like a good time to me!

Having established the narrative of the scene along with boundaries, rules, and expectations, we were ready to head upstairs to a room and get things started.

I left Mark with Lady Caterina at the front desk to take care of payment while I ran back to the dressing room to quickly change from six-inch stilettos into more practical four-inch thigh-high boots. In my ass-whoopin' boots, I was much less likely to cut the session short as a result of spraining an ankle while trying to overpower my victim. Knowing I would have my thighs wrapped around his head, I pulled on an extra pair of boy short underwear to offer an additional layer of coverage.

Once we got into the room, I didn't give Mark any more time to get nervous or overthink things. I called down to Caterina on the intercom to let her know we were starting the session, and we assumed our respective positions in the room.

Mark walked over to my "house" and knocked on the wall forcefully. I immediately answered the door.

"What the fuck do you want?"

He was taken aback by my abruptness.

"Well, I'm not sure that kind of language is necessary. I was coming over here to let you know that your music is just a tad loud. I'm sure you didn't know or you wouldn't be doing it, so I just thought I would tell you and see if maybe you could, uh, turn it down just a smidge?"

"No. I like it this loud. If that's it, I'm gonna go back in now."

"Look, I'm trying to be polite here, but if you don't turn it down I'll just have to . . . have to . . . umm, call the cops!"

"Just try calling the cops, you pathetic little rodent. Tell them how much of a pussy you are and see if they want to do anything about it. Maybe if you weren't such a fucking sissy, people would respect you more. I bet you're such a wimp that I could beat you up."

I slapped him in the side of the head and shoved him backward by both shoulders.

"Now hang on here just a second! I just don't think that violence is really necessary."

"Of course you don't, you worthless little shit."

My hand shot out and snatched his balls in a punishing grip. I could actually see all coherent thought flee his mind in that instant. I spun him around in a circle, leading him by the balls, and slammed him into the wall again.

Fantasy wrestling could be hard because it had to be forceful enough to be believable, but in most cases the clients didn't want to leave with stitches. I found that I was a small enough girl compared to most men that using almost full force worked just fine. I went for it, and if it was too much, they were pretty quick to let me know.

I took the opportunity that presented itself when he was off-balance and knocked him to the ground. I threw a few stray kicks at his chest and stomach for good measure, rolled him from his side to his back, and sat down heavily on his chest.

"What are you gonna do now, pussy boy? Call the cops? Tell them you got your ass kicked by a girl?"

"No, no! I won't call anyone! Just let me go home!"

"But I'm not finished with you yet," I pouted.

I slid up and to the side, and pushed one thigh under his head and wrapped the other up and over his throat, bringing my knees together to meet. We had agreed in the interview that if the pressure got to be too much, he would tap me twice and I would loosen my grip a bit. I decided it was best to get an idea of what level of player he was, so I pressed my left foot under my right calf and used the leverage to squeeze down on his throat and face. He thrashed and made desperate noises. I squeezed harder until he tapped me twice. Now I knew my range pretty accurately.

I shifted around without releasing any tension between my thighs to get comfortable. I was going to be here for a while. I picked up my cell phone, pretended to dial a number, and waited while the phone "rang." I pretended my roommate, Amelia, had answered and animatedly asked how her day was going and what her plans for the week were. Since I had missed her call earlier, it was easy to imagine what I would say when I called her back. After several minutes of chatting away, Mark tried to pry my legs apart, writhing and moaning between them. He was whimpering barely audible pleas for help and mercy.

"Please . . . I can't breathe!" he hissed with difficulty.

"Shhh!" I slapped him in the face and turned away pointedly, going back to my conversation and ignoring him.

"No, no . . . I'm not doing anything important at all," I said. "I've got all the time in the world to talk. Tell me all about it!"

Mark started to cry, wetting my thighs with his effeminate tears. Between the intensity of the moment and the tears rolling across my thighs, I was incredibly aroused. The power was a rush, but not just the physical power of having him at my mercy. It was that he was surrendering himself to me, allowing me to push him and take him to this crazy place. Trust is such a turn-on. So are tears.

"Please!" he sobbed desperately.

I laughed loudly at something fake Amelia had said.

"No way! Tell me more! I want all the details . . . really, take your time!"

I released some pressure to reposition my thighs, giving Mark a brief moment of respite to catch his breath and let the blood flow freely. When I leveraged my right foot under my left this time and squeezed, I could feel that now I had just the right angle. If I wanted to, I could knock him unconscious in a matter of seconds. His eyes would roll back and his body would go limp, but that wasn't my intention today. The first time I knocked a play partner out, I panicked thinking I had killed him. By the time I played with Mark, though, I could read the nuanced signs of breath play and knew precisely how to control the situation.

I continued to giggle and prattle on about nothing for a while. Mark eventually double-tapped me twice, indicating that we could stop and switch scenarios.

I let him sit up and catch his breath. I handed him a bottle of water, and he smiled.

"This is perfect," he said. "Just like that again. You're awesome."

We didn't want to break the moment too much, so we sat quietly for a few minutes to let him reset physically without detaching too much mentally.

In a stroke of genius, I text messaged the real Amelia to let her know that I was in a session, but I was going to call her. I told her we just needed to chat for a while. I could easily have called one of the girls in the dressing room and had just as much fun with it, but something about calling a vanilla friend who would be slightly confused by the whole thing seemed much more amusing.

Mark stood up, indicating that he was ready to go for round two. We repeated almost the exact same scenario, but this time I acted more childishly, calling him names and poking him once I had him on the ground. Instead of calling the cops, he was going to tell the teacher.

"What are you going to tell her, Mark? Are you going to tell her that you're a big baby? She's going to tell everyone that you got beat up by a girl!"

We had a good amount of time left, and I didn't want to leave him in the head scissors for too long, so I improvised and tried a more classic face-sitting move first. I squatted over his face, pressed my thighs together, and sat down, effectively cutting off his air supply and smashing his face with my cloth-covered lady bits. For most guys who are into smothering, this is a major part of the appeal. It isn't so much that they are being smothered as it is the fact that they are being smothered by the ass, pussy, and thighs of a woman they are attracted to. A pillow generally doesn't have the same effect.

He squirmed under me, but a boner check implied that he was rather enjoying this new addition to his fantasy. I lifted up occasionally to let him catch snatches of air, but took the opportunity to call Amelia.

"Hello?"

"Hey, girl, how's it goin'? We haven't talked in ages, so I thought we could catch up. I want to hear all about the new boy in your class and your new soccer team!"

"This is so weird. You're totally crazy."

"I just knew he would be cute! Why do you always get the cute ones in your class, and I get the lame ones?" I punctuated the last few words by bouncing on Mark's face.

"Are you really in a session with some dude right now?"

"Yep."

I lifted off his face, sat on the ground, and wrapped my thighs back around his neck. I let him pant for a minute or so before squeezing again. I pressed hard without warning, forcing him to expel a groan with his air supply.

"Oh, my God, was that him? Did you punch him in the balls or something?"

"No, I'm not in a hurry at all. We have another hour of recess today and then I get to go home, so I can talk for as long as you want. I'm not doing anything important."

Something about my total lack of concern while Mark thought he was going to die pushed him to the next level in his head. The tears flowed freely again, but he was palming his erection under his pants. I desperately wanted to make him use his tears as lube, but that wasn't for this scene.

"Please! I'm going to die. Please let me go!" he managed to hiss in a barely audible whisper.

When I kept chatting away to Amelia without missing a beat, he sobbed in earnest, but his stroking motions were getting frantic under his sweatpants. I squeezed just a bit harder, to match his heightened intensity, but had to be careful not to knock him out without meaning to in the heat of the moment. As I heard him alternately pant and hold his breath, I knew he was getting close. He groaned and came, shuddering in waves beneath me.

"All right, love, I gotta go. I'll see you at home in a bit."

"You are so fucking crazy. I'll see you soon."

I got Mark a towel and his water and handed him both as he sat up.

"That was seriously perfect. I loved the part when you sat on my face. I've never tried that before."

"Great. I'm really glad!"

"Man, you must think I'm a total weirdo for being into this shit. If we ever run into each other in public, you have to promise not to say anything."

"Of course! And don't be silly. Your fantasy makes perfect sense, and is actually really hot. It's not like you get off on someone pretending to run you over with a bike or from licking dirty brooms."

"You seriously have clients like that?"

"Oh, yeah. And you know what? They're fun to play with too. This is a safe place for whatever your fantasy is. There is no reason to feel ashamed of anything when you're here. As long as it's safe, sane, and consensual, there's probably someone here who's down."

"God, I just wish more people were that open-minded. I feel like such a freak most of the time. I can never tell my girlfriends."

"Maybe try meeting more people in the scene. Come out to some social events and you'll realize there are more of us kinksters out there than you would think. Or try introducing the idea to a vanilla girl. Sometimes they surprise you. . . . I was vanilla once too."

I never saw Mark out in the scene in L.A., but I hope he found someone who won't judge him for his fetish. I had a great time explaining the whole thing to Amelia when I got home. She is now in New York in her final year of medical school. And she's a pro Domme on the side.

2. HENRY

Let's rewind a year, shall we? Back to a period before words like *sub*, *flogger*, or certainly *head-scissors* would have meant anything to me—a time when the concept of a Dominatrix was nothing more than an archetype and maybe a Halloween costume. Oh, yes, such a time existed when I was uninitiated into the world of BDSM. I thought doggy style and blow jobs were pretty kinky. My mind was about to be blown open.

I was, by all accounts, a happy and successful recent college graduate. I had a decent job that was more than paying my bills while I sorted out whether a PhD was the right path for me. My friends were fantastic. In particular, my roommate, Amelia, was always there whether I needed a partner in crime or someone to watch a movie with on a Friday night. My family wasn't perfect, but really, whose is? But my sex life? Not so great.

On a typical Monday just a year before Mark, I awoke with a start, knowing immediately that I wasn't going to like what my watch showed me, judging by how much sunlight was streaking in the window. It was 9:32, which meant I had slept in dramatically.

Fuck it.

I rolled over and curled around my boyfriend, Wes, waking him. Wes was a law student, but most of the time he was more interested in extreme sports than law. He was medium height with long blond hair. He was handsome and charming and had a playful sense of humor that always managed to get me riled up.

I glared as I caught him looking at his watch.

"I know," I mumbled grumpily.

"I didn't say anything!"

"You didn't have to. I know I'm late, but my boss isn't on-site today, so I just need to get there soon and it won't matter."

"Well, I've got a few minutes before I need to get going, and someone is awake and ready to go," he whispered, guiding my hand down to his morning wood.

All I wanted to do was go back to sleep, but I giggled obligingly and began a stroking motion. When he decided he was ready, he spat on his hand, using it to lubricate things, rolled over, and thrust inside me. I was annoyed at the shortcut, but didn't outwardly protest.

If he had a floppy dick, I would hardly expect him to find a way to shove it in regardless of the obvious indicator that things weren't ready yet. Why is the reverse acceptable?

I could hear Amelia in the kitchen making breakfast and began to absently wonder whether there would be enough bread left for me to make toast.

Wes groaned, reminding me of my present duties.

We flipped positions, and it started to feel kinda good. I was driving a rhythm now that was slowly awakening my desires.

Maybe this was a good way to start the morning after all.

Six seconds later, he came.

Really?

I wonder whether I can get myself off while he's in the shower without him knowing.

Up to that point in my life, almost all of the sex I had made me want to burn a romance novelist's house down in frustration. I didn't have the confidence to get what I wanted.

Even more problematic? I wasn't willing to admit what I wanted. It's hard to blame your partner for not asking when you wouldn't have given him a straight answer anyway.

My basic understanding of intercourse was: It begins when the man is aroused and ends when he achieves climax. To ask for something else in the middle would be to risk both ridicule and rejection.

Wes grinned beneath me, and I hid my frustration with what I hoped would pass for a contented sigh. He kissed me and then headed for the bathroom to shower.

"Mmm, thanks, babe. That felt amazing," he said as he started the water.

Fuck it.

I rolled over and snuggled back into the covers, smiling to myself. In spite of its mediocre beginning, today was special. Today, I had a secret, and something about it was much more powerful than the orgasm I had just compromised on. Today was the day. I was interviewing for a job at the Dungeon. Deep down, I thought it was probably wrong to be hiding it, but it felt like something precious and embryonic, not yet ready to survive outside the careful nest of secrecy I was protecting it with. To speak about it would make it too real, and I knew I would be too intimidated to go. I had courage, but only because no one knew. There was nothing at stake until I told someone.

Before Wes, I had been deliberately single for a while. I needed a break after Henry.

Henry was short, with curly blond hair. He wasn't exactly handsome but had a charisma that drew people, so when he chose me it felt like the clouds had parted and the sun was shining for me alone. Such a giddy feeling can cause us to ignore the insidious voice that reminds us that our happiness should never be based upon the fickle favor of a man.

He was a fiercely intelligent creative writing student with a flair for the dramatic. He was also jealous to the point of it being absurd. And we were both stubborn and arrogant. As a result, our fights were spectacular. Long, passionate, and carefully articulated and reasoned disagreements were commonplace, but I always seemed to lose and be the one apologizing in the end.

My friends could only watch in dismay as I succumbed to the all-too-familiar "I made him do it" reasoning.

One particular fight over a game of beer pong sent things into a downward spiral.

Henry and I faced each other down across the battlefield, both equally determined to emerge victorious. As my team had slowly gained the lead, the vibe had turned from a friendly game of beer pong to something more serious. Admittedly, my partner Colin was the reason we were winning. Of the eight cups we had cleared from the table, I had accidentally bounced one in without meaning to when I dropped the ball. The other seven fallen soldiers belonged to Colin. Eye-hand coordination had never been a strength of mine, something I would be forced to address once I had a whip in my hand. It's amazing how quickly those skills improve when there's something at stake besides sobriety.

Henry's team had only made two of their ten cups, so they had a long way to go. It was my turn to shoot.

"C'mon, Jen, you got this. Make one and I'll make the other," said Colin from behind me. His patience was encouraging as I had thus far been a useless partner.

From across the table, Henry rolled his eyes.

"Jen? Is that his little name for you? He only wants to play with you so he can stare at your ass. You fucking suck at beer pong, baby. Maybe you should just suck Colin's dick while he plays. At least you're good at that."

Shit talk in a college drinking game was normal, expected even. But this was stunningly inappropriate and seemingly out of left field. I knew it was his wounded ego lashing out. I had seen it before.

Colin had been a close friend of mine for years and I didn't want to make him any more uncomfortable, so I ignored Henry and threw the ball.

It landed in the left cup with a satisfying splash, and I threw my arms in the air, victorious.

Colin swept me into a bear hug as cheers went up from the watching crowd.

"That's my girl!" Colin shouted.

"No, bro, that's my girl. Get your fucking hands off her."

I could sense all six feet three inches of Colin bristling in my defense, but I gave him a look that begged him to let it go. For months he had been pushing me to break up with Henry, but I wasn't there yet.

"Whatever, man," he said and stepped back to let me shoot again.

As usual, my previous shot had just been a lucky fluke, and this one made up for it. The tiny ball soared over the table and nailed Henry in the shoulder. It wasn't deliberate, but he took it personally.

"Nice shot, baby!" he said sarcastically. "But you know the rules . . . miss the table and you have to play with your pants around your ankles until someone makes a cup."

Colin came to my defense.

"Dude, we haven't played with those rules all night. We'll just pull one of your cups and call it good."

"House rules, Colin, and it's my house. Drop your pants, baby."

He laughed hysterically and high-fived his partner, like a frat-boy douche bag.

Colin pulled one of their cups and slammed it.

"We're good now. Your throw."

I was blushing furiously and considered running inside, but my pride planted my feet firmly to the ground.

Henry was drunk and wasn't going to let it go.

"What, now all of a sudden she's a prude? You've been acting like a slut all night—laughing and hugging this guy, but now you're gonna pussy out? He's been imagining what's under those sweats this whole time. Why don't you just show him?"

It was a game for Henry. He would push and push me knowing that I wouldn't do anything about it until we were in private later. He was getting humiliated at the game, so he needed to turn it around on me. I knew he didn't actually want me to drop trou. He was way too possessive for that. He was just being an asshole. This time I snapped.

Without saying a word, I dropped my sweats to the ground where they pooled around my ankles.

At the sight of my green thong, the crowd erupted with astonished yells and clapping.

I pushed my chin up, looked Henry in the eye, and said sweetly, "Your turn."

Colin started to say something, but I turned and silenced him with a glare and a shake of my head.

Henry's pride was evidently an obstacle as well because he was no longer talking and he obediently threw the ball. It struck the rim of one of the cups and Colin snatched it before it could bounce away.

Quietly, so only I could hear, Colin said, "Okay, that's enough, Jen. You can pull your pants back up. You've proven your point."

I was not as quiet with my response. "Just make the cup and then you get to be my hero."

This sent Henry into a rage. He violently smacked the last remaining cup in front of him, knocking it flying from the table and covering the people around him with beer. Now I was worried that I had pushed things too far. The last thing I wanted was for an actual fight to break out, though in hindsight, an ass whoopin' was exactly what Henry needed.

As he took angry steps toward our side of the table, Colin protectively swept me behind him with his arm.

"Move, asshole," yelled Henry. "And pull your fucking pants up now. You really are a slut. I can't believe you would embarrass me like that."

"You embarrassed yourself, Henry. And you made it perfectly clear that I couldn't pull them back up until someone made a cup . . . but now you've ruined the game, so I guess I'm not allowed to."

Stubbornness prevailed over logic.

Henry tried to move around Colin, but he blocked him.

"This doesn't concern you, Colin. I want to talk to my girlfriend!"

"She shouldn't even be your girlfriend. I don't know why she puts up with this shit."

He was right, but he had taken things too far.

"Colin, shut up. That's not helpful."

Henry lunged forward, but Colin pushed him back by the shoulders. I jerked away instinctively and tripped over my pants, landing on my bare ass in a mortified heap. I wanted to cry at how ridiculous the situation had become. I could feel the tears stinging my eyes, but crying would only make it worse.

As though he sensed that he had turned the tables again, Henry leaned over and spat, "You want her, Colin? You can have her. She's fucking trash to me."

He stormed into the house.

My stomach dropped.

Oh, my God, is he breaking up with me? I hadn't meant for it to go this far. I need to stop him and apologize. This was stupid and it's all my fault. I should've stayed calm. Why did I have to call his bluff? Fuck! I'm going to lose him.

I started to cry. I pulled my pants up and Colin helped me up from the ground. He wrapped me in his arms to shield me from the awkwardly staring faces around us. He couldn't understand that I was too head-fucked to accept his sympathy. I still wanted to be in Henry's arms, not his.

Years down the road, Colin would still be trying to "save me" . . . but that comes later in this tale.

I tried to push him away.

"Stop! This is your fault! Why did you have to say that?"

He fought to keep me against his chest as if I were a child who would calm down eventually.

"That guy is an asshole, Jenny. You deserve better."

"Let me go!"

I broke free and chased Henry to his room to continue the melodrama.

I can't bring myself to detail the sobbing, pleading argument that followed. I was pathetically desperate to make amends, apologizing and assuming responsibility for the entire situation. He tormented me for at least an hour.

He stood by the door and said, "It's over. Get out."

I went to him and tried to wrap my arms around him. "But I love you!"

I was devastated when he reached around me for the door handle, but at the last second, he pulled me into a passionate kiss instead. He acted as though it was impulsive, but I'm sure he had been planning it the whole time. He pulled me toward the bed with him and my relief was palpable. It seemed so passionate and romantic.

He pulled out his dick, once again removed my offending sweatpants, and managed to drive it home. He thrust hard against me for a few minutes and then abruptly pulled out and came all over me.

The underlying message was pretty clear to me.

The trend continued like this for months.

He locked me out of his house in the middle of the night and left me to find a ride home . . . but I had brought it on myself by questioning his relationship with a female friend. I needed to be less jealous and trust him more.

He reduced me to tears on a regular basis for what he perceived as my flaws, and then he would explain that he was just trying to help me to grow, to be honest with me about what I was doing wrong.

No matter what happened, I saw the fault in myself because I desperately wanted our love to be real, needed lightning bolts and fireworks in my life. Blame daddy issues or whatever else it could be attributed to, the outcome was the same: I was willing to overlook almost any fault to make it work with this handsome, intelligent, larger-than-life creature because I was pathetically desperate for my happy ending.

The first time we had sex, I remember sitting on the bed and watching as he stripped his pants and shirt off. He stood before me in his gray briefs and black socks.

There was a moment of slightly vulnerable eye contact, and then he hooked his thumbs into the waistband of his briefs and slid them off.

Why do they always leave their socks on? I thought with a giggle.

Determined to be seen as the desirable vixen I wanted to be, I pushed him forward and slid to my knees in front of him. With no hesitation, I took him in my mouth and began servicing him like a seasoned porn star. My fake noises of pleasure had been practiced in the shower for years to sound appropriately naughty but sexy at the same time. I used them now, hoping to show him just how wild I was.

He eventually stopped me with a touch and pulled me up from my knees. We stood chest to chest, and I leaned in for a passionate kiss, missing his mouth as he turned away and offered me his cheek.

Are you fucking kidding me? He really won't kiss me after I've been down there?

Now such disrespect would be a deal breaker, but I hadn't yet found enough respect for myself to demand it from others. Rather than questioning the behavior, I flopped back down on the bed, sliding my dress up and over my head.

Henry knelt in front of me and planted a kiss on my satin-covered mound, and I began to writhe, thinking things were about to get good, while simultaneously worrying about whether anything smelled/tasted/looked bad to him down there. He licked slowly up and down the satin, repeating the motion one more time before abruptly standing up again. He slid my panties to the ground and pushed me farther back up the bed, climbing on with me. I was still trying to figure out what had caused him to stop, internally crawling into a hole of insecurity, when I felt him pressing at my entrance. He entered with a quick thrust and a grunt.

I mentally freaked, realizing he wasn't wearing protection, but again, I didn't have the confidence, self-respect, or presence of mind to say anything. Absurdly, it seemed somehow impolite now that he was already doing it. I had been repeatedly told that condoms don't feel as good for the guy and if he just assumed it was okay, then clearly others had let him ride bareback. So on the one hand, I didn't want to be the lame girl who forced the issue and made the experience less pleasurable for him . . . but on the other hand, by my own argument, the fact that he automatically deemed it acceptable meant that he was irresponsible and was the guy I should be forcing the issue with. As always, my eagerness to please prevailed and I let him keep going.

As Henry began to thrust in earnest, he grabbed the headboard and pounded, our hips slapping together rapidly.

I braced myself against the headboard with my hands, but I was bouncing closer and closer to it until I was bracing with my head, neck turned awkwardly sideways. I had given up all pretenses of enjoyment. Had he taken a moment to absorb my expression, he would have been faced with incredulous disgust and a cocked eyebrow.

You have got to be fucking kidding me.

To my relief, Henry began to make strangely feminine guttural grunting sounds.

"Oh, God. Oh yeah, baby! Come with me. Come with me, baby! Come with me!"

I was tempted to ask him where we were going, since he surely couldn't be referring to an orgasm, but I wasn't given an opportunity. No sooner had he issued the invitation than he went rigid, gave an effeminate, drawn-out moan, and collapsed his weight down.

As we lay in a post-coitus heap, he kissed me sweetly on the shoulder and nuzzled my neck. When he made his way to my ear, I expected him to whisper a sweet nothing. Instead, I got, "You know that they can do a surgery to trim off your labia so that it would be easier to get my dick in and you would get wetter on the outside? You don't get wet like other girls do."

I thought my head was going to explode. He wanted me to surgically remove pieces of my female genitalia, which for the record are perfectly fine, so that he could insert his dick more easily without foreplay? Thinking about it now makes me want to surgically remove his dick. Back then, I almost died of embarrassment. I had never thought vaginas were a particularly sexy part of the anatomy, but I also never felt like there was anything especially unattractive about mine—or worse, something wrong with it. Now I was insecure about the most basic part of my female body—and would be from that moment until the first time a woman made love to me years later.

Henry was consistently selfish and I didn't put my foot down until the very end of the relationship, when that dormant Mistress that lives inside every woman eventually began to stir in frustration.

In our final fight, I distinctly remember giving up and admitting,

"I have never had an orgasm in your presence and you don't even care!"

Henry was part of an obvious pattern that I couldn't yet see. My identity was based upon whomever I was in a relationship with. My outlook on life slowly morphed to match my boyfriend's. Todd was a hustlin', drug-dealin' thug? Suddenly, I was listening to rap music, lying to the cops for him, and dressing like trailer trash. Henry was an aspiring writer who loved smoking weed all day? I was reading avant garde books that made no sense to me, wasting my life in a haze of smoke, and trying to fit in with the hipsters. Wes was commitment phobic? I was pretending I didn't want a serious relationship. If I had stopped to question it, I wouldn't have been able to answer what was really me and what was constructed to please someone else.

A year before Mark, I was lost and terrified to admit it.

So I began an internal odyssey to find my way back to my authentic self, starting with the source of my greatest frustration—sex.

3. JENNY

Prior to actually engaging in intercourse at the ripe age of seventeen, I had a pretty clear, if limited, idea of what turned me on. Before anyone else was involved, I was free to simply let my mind wander where it would, without judgment or distraction. As soon as there was a man involved, I felt pressure to please and be pleased by the same things he was into. It sounds pathetic, but is more common with women than you would think. I felt like I was somehow failing if I couldn't enjoy it the way my partner did. After all, women aren't just supposed to enjoy sex, they're supposed to enjoy it the way the man does, bringing them to a pornographic simultaneous climax.

And it wasn't just something I was constructing on my own. I encountered disappointment and frustration when I attempted to communicate or demonstrate my needs, as though they were failing as men because I couldn't get off from exactly what they were doing. Even those who were initially turned on by me taking charge eventually just wanted me to be able to get off from whatever they were in the mood for.

More than once, I was asked, "The other girls I've been with didn't take this long to come. Why is it so difficult for you?"

Oh, I see . . . I'm the one with the problem. . . .

Part of me wanted to scream, "They were all faking it, asshole!"

But instead I retreated inward, coming to accept that sex for me would be about connecting with and pleasing my partner and masturbating would be about pleasing myself. It was bullshit.

At least I was in the category of women who knew how to please myself. I learned that trick when I was only twelve. I didn't even understand what I was doing. I got my hands on one of my mom's forbidden romance novels. It was some bodice-ripping tale of a colonial woman who finds herself in the clutches of one of the native savages. He takes her as his woman and somehow it all works out well in the end. Her blushing virgin reluctance was close to nonconsent the first time he ravages her, but she enjoys it, so it's okay. Right?

The characters in the novel graphically made love multiple times throughout the book, but it wasn't the tender or even the raunchy parts that made me feel funny in my lady bits. It was the scene in which Nicole, the demure Irish redhead, was being borderline raped by Tipaake, the wild savage, that had me agitated. I read it so many times that that section of the book fell out of the bindings and I stashed it between my mattress and the wall, no longer needing the rest of the novel.

The day my mom brought my now wonderful stepdad home to meet us was the first day I actually achieved orgasm. I had been locked in my room all afternoon obsessing over that scene, frantically touching myself like an inept frat boy when eventually something explosive and life changing happened. The novel had referred in loose and poetic terms to Nicole achieving release, but the whole exercise wasn't clear to me, and I certainly didn't realize I could reach such a pinnacle without my very own Tipaake.

After coming once, there was no fucking way I was going downstairs to meet some dude my mother brought home. What if I stopped and couldn't do it again? I kept my door locked and refused to emerge. I must've come ten more times that day. My mom assumed it was just the prospect of a new man in her life after my dad that had me upset and unwilling to come down, so she left me alone.

Some would argue, after first confirming a total lack of abuse in my past, that my current perversions are somehow related to reading that scene at such an impressionable age. Why did I fixate on that scene in particular, though, when there were other more traditional ones I could have chosen? And why—long before that—did my Barbies somehow always end up tied to something, helpless and tortured? Why since childhood had I been orchestrating epic playground battles between the genders, which had resulted in more than one trip to the principal's office? These were the questions that I had to consider to reclaim my identity.

At the tender age of five, my parents moved us from a small town in Scotland to an equally small village in France. They had been told that the best thing to do with kids in that situation was to simply start them in school and they would learn the language quickly: a typically French sink-or-swim approach. Thus my two sisters (who were four and seven at the time) and I were dropped off at the village school, literally able to say four things in French: "yes," "no," "please," and "thank you." Heaven forbid we had bad manners as a result of the language barrier. This proved a traumatic experience for my introverted older sister. My younger sister simply refused to participate in the silliness. When the other preschoolers were told to sing French songs, she sang "It's a Small World" in English as loudly as she could. My parents received a distraught call from her teacher explaining that she had essentially staged a preschool coup resulting in all of the children refusing to sing anything but "It's a Small World" in English.

I had an altogether different approach. Even at such a young age, I was aware of the attention I was receiving as the new girl in the village, and I liked it. Two boys in particular seemed to be endlessly fascinated by me and tried repeatedly to engage me in conversation. I had absolutely no idea what they were saying, but responded at what seemed like appropriate moments with either "oui" or "non." They quickly caught on to the game. When I would say "yes" to one and "no" to the other, they would laugh and point at each other, but then I would quickly turn the tables and give the other an affirmative and devastate his friend with a negative. To this day, I don't have a clue what we were saying, but it is my earliest memory of learning what feminine power over men can feel like. At a Sunday afternoon village lunch about a year later, one of the boys, Francois, pulled my dad aside for a man-to-man talk. He explained that he was seeking my dad's permission to marry me in a few years—you know, when we were like eight or nine and of a more appropriate marriageable age. My dad still tells this story and relates that it was the moment when he knew that of his three girls, I would be the one to give him the most trouble. He had no idea.

I have always had a villain complex. While other little girls were running around pretending to be the princess, I was fascinated by the antagonists. Growing up with two sisters, we were always playing imaginative games, and in any of our make-believe worlds, I was the villain, the male characters, or an occasional ass-kicking heroine thrown in for good measure. My villains were spectacularly bad and particularly preoccupied with rendering my sisters' damsels power- less and at their mercy.

They were never especially violent or homicidal characters, which I assume would have raised warning flags with my parents who, rather amusingly, were more worried that I was a lesbian than a serial killer in the making. My mom has recently said that she just figured some- one needed to be the villain in our games and it made sense that it was always me since I was the most assertive of the three of us. The fact that I always wanted to be the guys and my female characters were curiously masculine evidently led to many a bedtime conversa- tion between my parents about how they would eventually handle it when I came out to them. Little did my mom know that when I even- tually did come out to her, it would have little to do with my gender identity, and a great deal to do with that early obsession with power and control.

A typical scene of the three of us playing looked like this:

Fiona, the oldest, with her straight black hair and serious demeanor, was generally cast as the leading female characters who in my eyes were weak and prime for the taking. Jane, my hilarious little sister, was cast as the secondary characters—the sidekicks, eccentric friends, or periphery cast. It must suck being the youngest, but she delighted in her role.

"Make it" was our term for "let's pretend that . . ."

Fiona would start with, "Let's make it that Barbie is seventeen and she's going on a hot air balloon trip with her friend Kelsey [Jane's doll]."

I allowed this utterly boring hot air balloon trip to begin and followed Fiona's plan until I felt my villain could make the maximum impact.

After twenty minutes of their balloon ride sweeping us around the house, Fiona continued, "Make it that their hot air balloon has found a floating cloud island paradise. . . ." Jane and Fiona whipped their Easter baskets filled with Barbie, Kelsey, and girly rainbow-colored dreams through the air and up onto the top bunk.

"But little do they know that this is the Unfindable Floating Lair of Dragar from whom there is no escape!"

Yes, I really spoke like that as a kid. I was a little obsessed with Tolkien.

Dragar, who was a Ken doll that I had cloaked in black and Sharpied his surfer-boy hair to a more acceptable color, flew through the air and before my sisters could protest, had snatched Barbie and Kelsey and dragged them down to the bottom bunk.

While holding Dragar as though he was the perpetrator, I rapidly used loom loops to tie Kelsey and Barbie's hands to the slats of the top bunk.

"You have landed upon my plane and are now mine to do with as I please!"

Fiona was not yet ready to concede to this turn of events.

"But then Prince Phillip arrives on his flying white unicorn—"

"Only to be caught by Dragar's pet dragon and brought before the evil lord Dragar!"

Poor Phillip was quickly emasculated and his rescue mission foiled now that he too was bound at the wrists, dangling above molten lava filled with lava sharks.

"Dragar, let us go! You can't do this!" came their helpless pleas.

"Your begging will get you nowhere. Setting you free would anger my queen whose wrath I hope never to incur. You will be my gifts to her."

Interestingly, tied up or trapped is as bad as things ever got for the helpless damsels. It was as though my villains didn't know what to do once they had them at their mercy. Which I now think was precisely the case. I had no concept of sex but, even at that age, deep down there was something alluring about being on the winning end of a power exchange.

As I got older, villains filled my fantasies. I don't mean uncouth or disgusting villains, but if he's the sophisticated, clad-in-black, criminal mastermind—I'm in. Most women flock to the bad-boy figure. I like the bad guy. I like him for his power, ruthlessness, and ambition. A British, German, or Russian accent doesn't hurt either. Picture Alan Rickman in *Die Hard* or as the Sheriff of Nottingham in *Robin Hood*. (Alan Rickman passed away after I wrote this, and we debated changing it, but no one does a bad guy quite like him.) And it's not that I want to save or fix him like many women want to do with the bad boy. I'm totally fine with him being a maniacal criminal, but he will bow down to me and only me.

In high school, I began to participate in our theater program and now realize that I was typecast. I know it will come as a shock to learn that if there was a sophisticated, sexual, domineering bitch to be played, I had the part. The first was Titania in *A Midsummer Night's Dream*, the fairy queen who toys with everyone for her own amusement. Next I played Antigone, the tragic ancient heroine who is put to death for defying her king. When I was a sophomore, our director announced that we would be doing *Medea*, an ancient Greek tragedy and the single biggest female role in theater. It is about a queen who goes on a murderous rampage to get back at her estranged husband, Jason, after he uses, betrays, and abandons her—going so far as murdering her own offspring to punish him. I went to a progressive high school. Medea is the baddest bitch of them all and I wanted the part.

During the auditions, the director had narrowed callbacks down to about a dozen girls who were competing for the lead role. He had us all stand on the edge of the stage in a line and then threw his keys out into the auditorium. We stared at him in confusion.

"Whoever retrieves the keys gets the part."

The girls launched themselves off the stage and wrestled one another as they crawled between the seats to find the keys. The director turned back from the hair-pulling bedlam to find me sitting on the edge of the stage observing the madness.

"Why aren't you trying to get the keys?"

"Medea would never debase herself with something like that. She's a fucking queen."

I got the part.

Now, I can cackle quietly about all of this because I understand how it all comes together and have embraced it, but back then there were desires inside of me that I didn't want to acknowledge.

Over the years, I had heard many women admit to having "rape" fantasies, not having any better vocabulary with which to describe these images of power exchange and submission. *Fifty Shades of Grey* hadn't been written yet, but it is certainly proof that more women are into it than anyone had realized. But up to that point, I had never heard a woman admit that in these fantasies, she was the aggressor— the one in control. Deep down, I wanted to make other people do things. And I was terrified of what that meant. I sometimes fantasized about being the man in these scenarios, but didn't really want to be a man in life. Did that mean I was confused about my gender identity? Did it mean I was gay? It was too overwhelming to process back then, so I buried it all deep, didn't tell anyone, and went about pretending to be an average teenage girl.

My high school years were marked by the same angst and insecurity that I'm sure everyone experiences at that age. I was a model student, competitive athlete, and participated in far too many extracurricular activities: speech and debate, theater, academic decathlon, honor society, mentoring programs, and the like. I think I was avoiding spending too much time at home with nothing to do. I was in the phase when you need your parents the most, but want to spend time with them the least. It didn't help that things were rocky and a little confusing at home. After my parents' divorce, everything had been great—for a while. They separated and only lived a few miles apart in the suburb of Houston that I grew up in. Initially, our custody arrangement was informal and we moved back and forth as we pleased, but that didn't last long. When they both remarried, things got a little more complicated. I can't extricate the bullshit from the truth now. I was just a kid, and I'd like to think that everyone meant well. There must have been blame on both sides. Custody arrangements aren't natural, and when the kids being passed back and forth are teenagers, feelings are bound to get hurt.

Normal divorce stuff is one thing, but after my dad remarried, things took a turn for the strange with my stepmom, Eleanor.

I can see why my dad fell in love with her, particularly looking at it now through adult eyes. She was brilliant, kind, and poised in a way that made her seem like she came from another time, a time when women held themselves differently. When people are afflicted with mental illness, as she was, we seem to forget they weren't always like that. The change can happen slowly, so slowly that it takes those closest to them a long time to realize something isn't right. Once the realization has struck, it can take even longer to actually accept that the person you love is being consumed by their disease. Initially, it makes more sense to believe their delusions are real.

It started with her becoming irrationally upset about little things— me using the wrong knife to prepare something in the kitchen, opening the bathroom door while the toilet was still flushing, arriving ten minutes later than expected. I was a teenager, so I'm willing to accept that some of it must have just been me being a royal pain in the ass and her struggling to find her footing as a stepparent. But then it got weirder. My dad sat me down and explained that they knew I had been stealing teaspoons and towels from their house and that I would have to either do chores to make up for the cost or return the "stolen" items. I denied any wrongdoing, but swallowed my pride and did the chores for the sake of peace. Maybe I had accidentally taken a towel to swim practice and left it at my mom's once or twice. My sister liked to eat yogurt on the way to school. I suspected there were a few teaspoons in her car. There were explanations that mostly made sense.

When they got pregnant, I was pissed. I liked the idea of a new sibling and I wanted them to be happy, but I felt like they maybe should have mentioned to me that they were even considering expanding the family. It wasn't exactly an accident. Being an angsty teen, I wrote them an angry letter informing them precisely how unhappy I was with their conduct. It wasn't the reaction they had expected, and things got even more tense.

She gave birth to my half brother just before my senior year of high school started. They called him Danny, and with his baby charm, he made me fall in love with him and forget all of the anger over his conception.

Looking at it now, I think it must have been the hormone swing from pregnancy or postpartum depression or just the overwhelming stress of being a new parent, but shortly after Danny's birth, things between Eleanor and me reached a new level of crazy. I was accused of breaking into their house and tapping a flashlight on their antique headboard to leave small damaging marks as some sort of bizarre act of rebellion. I didn't have keys to their house. They had a security system that I didn't know the code to. But I had somehow used my criminal mastermind powers to break in . . . and my crime of choice was damaging an antique headboard. Made a whole bunch of sense. It was so absurd I actually laughed. Why bother applying for scholarships when I had mad ninja skills and could just rob people instead? They were understandably not amused.

The next major accusation came with a phone call from my dad. I had just finished a rehearsal at school when he called. I answered with the usual pleasantries, but he cut me off immediately and said, "Jenny. We're at the hospital. Eleanor has cut her hands on the glass you put in her hand cream and we need to know what we should be testing for."

I started to cry.

"Dad? Are you serious? I have no idea what you're talking about. I don't underst—"

"Not interested in hearing that right now. Just need to know the extent of what you've done."

I couldn't get another word out over my sobbing. He hung up.

When I had stopped panicking long enough to think through what was happening, I went and found a younger teacher who I was close to and explained what was going on. I was terrified the police were going to show up at school and arrest me and I needed someone to know what was happening who could be my advocate. I was rattled, but the magnitude of it hadn't sunk in for me yet. As an adult outsider, she was able to see the situation much more clearly and knew how deeply wrong it was.

"Jenny, you have to stay away from there. I think she's sick and from what you're telling me it has been escalating. I'm worried that if you don't stay away, she's going to do something to harm the baby and find a way to blame you for it."

That seemed a little overdramatic. This wasn't a Lifetime movie after all.

Talking to my teacher had allowed me to shift the burden I had been carrying on my adolescent shoulders to an adult authority figure, and it felt good to surrender control to a grown-up. Underneath my teenage swagger, I was overwhelmed and out of my depth, but I never would have admitted it. I trusted her and followed her advice. I didn't see or speak to my dad or Eleanor again and the accusations stopped.

I grieved for years. I had lost a parent because he had chosen his other family over me. Not only that, but he actually believed me to be the person Eleanor had portrayed in her wild stories, capable of callousness and cruelty. I went through a brief spell of wondering whether this was what crazy people felt like. Maybe I had done the things they said I did and I just didn't remember them. Was I dangerous? Did I need help? Working through those thoughts was terrifying, but I kept reaching the same conclusion: It wasn't me. There were no periods of time I couldn't account for or any other warning signs in my behavior. I didn't have access, and on the occasions in question I knew exactly where I had been and who I was with when I was supposedly committing deviant acts. I should have been reassured, but if it wasn't me, then it was her, and that didn't make me feel any better. It must have been even harder for my dad to be in the middle of it.

4. SCARLETT

With some distance and some time, I began to heal and move on from it all. I started college at USC, loving the freedom and fun of student life. I tried to act like my peers, experimenting with relationships and casual sex. None of it was particularly satisfying, but I was too scared to push any boundaries. And now there I was repressed, frustrated, and insecure—and just as terrified of it all as I had been as a teen.

Scared or not, I had resolved to probe these questions, so I dug through the Internet, desperate to find a way to understand and accept what I had been blocking out in any of my sexual experiences.

After sifting through heaps of porn and lots of disturbing awkward-cat-lady BDSM fan fiction (you can't unread a story about Dumbledore spanking Hermione), I stumbled upon something intriguing: a working dungeon in Los Angeles. There was evidently a place of business not ten miles from where I lived where women worked professionally as Dominants and submissives. It was a house of fetish that catered to adult desires without being a brothel. It was a dungeon that also happened to be called the Dungeon.

I read through all of the pages and profiles with fascination, wondering who works in such a place. Then the banner on the side of the page caught my eye.

"Now interviewing subs, Switches, and Dommes. No experience necessary."

What better way to learn than to do? It was the universe calling my bluff.

She seemed to whisper, "Here it is, your chance to do something wild and forbidden." I didn't think. I just picked up the phone.

When a real woman answered, I was shaken back to reality. I stuttered my way through an explanation of why I had called and hung up the phone with an interview scheduled at six the following evening.

I sat on my bed, mind racing. What the hell had I just done? Was I really going to go? I knew the answer was yes before the question had even finished forming in my mind.

I struggled with the question of what to wear to the interview so much that I actually called back to ask. I couldn't very well ask my mom for advice. The lady on the phone explained that the Dungeon keeps an extremely low profile, so I should wear whatever I would wear to a normal job interview and nothing that would raise the eyebrows of the neighbors. The term *dungeon*, to me, implies a menacing stone building, but in reality, this dungeon was an unassuming house in a mostly residential neighborhood.

Walking in, I was totally confident in my pencil skirt, blazer, and Mary Janes. Once inside, I felt matronly and prudish. Lady Caterina was busy when I arrived, so I had been seated in the interview room to wait. The girls who were working flitted past the open door like curious butterflies assessing the new prospect. They were dressed in a scintillating array of lingerie and costumes. Shiny leather and latex hugged their curves and fishnet stockings left flashes of bare thigh beneath scandalously short skirt hems.

An alluringly androgynous woman with a black faux hawk and equally dark eyes strode into the room, wearing a leather minidress and impossibly high boots. There was a challenge in her eyes that I didn't yet understand. She looked me over with a smile that hinted at something secret and then began rummaging in the wooden chest on the far side of the room. Once she had turned her back to me, I couldn't help but stare at the slit up the back of her dress, which reached her waist. And as she was currently bent over, I had a stunning view of her black thong and perfectly shaped derriere.

She didn't even turn around when she said, "Are you checking out my ass?"

Lady Caterina saved me from having to answer. She entered the room and swatted the girl on the behind.

"Mistress Erin, stop flirting with the new girl!"

Mistress Erin chuckled and winked at me as she left.

Up until that moment, I would've said that, without question, I was strictly heterosexual. I had never even considered being with a woman. Now I had an undeniable crush on a Dominatrix named Erin. My heart was fluttering and I was blushing like a schoolgirl who had been asked out for the first time.

I was confused and out of my element when Lady Caterina, an older woman who looked like an archetypal bohemian with completely white hair, perched on a stool across from me and started working through a list of questions over the top of her glasses.

It is hilarious now to remember how naive I was, but I confidently bluffed my way through the whole thing. When it seemed that I had answered all of her questions favorably, the tone shifted and she focused on explaining the mechanics of working there.

We took a tour of the Dungeon and as we went from room to room, she reviewed the rules and what would be expected of me. I began to notice that there was some understood flexibility between the legal rules that were posted in every room and the unspoken rules of the Dungeon. Rules such as no penetration and no exchange of bodily fluids were fixed and fireable offenses. Not to mention felonies. But there was an understanding that a client was allowed to be fully nude and could orgasm as long as we didn't assist. In other words, I can't stop him from doing it, but I can't be the one stimulating. Panties were never to be removed. Toplessness was at our discretion. Some of the nuances of the rules would take me months to understand, but the core of it all was to protect us from the law and from potential exposure to disease. For instance, technically we were not allowed to interact with a client's genitals. But I could kick him in the balls with boots on and it was acceptable, assuming said gentleman was expecting ball torture of course. Caterina did her best to talk me through what I would encounter and how to handle it, but most would have to be learned through experience.

Every room we walked through had a different theme and the attention to detail in each would have made Disneyland proud. There was a space for almost any fantasy I could come up with, and I'm sure a number that I couldn't. The themes varied from a menacing dungeon like the one I had initially pictured, complete with stone walls and medieval-looking torture racks—to a fully equipped classroom. There were cages and crosses, medical tables and frilly couches. Implements and erotic posters adorned the walls. I felt dark and naughty just being there. And I liked it.

There was an entire hallway dedicated to implements and toys that could be taken into a session. Rope in every color imaginable was neatly coiled and hung next to paddles, whips, floggers, chains, ball gags, gimp masks, blindfolds, and a vast array of items whose purpose I could only imagine. It was overwhelming, but intriguing.

I was struck by how immaculate absolutely everything was. It was clear that everyone adhered to extremely high standards for hygiene.

Nothing about the place felt dirty or wrong. After a little while inside the walls of the Dungeon, it was easy to forget that the outside world even existed. There were no feelings of guilt or shame here, no preconceived notion of normal. It was a place where pleasure and fantasy were sacred.

I left feeling electric and energized.

I got the call the following afternoon to let me know I had been hired. The only catch was that I would have to start as a submissive since I didn't have any training in domination, even if that was where my proclivities lay. That meant I would need to be the one receiving spankings, being tied up, and role-playing as the meek little schoolgirl when necessary. I wasn't excited about that idea, but it was still a challenge and the end result would be the same. On a logical level, it made perfect sense that I couldn't just walk in and start dominating people without any concept of what that meant or how to do it.

They wanted me to start on Monday. I knew I wanted to keep it a secret, but I felt that I needed to tell someone what I was up to or I was going to explode. The obvious choice was my roommate, Amelia. We had lived together for nearly four years, and we always supported each other.

At first, she was stunned.

"What the hell is a dungeon?"

"It's a similar idea to a brothel, except no sex happens there and it specifically caters to fetishes."

"So will that still make you a prostitute?" she asked with more excitement in her voice than she probably intended.

I had to laugh. "That really depends on your definition of a prostitute. Technically, I won't be doing any traditional sex favors for money, so no. But at the same time, there are acts that have an overall sexual connotation, even if they don't fit the normal bill, so in that sense, yes. I think the real question is whether I'm comfortable if someone thinks I'm a prostitute regardless of technicalities. The answer is yes. The only difference between a prostitute and one of the girls who's sleeping with a new guy every weekend is that one is smart enough to get paid for it."

"Does Wes know?" she asked without meeting my eyes.

"No." I hesitated. "I didn't want to tell him before I knew whether I got the job, but now I don't know what to say."

"Kinda seems like it's now or never. It'll only get harder once you're doing it. Are you actually into this . . . stuff?"

"I think I might be. And that's part of what I want to find out."

She tactfully changed directions with, "Is it even legal? What if you get arrested?"

"From what I can tell, it falls in a gray area. I mean, the Dungeon has been there since the eighties and no one has gotten arrested, so it must not be too bad. I think as long as I follow the rules and don't do anything stupid, the risk is low, but I'll admit it's a possibility if the cops decide to crack down or something. Every time I do a session,

I'll have to decide whether I'm okay with it. I think this whole situation is going to be about evaluating risks and deciding how far on the edge I'm willing to go before it becomes too much."

"What if someone tries to rape you?"

"That could happen anytime. We live in the fucking hood. Girls get raped at frat parties or on their way home from a night out, but that doesn't stop us from going. It just means we try to be smart about it. Similar idea here, but I actually think it's less likely to happen at the Dungeon for a few reasons. In theory, there are no drugs or alcohol at play. It's in a secured building with cameras and lots of witnesses, so it's a pretty sure thing that they would get caught and be prosecuted. For most of these guys, this is the one safe place for them to get their outlet, so they don't want to fuck it up or they'll never be allowed back. And I'll only be taking clients I'm comfortable with and laying the ground rules for the session ahead of time, so I can be careful. But again, yes, I admit it is a risk."

"What would you do if your mom found out?"

"Drive my car off a cliff. I don't know. I don't see how she would find out."

Amelia shrugged and shook her head. "Fair enough. I wanna see the Web site!"

As we laughed and clicked through all of the pictures and profiles, I felt a weight being lifted. Secrets can be such a burden.

We spent the weekend shopping for scandalous new outfits. I was in the car with her on our way back when Lady Caterina called to find out what I wanted my name to be. I had given it some thought and decided that I wanted to be Thalia, named after the ancient Greek muse of comedy.

"Thalia? Yeah, that's not going to work. We're dealing with men here, and men are dumb. Keep it simple; something they have heard before and can pronounce."

I was totally unprepared. It hadn't occurred to me that she would reject my choice.

"Okay. Can I think about it and call you back?"

"I really need an answer now. The Webmistress is about to leave and Lady Leah said it had to be up on the Web site today."

"Okay, two seconds . . ."

I covered the phone and shrugged at Amelia. "She said Thalia won't work and I have to pick now. Ideas?"

"Diana?"

"Boring."

"Caroline?"

"Lame."

"Natasha?"

"Already taken."

"Marilyn?"

"Taken."

"Mufasa!"

"Not helpful."

"Destiny?"

"Stripper name."

"Scarlett?"

"Lady Caterina, what about Scarlett?"

"Scarlett it is."

I didn't realize it at the time, but my alter ego had just been born.

5. TICKLE ED

I awoke in the early morning hours of darkness on Monday with the immediate knowledge that today marked a delineating point in my life. There would be a before today and an after today. This morning I was a bright, successful recent college grad walking a typical path in life that would make any parents proud. With that thought, though, I was reminded that I didn't have parents anymore. I had a mom. And the typical path had left me hollow and frustrated. The next time I lay down to sleep in this bed, I would be a different woman in ways I knew I couldn't yet imagine. I would be a bright, successful recent college grad with a dark secret. I would be a sex worker. My stomach danced in circles at the thought. But from the nerves and that knowledge, a wicked smile appeared. I could do this. It felt right.

I made it through my work day at my vanilla job, and quietly left a little early to make the drive up to the Dungeon.

After parking on a side street, I approached the ivy-covered house, wondering again how it managed to be so conspicuous yet draw so little attention. It was like something from Harry Potter. Once you know it's there, you can't understand how it didn't strike you as strange before, but until you're standing in front of it staring, it fails to capture your attention. What is a sprawling two-story gothic house doing among the businesses of this trendy, upscale area? Why are all of the windows covered? Why are there strange noises coming from within?

I stood at the front door and waited for the buzz before I opened it. As I crossed the threshold, I was struck by how a place can be so dark and so charming at the same time. I suppose it's appropriate. In the shadows is where our secret side gets to play.

I had my chin up and felt confident and ready for anything. I stood as unobtrusively as I could in front of the reception desk and waited for Caterina to finish the phone call she was on.

". . . I'll have to double-check with the girls who are working tonight, but I'm sure at least one of them would be happy to smash tomatoes with her toes for you."

She looked up and smiled apologetically and held up two fingers. I dismissed the gesture and mouthed to her that there was no rush.

"She is working tonight and she has an opening from seven to eight thirty if you'd like to come in and meet her. . . . I can't tell you offhand whether her second toes are longer than her first, but that's something you could investigate if you'd like to come in. . . . I wouldn't describe any of our girls as heavy, but she does have ample curves. . . . I would think she'd be fine with you wearing a diaper, but you'll want to confirm all of this with her when you interview. . . . Great. So we'll see you around seven? . . . Wonderful. See you then."

She hung up the phone and looked up at me shaking her head.

"Hi, Lady Caterina."

"Hi, Scarlett! Ready for your first day? I've got a client booked for you in about an hour—Tickle Ed. Should be an easy intro. I'm trying to get some others for you too. New girls are always an easy sell. Raven will be your mentor today, but she's running late, so just head back to the dressing room and get ready and hopefully she'll be here before your first client."

I nodded and smiled feeling off-kilter, but still committed. My first client . . . this was getting real. Tickling?

———————

I walked in the door as Jenny in my USC triathlon team jacket and a pair of jeans, and proceeded to the dressing room past rows of torture implements on the walls. There I shed layers of myself as I stripped down to a thong, and replaced my street clothes with lace and frills. It wasn't me. But I wasn't me anymore either. I was Scarlett. The same blue eyes stared back at me. I still had my mother's high cheekbones and vampire-pale skin. My hair still fell in red waves to my shoulders. The features were identical, but I already felt different.

Getting dressed gave me something to focus on, but now that I was ready, I wasn't really sure what to do, so I sat on the couch in the dressing room and tried to look comfortable, like I belonged there. The reflection that stared back at me from the opposite wall mostly looked nervous.

Then Erin walked in and I got to see the genuine version of what I was pretending to be. She dripped easy confidence.

Fuck, she was sexy. Just watching her made me picture things that had never crossed my twenty-two-year-old heterosexual mind. I wanted to know what it would be like to be touched by her. Could she possibly be as soft and sensual as she looked?

I'm straight. I'm straight. I'm straight.

I mentally smacked myself. I was a cute chick. I could play this game too.

I didn't bother to get up, but extended my hand and said, "Hi, Erin, we weren't properly introduced the other day. I'm Scarlett."

It gave me a thrill to use my new name.

She ate a fry from the bag she was holding, and licked the tip of her index finger clean, before extending her hand and grasping mine.

"Mistress," she said.

"Ummm, no, I have to start as a sub, but I think I'm really a Domme. I just need to learn the ropes first."

She smiled indulgently.

"Mistress Erin."

"Oh. Got it. Sorry. Mistress Erin."

"Caterina said to tell you your first client is here."

"Okay, great. Raven was supposed to be mentoring me today, but she's late. Should I just go ahead?"

"Yeah, you don't want to keep him waiting. It should be a simple interview. He's a younger dude—lucky for your first client. He likes a sub who observes protocol, so stay on your knees after you go in, but be flirty. He sometimes likes to role-play that he isn't a client, so just use your imagination and roll with it. Should be easy. You got this."

Erin's confidence bolstered my own. How hard could this be? I gave myself one last look in the mirror and turned to thank Erin for the help as I made my way back down the hall. I could hear Caterina on the phone again.

". . . I'm afraid we don't use strap-ons here at the Dungeon. We don't allow any kind of penetration, but I'm sure there are other ways we could fulfill the fantasy. . . . Well I suppose if you were already wearing a butt plug and we didn't know about it, there wouldn't be much we could do, but if she saw it, she would need to end the session. . . ."

Instead of interrupting her, I bypassed the desk and entered the interview room. The guy standing there couldn't have been more than a few years older than me, but looked significantly more nervous. He was standing so awkwardly, I felt bad for him.

"Hi, Sir, I'm Scarlett," I tried in my subbiest voice. "Feel free to have a seat on the couch."

He didn't say anything, but sat obediently, looking a little bit like he thought the couch might swallow him if he relaxed.

I knelt on the ground a few feet in front of him and folded my hands in my lap. I wasn't really sure what sub protocol was exactly, but this seemed about right.

"So sorry to have kept you waiting, Sir."

"No problem," he said so quietly I almost didn't hear it.

Now what the fuck am I supposed to do?

"Would you prefer I call you Ed or Sir?"

"Umm. My name's Fernando. I'm just waiting to be paid."

Role-play? What kind of role-play was this? I am not going back out there to ask for help. Erin said to use my imagination. I can do this.

"Oh, I see, Fernando. Have I been a bad girl and I owe you money? Maybe you would take some other form of payment?" I asked playfully, really wishing I had mastered a seductive wink instead of looking like I had been poked in the eye when I tried to wink.

"No, thanks," he said with an uncomfortable laugh. "I really just need the money."

I was beginning to panic. Something felt off. This dude wasn't pretending. He looked like he was two seconds from running out the front door. How could I be fucking up this bad with my first client?

"Oh, but, Sir." I pouted. "Surely we could come to some kind of—"

Erin walked in and glanced down at me with an eyebrow raised in judgment. She had cash in her hand.

"How much do I owe you for the food?"

Fernando looked immensely relieved. I wanted to crawl into the broom closet.

"Twelve fifty-six," he said, springing up from the couch.

Erin handed him some money and he fled, letting the front door slam.

"Welcome to the Dungeon." Erin grinned as she left the room.

I got off my knees and took a deep breath. I could feel the blood pounding in my ears.

Very fucking funny. What a bitch. Fuck her.

Caterina was still on the phone arguing about butt plugs, but raised her hands in question as I got to the desk. I made a dismissive gesture and smiled, continuing to make my way back to the dressing room. I could hear multiple women laughing, and assumed Erin had gone back to share the results of her prank, but when I entered the room, no one took notice.

A tall, dark-haired woman who looked strikingly like a Latina Wonder Woman had obviously just arrived, and I guessed she had to be Raven. She was in the middle of telling the three other girls in the dressing room a story when I walked in.

". . . Going to the post office is bad enough, but then there was no parking anywhere. So I do the logical thing and go creeper on some old dude walking out to his car. I follow him to his spot and sit there with my blinker on for like three years while he gets in the car. He finally pulls out . . . and some skank in a Porsche zips in and steals my spot!"

"I hate it when someone pulls that shit!" yelled a voice from the bathroom.

"Right? So I lay on my horn for like fifteen seconds, but bitch isn't moving, so I roll down the window and *politely* [laughter from the group] let her know what she just did. She flips me off and keeps walking. I waited until she was inside and then pulled my bloody maxi pad off, got out of the car, and stuck it under her door handle. I wish I could've waited around to see her face, but I was already late, so I left."

The laughter, groaning, and clapping took a moment to subside.

Note to self: Don't cross Raven. Who the fuck are these women?

The answer to that question, I would learn in the coming months, was that these are the women who are wickedly smart, completely comfortable with their sexuality, and not remotely interested in any of the boundaries that have been set by society. Raven is what it looks like when a gorgeous psychology PhD fucking owns both her intelligence and her sexuality.

Raven was born in East L.A., in one of the neighborhoods that would make you lock your car doors if you accidentally drove through it lost and looking for a way back to the freeway. She was the first person in her large extended family to graduate high school. And then college. By the time she got her PhD, she had become a sort of legend within the community. Because of her humble beginnings, she didn't fit the stereotype of a higher-educated thirtysomething woman anyway, so she wasn't constrained by the expectations that went along with it. She had spent her entire life not giving a fuck what anyone thought, and she wasn't about to start just because she was a professor. I think the university had caught wind of her "other job," but she was well liked as an educator, and as a minority female was difficult to fuck with. She wasn't someone you fucked with in general, but as a friend she was as supportive and loyal as they came. Her clients adored her sharp mind and enthusiasm for absolutely anything they could come up with. Raven's downfall was that she was inexplicably drawn to worthless men who were neither as intelligent nor driven as she was. She didn't put up with nonsense from anyone except whatever douche bag she happened to be in a relationship with. It was infuriating to watch, but there was no reasoning with her.

Mistress Erin popped her head around the dressing room door and smiled a coy smile. I wanted to knock the dimples off her stupid face, but I forced myself to smile back, not willing to let her see how embarrassed I was.

She turned her attention to Raven.

"Hey, Raven, this is the new chick you're training today. Cat said she has Tickle Ed in a few, so run her through the basics."

I squared my shoulders and addressed her myself, not wanting Erin to be involved in the exchange anymore.

"Hi, Mistress Raven. I'm Scarlett. It's really nice to meet you."

She shook my hand and gave me a warm smile.

"Just Raven is fine. I'm not a Mistress. I make more money as a Switch," she said, giving her gigantic, perfectly rounded ass a slap.

Damn it. When am I going to get something right?

"No biggie, though. I can explain the difference between the three as a good starting point for our training. The Dungeon is divided into subs, Switches, and Dommes—which can all be called a variety of other names, but let's keep it simple for now."

"Okay . . ."

"Everyone starts as a sub unless they have an already impressive résumé as a Domme. Outside of the Dungeon, it's not as common for Dommes to sub initially, but almost everyone will tell you that the best tops always started as bottoms. How can you really get inside a sub's head if you don't know what it feels like?"

"Makes sense."

"So in here, subs are generally on the receiving end of whatever the client wants to do. They are the ones getting spanked, tickled, tied up, flogged, hypnotized . . . you get the picture. You may not actually be into any of that, but for the sake of the session, do your best to fake it. You get to dictate in the interview how heavy a player you are and what your boundaries are, so never be afraid to speak up in there. Better to make sure you're both clear before going to a room. Subs aren't allowed to wear black and are supposed to look girly. Oh, and subs wear a collar—I have one you can use. Switches don't wear a collar unless the scene specifically calls for it and they can dress like Dommes or subs. Dommes are the ones dishing out different kinds of beatings, head-fucks, and humiliation. From the smirk, I'm going to assume that's more your inclination, but don't underestimate how much you can learn outside of your comfort zone. Switches, as the name would imply, go both ways. That can mean they take sessions that are one or the other, or sometimes a client wants to switch roles within a session. There is a practical skills test before becoming a Switch and another one before you can be a Mistress. We can get into all of that later. Right now . . . your first client is Tickle Ed. He's like eight hundred years old and as harmless as they come. He's mostly into tickling. Are you ticklish?"

"Not really."

"Doesn't matter. Just squeal, giggle, and squirm. That's all he's looking for anyway. He likes a little light bondage to add to the helplessness. Are you comfortable with that?"

"I think so."

"Cool. I'll let him know in the interview that wrist cuffs are fine, but I'll pick ones that are a little big, so you'll know you could get out of them if you really wanted to."

The intercom on the wall crackled to life.

"Scarlett, your client is here."

I barely remember the interview now. Raven went with me and did most of the talking. Before I had really processed what was happening, I was following an elderly man upstairs with a bag slung over my arm that contained rope, cuffs (a size too big), feathers, and clean towels and blankets to replace anything we used while up there.

We stopped outside of the den, and I tried to keep my hands steady as I found the right key on the ring and fumbled with the lock.

The den was a large room with a dressing area at the back that I would come to learn was specially designed for playing with cross-dressers. The room included an attached bathroom and stairs that led up to a loft where we weren't allowed to play, but where a house slave named Margaret sometimes slept and secretly hung out during sessions. There was a large leather table with restraints attached, a spanking horse, and a black leather chair that looked like a throne. Mirrors adorned most walls, and a Saint Andrew's cross stood menacingly in the corner. There was so much attention to detail that it felt a bit like kinky Disneyland. It looked naughty without being scary, which made it one of the most popular rooms to play in.

Once we got inside, I closed the door behind us and pressed the button on the mic, as I had been instructed.

"Yes?" came the reply from Caterina, as though she didn't already know why I was pressing the button.

"We're starting," I said in my most confident voice, now feeling a little unsure. I wasn't worried about Ed. I just didn't know what to expect.

"Thank you," responded Caterina, then the intercom went silent. *Okay. Thirty minutes. I can do this.*

That's about the time I realized I hadn't worn a watch, a mistake I wouldn't repeat.

Ed and I stared at each other awkwardly for a moment.

"Should I maybe get on the table?" I asked, offering up the wrist cuffs and rope.

"Yes, my little prey." He giggled. "Let's start there."

I hopped up on the table, lay down, and spread my arms above my head obligingly.

Ed fumbled with the first wrist cuff until I took it from him and put it on myself. I tried to take the other one and do the same, but he was already feeding rope through the metal O-ring and looping it through the D-ring on the table. I think he was trying for some kind of elaborate knot, but got tangled somewhere and ended up with a rat's nest that would serve its purpose for the time being. With one wrist tied, I couldn't help him with the other cuff, so I lay there as he struggled with it. He eventually gave up and just tied the rope with shaking hands directly around my wrist.

I wondered if I should protest this since it wasn't technically what we had agreed to, but it wasn't too tight and I knew I could get the other wrist out if I needed to. I decided I would pick my battles and left it alone.

"Okay, now we're in business," said Ed, rubbing his knobby hands together.

"Are you ticklish, little girl?"

"Yes! Please, please don't tickle me!"

The image of Ed in that moment will stick with me forever and will probably never fail to make me laugh. Approaching with gleeful menace was a terribly old, frail-looking man with the gleam in his eyes of a fifteen-year-old boy who has seen boobs for the first time.

He raised both of his gnarled, arthritic hands in the air, grinned like a madman, and said, "Here comes the tickle monster!"

He wiggled his fingers as he got closer and closer, repeating, "Here comes the tickle monster! Here he comes!" I squealed and shrieked with fake laughter all too aware of the absurdity of the situation.

I am not even remotely ticklish anywhere except my feet, and he wasn't interested in tickling me there. I learned that day just how exhausting it is to pretend you are, but it wouldn't have mattered whether I really was or not. Ed didn't so much tickle as dig into my ribs with his fingers.

The more I squealed and squirmed and shrieked with mock terror, the more animated he got. It was the first but certainly not the last time I would wonder what would happen if one of my elderly clients had a heart attack or a stroke from the excitement.

To me, it felt monotonous and the half hour seemed more like two, but to Ed, it seemed to be a nonstop thrill.

Am I really getting paid for this? Does he do this with his grandkids? Are his grandkids older than me?

The questions were endless, but regardless of whether I was into the session or not, I recognized something that day. I was getting to see a side of another person that he doesn't show to the world. This man walks around every day and people simply see him as a nice old guy who is probably past all the "sexual stuff." They have no idea that he not only fantasizes about tickling young girls, but goes to a dungeon on a regular basis and pays for the privilege of doing so. It was intriguing and unsettling at the same time.

What else don't I know about people?

Caterina's voice eventually broke the moment and let us know that our session had ended. As we cleaned up the room and got ready to go back downstairs, I tried to assess how I felt about the experience. Was I uncomfortable? Did I feel cheap or dirty? Surprisingly not. What I did feel was a strange intimacy with this man who had been a complete stranger less than an hour earlier. We had shared something: a secret, a moment, the broken barrier of touch . . . I couldn't exactly place my finger on what it was, but some thread now connected me to Tickle Ed.

I was still trying to process this when I got back to the dressing room, but instead of acknowledging it when Erin asked how my session had gone, I fell back on the comfortable judgmental cynicism that we all carry around as a shield.

"That was so creepy! I mean, he's old enough to be my grandpa and he's pretending I'm super young. And tickling? Really? Who gets off on that?"

I was stunned when Erin's response was, "What's your fucking problem? Why are you here if you're just gonna judge people? Is he your grandpa?"

"No."

"Are you a consenting adult—who I might add is being paid for the experience?"

"Yes."

"So no issues there. You got a problem with him being into tickling? What are you into that's so much better?"

"I don't kn—"

"Yes, you do. You're just too much of a pussy to admit it. This guy, on the other hand, knows what he wants and what he has to do to get it and probably doesn't give a fuck that you're judging him for it. And he's old . . . really? You think you're gonna stop thinking about dirty shit because you get old? Maybe. But I sure as fuck hope I don't."

She got up from the couch and came to stand behind me in the mirror. I could feel her breath on my neck as she whispered, "Open your mind, Scarlett. I promise you'll like it."

She chuckled as she walked away.

I didn't think I had ever met anyone more infuriating.

6. RICH

The next morning, I went back to my day job at the construction site of a new hospital in Orange County. The company my mom worked for had been hired as the medical equipment consultant for the building of the new tower and she helped me to get a job that I could do while I figured out whether to go to grad school. Essentially, an architect designs the building, a general contractor builds the building, and someone has to figure out all of the stuff that goes in the building. So the team I worked for would help the clinical staff to determine all of the equipment that needed to be purchased—from scalpels to MRI machines. They would then implement a plan for things such as installation, seismic anchorage, and delivery priority. After that, we would actually purchase the roughly $54 million of equipment. With a degree in archaeology, I naturally came to the table with a full understanding of all of this and was ready to hit the ground running from day one . . . or not.

I had been doing the job for a few weeks, and to my dismay had essentially been relegated to the role of bimbo secretary. This was disconcerting not just because of the blow to my college-educated ego, but because I was totally unqualified to even be a secretary. I didn't drink coffee and thus understandably had no idea how to work a coffeemaker. As in I had literally never made a cup of coffee in my life.

Turns out, there is more than one way to catastrophically fuck that up and have the entire jobsite trailer judge you. There had been brilliant moments like the one where I decided I would take some initiative and ask Mary, another admin, instead of someone from my own team how I would go about FedExing something:

"Call them and schedule a pickup."

"Okay, great. Do you happen to have their phone number handy?"

"1-800-GO-FEDEX." I walked away dripping in the disdain she threw at me with that one.

I didn't know how to use a fax machine. Didn't know how to read an architectural drawing. Had never scheduled a meeting. I basically sucked. The most I could do was keep my chin up and try not to make the same mistake twice.

That first morning back in the office after starting at the Dungeon was uncomfortable. I felt different, so I was sure people could somehow tell that I was a changed woman. I guess it's a bit like being high and being convinced that everyone knows when they really wouldn't if you would just chill out. With that in mind, I was trying to play it cool.

I needed to talk to my project manager about changing my work schedule on the days that I would be working at the Dungeon so that I could start at 6:00 and be on the road by 3:30 to arrive at my other job by 4:15. This wasn't an abnormal request in L.A. since those hours would help to avoid traffic, but I knew if that was the reason I gave then if something came up (and something always comes up on a jobsite) then he would ask me to stay late and I wouldn't have a good reason to leave. My solution was to devise the first of many lies that would tumble from my lips in order to preserve the secrecy of my double life. It wasn't something I had much practice at, so I didn't know yet to keep it simple and stick as close to the truth as possible, lest I get tangled in my own web.

I cycled through a number of managers on that job, but my boss at the time was a guy named Rich. He was a former chef who had gained moderate fame in the restaurant scene for his cooking, and celebrity status for his success with the ladies. Back when Bourdain was still working brunch, Rich had groupies. Women would lurk outside whatever restaurant he hadn't been fired from yet waiting to accost him when he would sneak out to smoke a cigarette. His smoke breaks were just as likely to turn into a blow job next to the Dumpster. He was the hard-partying, tattooed bad boy of the L.A. food world before it was cool. He claimed he got older, couldn't keep up, and the kitchen life lost its luster, but I suspect after a certain point no one would hire him and the drugs took their toll. He had lived such a colorful life that he seemed a little confused that at forty-eight, this was where he had ended up. He had severe high blood pressure, but subsisted on a diet of coffee, doughnuts, and booze. He was still rail thin with a shaved bald head, still rocked a leather jacket, and still showed flashes of the boyish charm that had made him so popular. He often came into the trailer still hurting from the night before, and that particular day didn't appear to be any exception.

He trudged in past my desk after his first morning meeting, sweating through his shirt, and didn't address me until he had refilled his coffee cup.

"A sub stopped by to see you earlier."

What. The. Fuck.

"Excuse me?"

"A sub came by earlier looking for you to schedule something for this afternoon."

I must have looked like a deer in the headlights and was trying not to panic. No one knew. How could my worlds be colliding this quickly? I didn't know what to say, so I continued to stare at him blankly.

"Jen, you all right? It was a subcontractor, but I don't remember who he works for. Maybe low voltage? Anyway, he said he'd stop back before lunch and catch you then."

". . . cool, thanks."

Sub . . . subcontractor. Not sub . . . submissive. Got it. I had the feeling that one was going to take a while to get used to.

I took a deep breath and walked through to Rich's office.

"So, Rich, I've gotten myself into kind of a stupid situation and

I'd rather not go into all the details, but I have mandatory community service three days a week for the next while in the evenings. Do you think those days I could come in and leave early so I can get up to L.A. on time and not get myself into more trouble?"

He looked up at me skeptically and for a moment I was concerned that he was going to pry. I didn't have an explanation of why this was supposedly happening or what I had done wrong. I overheard a Switch named Lexy talking about her court-mandated community service the night before and borrowed the story. My instinct was that with what I knew of Rich's background, he had been in trouble before and would respect the boundary I had implied. The man had a tattoo he told me had been made with a safety pin in prison, so I was banking on him being understanding of the fact that sometimes young people do stupid shit. I had never so much as had a speeding ticket in my life, but felt like he would appreciate the bond.

"That shouldn't be a problem. Anything I need to know about?"

"It's all old news. Stupid college stuff that's not even worth getting into. I just need to get it resolved and put it behind me."

"I hear ya. I take it I'm not mentioning this to Lorna?"

I hadn't really worked out what I was going to tell my mom since she would likely know this story was bullshit. I knew she wouldn't be on-site for a while, so my plan was to deal with it when I needed to.

"I don't want to put you in a position where you have to lie to your boss, but if you could just not mention it, I would really appreciate it."

"Sure thing. Not like I haven't seen my fair share of trouble."

"Thanks, Rich. I'll leave you to your conference call."

"What call?"

"The one you were supposed to be on four minutes ago."

I sat down feeling quite smug. I now had a clear path to working both jobs and no one needed to know.

It may sound stupid, but one of my main responsibilities on the jobsite was supposed to be traffic control into the trailer. There was a steady stream of people coming in and out throughout the day and Rich had a total inability to tell anyone no when they asked for something. That meant he spent every day running in circles instead of staying focused on the task at hand. Most people meant well and were busy themselves, just looking for answers. Vance, the architect, however, was just a disrespectful dick who thought his time was more valuable than anyone else's. He was particularly bad at interrupting other people's meetings over trivial matters that could have been answered via text or e-mail. Upon starting my job here, he had been pointed out to me as someone I needed to manage so that the rest of my team could get their jobs done. Thus far, I had failed abysmally. He was from somewhere in Eastern Europe, and I don't know whether we had some cultural differences going on or he was simply a chauvinist pig, but my existence didn't appear to be relevant to him.

He chose that moment to walk into the trailer, so I jumped up and tried to engage with him.

"Good morning, Vance. Rich's on a call, but I can—"

He didn't even make eye contact. He waved his hand dismissively at me and kept walking straight back into Rich's office. I sighed and sat back down.

I guess you can't win them all. . . .

He was in there long enough that Rich must have cut his call short to deal with him, which is exactly what I was supposed to be preventing. Vance didn't look at me on the way out, but stopped at the coffeemaker and filled up his cup, emptying the pot.

"Might want to make more coffee, Janine," he said on his way out the door without even looking up at me.

I considered chucking my stapler at him, but instead got up and obediently made more coffee like a good Janine would do.

7. SISSY HARRY

"Scarlett! Ready for day two? You're almost totally booked tonight—you've got three sessions with regulars. I've tried to give you enough of a break between them that someone can talk you through what to expect."

"Thanks, Lady Caterina! Will it be Raven training me again?"

"When she can. But she's pretty booked tonight too, so it might need to be someone else. The other tops tonight are Erin, Serena, and Dom. You've met Erin. Serena's in a session right now. . . . Dom!"

I had seen on the Web site that there was one male Dominant who worked here, but hadn't paid his page any attention. From the back emerged a tall, handsome, blond man who reminded me a lot of Eric Northman from *True Blood*. He oozed old-world charm and sex appeal. He extended his hand and smiled, revealing canines that were just a little long. They made his smile look delightfully wolfish. I looked down at his hand, and for a moment forgot what I was supposed to do. I half expected him to kiss my knuckles, but thankfully that thought merely came from my romance-novel fantasy imagination, and he simply shook my hand. I say thankfully because I may have done something embarrassing like fan myself . . . or try to have sex with him in the lobby otherwise.

"I'm Dominic. Pleased to meet you."

Well, fuck me. Of course he has a German accent. He looks like Hitler's fucking wet dream.

"I'm Scarlett."

"Dom, once Scarlett's dressed, can you give her a heads-up on Sissy Harry please?"

"No problem. I'll be smoking a cig on the patio. Come and find me when you're ready. Sissy Harry likes frills and lace if you have anything really girly."

Moments later, I stood clad in a pink mini tutu and a white corset with white fishnets—feeling a little bit like a six-year-old going to her first ballet recital. I felt marginally better when Dom looked me over and gave a thumbs-up with a wink.

I find smoking a major turnoff, but of course when he did it, it was attractive. I sat across from him at the patio table.

"So what's Sissy Harry into?"

"He's a funny one. His is technically more a session for a Switch or a Domme, but he'll only play with subs because he wants everything gentle and girly. I suspect he also likes the more genuine reactions he gets out of newer girls."

Dominic spoke with his hands and I had the distinct impression those elegant fingers knew how to please a woman.

Focus, dumb-ass.

"He's been coming in multiple times a week for the last decade and does basically the same scene every time. It'll be more spontaneous if I don't tell you every detail . . . but he's into role-play that you're a schoolgirl and he's a family friend who's been asked to prep you for your first day at the academy. You ask him about boys and tell him you've never seen a penis. He'll show you his and then he wants to be humiliated for it. Whine about how you thought it would be bigger and ask him over and over again whether he can make it bigger and thicker. If in doubt, just keep saying those two words. Then he wants you to force him to wear drag and do some more humiliation. And then he'll probably wank off."

"That's allowed, right?"

"Our unspoken rule is that you can't participate in it . . . but that you're not going to try to stop him. Don't worry," he said with a grin, "he cleans up after himself."

"Okay . . . that all I need to know?"

"Should be. He's harmless and knows what he wants, so he'll guide you through it.

"Heads up that Margaret is probably sleeping in the loft part of that room at the moment, so if you hear her up there, don't worry. We'll have to introduce you later. She's the house slave who lives here and does cleaning and odd jobs in exchange."

"Good to know. Thanks for all the help!"

"No problem. Break a leg!"

I met Sissy Harry in the lobby and was stunned by how utterly normal he looked after hearing a summary of his perversions.

He was a middle-aged, average-height, average-build, average-looking white dude with dark hair and brown eyes. He was wearing Dockers and a polo shirt. I wouldn't have given him a second glance in line at the bank. He carried a duffel bag, which I suspected wasn't allowed, so I looked to Caterina for guidance.

"We don't normally let clients bring their own equipment or toys, but Harry is a longtime trusted client, so we make exceptions for him."

He seemed pleased by this description. I also noted that she just called him Harry instead of Sissy Harry, and was careful to do the same.

I started the scene when we got upstairs to the den while Harry laid out the contents of his bag. I glanced at my watch. We had an hour to play. At least this time I would know how much time was left.

"Come here, Scarlett. Let Uncle Harry get a good look at you."

I stood before him with my hands on my hips.

"Now, young Scarlett, your parents have asked me to make sure you're ready for your first day at the academy. Is that what you're going to wear?"

"Yes, Uncle Harry," I said in a stupid girly voice and added an impromptu twirl.

"An outfit like that is going to make the boys drool over you."

"But, Uncle Harry, I don't know anything about boys!" I said, wringing my hands and biting my lip in a spectacular display of over-acting.

"Well, have you ever seen a penis?"

It was such a jump that I had to swallow a laugh. No wonder the dialogue in porn is so terrible.

"No, Uncle Harry. Never!"

He hesitated, so I took a guess at what was next and said, "Do you think you could show me yours? Just so I know what they look like and the other girls don't laugh at me!"

"Well . . . maybe. We wouldn't want the other girls to laugh at you. But what if your nanny comes in and sees?"

"She won't! She's in Costa Rica visiting her daughter."

Costa Rica? No idea where that came from . . .

With no further ado, Uncle Sissy Harry dropped trou . . . and his monster dick sprung forth.

My stunned reaction was probably spot-on for young Scarlett, who was seeing her first penis.

"But why is it so small?" I choked out. "I thought it would be bigger and thicker!"

Any bigger and that thing would be a baseball bat. I would run the other way if it came at me in a dark alley.

He brandished it in one hand and said in a timid voice, "You want it to be bigger . . . and . . . and thicker? Uncle Harry can try."

"Maybe it would look bigger and thicker if you put those panties on?" I pointed to the frilly pink pair he had laid out.

He wiggled into them, but let his penis hang obscenely out of one side.

"Now the bra and stockings, Uncle Harry!"

He took off his shirt and did as he was told, attaching his stockings like a pro to an elaborate garter belt that I would have struggled with.

"Does it look bigger and thicker now, young Scarlett?"

He posed from different angles.

"Hmmm . . . maybe a little. I bet it would look even bigger and thicker if you put those heels on."

He sat down and put on a pair of massive, strappy red pumps. I had the absurd thought that they clashed horribly with his pink panties and orange bra. As though that was what was out of place in this scene.

He strutted back and forth across the room. For all the practice he must have had in those shoes, he still walked with all the grace of a newborn giraffe, his legs moving at odds with the rest of his body.

Next, we did a full application of garish makeup while he pretended to protest. I had never put makeup on a stranger or a man before and found the experience oddly intimate. Touching another person's face and sitting much closer than you ever would in normal circumstances is odd. I was also hyperaware of the fact that his dick was still flopping around, now slightly less big and thick since our attentions were focused elsewhere. Totally normal working conditions, right?

It turned out I did not have a future as a makeup artist, but he wanted it over the top, so my heavy-handed, smudged blue eye shadow was spot-on.

He tottered back to a standing position from the makeup stool and strutted about posing, now in full drag.

"But, Uncle Harry," I whined, "you said this would make it bigger and thicker! But it isn't! I want it to be bigger and thicker!" I stomped my foot angrily.

He grabbed a towel from the bathroom, placed it on the leather table, and lay down on it.

"Scarlett, tell me about the first time you saw a penis. Did it get bigger and thicker?"

I was caught off guard. I guess I was now me Scarlett and not young Scarlett. The first time I saw a penis? I was drawing a blank. Living in France as a kid, things were pretty liberal. I don't remember there being a defining penis revelation for me, but Harry was looking at me so intensely through his clumpy eyelashes that I felt obligated to make something up.

"I was in a tree house with a boy named Seth, and he agreed to show it to me."

"Yeah? He showed you his penis? Just like this?"

Harry had started "wanking off" as Dominic had put it. Now I felt the same pressure as I had in the past when asked to participate in phone sex. Talking dirty to someone who is beating it had always seemed really uncomfortable, but I figured I just needed to get on with it.

"How old were you Scarlett? Was it scary?"

"I must have been thirteen. I was so surprised. I didn't know it would look like that. And then he started rubbing it. Yeah, just like that. And when he rubbed it, it got bigger and thicker. Much bigger and thicker than yours!"

"Bigger and thicker?"

"So much bigger and thicker."

I'll spare you. It went on like this for a while with my story getting more elaborate and Harry's movements more frantic. My elaborately made-up story would backfire in later sessions with Sissy Harry. I underestimated his ability to remember what I was describing since he was a little distracted. He remembered it word for word. He must have gone home and obsessed over my tale of Seth in the tree house.

"Oh, young Scarlett! Tell me how disappointing it is! Tell me you want it to be bigger and thicker!"

He rolled his legs up and flipped them behind his head in a move of remarkable flexibility. His back was still on the table and his knees nearly rested on either side of his head. He kept wanking, though, so I kept talking.

"It's so little, Uncle Harry. You told me I would see a real penis! Make it bigger and thicker!"

With that last repetition, he aimed his dick down and came in his own mouth. He had swallowed it before I had even accepted what I had seen. I was shocked, but not appalled. I felt like I had just seen a really fucking crazy magic trick.

"Thanks, Scarlett. That was fantastic."

He got up and I was a little worried he was going to try to give me a sweaty hug with penis fingers and semen mouth, but he didn't.

We had about ten minutes left, so I quietly sanitized the room while he cleaned up his face and got changed back into average-dude clothes. He went into the bathroom, and I let Caterina know we were finished a little early and were headed down. As we parted ways at the bottom of the stairs, he gave me a hug and slipped a $60 tip into my hand. Then he looked at me earnestly and said in such a vulnerable voice, "It isn't really small, is it?"

"No, Harry," I said with a reassuring smile. "Biggest and thickest I've seen in a while."

And by a while, I mean ever. Or at least so far.

I suspected if I stayed in this line of work long I was going to see a startling array of male genitalia.

Caterina buzzed me back in the front door and I was greeted by Erin, Raven, and Dominic all standing around the desk with shit-eating grins on their faces.

"He came in his own fucking mouth!" I blurted, and they dissolved into laughter.

"I wanted to warn you, but he loves getting a reaction out of new girls! Did I not tell you he cleans up after himself?"

Erin had the most contagious laugh, and she was smiling at me like I was one of them now. I felt giddy.

We kept breaking into new fits of laughter as I straightened my outfit in the dressing room and met the three of them at the patio table for my next client debrief.

Raven offered me a cigarette and shrugged when I declined. The other two each took one.

Apparently all the cool kids smoke.

"You have Yoshi next. He should be pretty tame after last session's fireworks," said Raven.

"I hate that fucker," muttered Erin.

"C'mon, he's not that bad. A little gross and grabby sometimes, but manageable," argued Raven.

"Okay, time-out," I stopped her, still trying to process the last hour.

"What the fuck is Sissy Harry's deal? I guess I was expecting more textbook stuff: guy was spanked as a kid, now he likes to be spanked. But how the hell do you explain where that shit came from?"

"Why do I like licking assholes?" asked Raven, and I started to laugh before noticing she was totally serious.

"It's rarely that simple, Scarlett. The brain is much more interesting than that. You'll learn to go with it. Around here, we see less cause and effect, and more patterns . . . guys who are into the same shit, weird as it may be. Stinky feet, repeated specific phrases, toenails painted a certain color. It makes sense after a while." Raven shrugged and took another drag.

"Do you think he actually shows his dick to little girls?" I asked, voicing something that had been nagging at me for most of his session.

"I don't," said Dom. "I think he comes here to play out a specific fantasy, but I don't see any reason to assume he's taking it any further than that in the real world. I'm into fantasies of nonconsent . . . rape fantasies," he said with a wicked smile, "but you don't need to worry about me accosting unsuspecting women in public. I like my partners to enjoy themselves. Fantasies for most people are just that. Even if they act them out, it's with consenting participants."

Would I ever be that comfortable talking about my own fantasies? I had to admit the image of Dom bending me over had a certain appeal, but it was the knowing look in Erin's eyes that made my stomach flip. The idea of being the one with the power was tantalizing.

"A little like anal sex, then?" I asked. "The idea of it is super hot, but I really don't want a dick in my ass."

"Speak for yourself!" laughed Raven.

"Scarlett, your client is here," came Caterina's voice from the intercom.

Raven stood up with me.

"Don't stress about Yoshi. He only plays for thirty minutes. He'll say a bunch of stupid shit and probably try to touch you inappropriately, but just hold your ground and you'll be fine."

8. YOSHI

I went to meet Yoshi feeling amped up with a combination of nerves and excitement. Each of these new clients had the potential to be a fascinating adventure into the human mind. Some of them might even let me explore my own.

Yoshi was waiting in the interview room, so I went in and introduced myself. He was an Asian guy who was roughly my height and was wearing blue scrubs. He didn't seem lecherous if I overlooked his roving eyes, but we weren't exactly in church so a little leering didn't seem out of place. We set boundaries for touching: he couldn't touch my breasts, but some light spanking was okay. I didn't really have a good sense of what he actually wanted to spend half an hour doing, so I didn't know what to ask or set as a limit. He kept just saying he wanted to get to know me . . . which sounded ominous.

Yoshi took care of payment at the desk and asked for a five-minute warning before the session was over. We went back to a small room next to the dressing room called the cell. It had a kind of futuristic, metallic prison feel to it, but there was a cushioned table on top of a cage, so I jumped up and sat on it. The room was close enough to the desk that there was no need to formally start the session. The desk Mistress could hear when we started. I didn't know it at the time, but anyone in the dressing room could also easily hear what went on in the cell.

He came and stood next to me and took my hand. I wanted to pull it away, but decided it was harmless enough. I could put up with it for now.

"*Oh*, Scar-rett . . . you been killing me. I been looking at your picture online. How many time you think I get off to your picture today already?"

"Ummm . . . twice?"

"Eight time. Eight time I get off to your pictures, Scar-rett!"

"Oh. Well isn't that charming?"

How the fuck is one supposed to respond to that?

I pulled my hand away and tried to keep the disgust off my face.

He then undressed. Before exposing his genitals, he made me play the numbers game again.

"How big? How big you think it is, Scar-rett?" he asked with an eyebrow wiggle.

I sarcastically responded, "Two inches," without hesitating.

I don't like playing the guessing game with cock size. You never win no matter how you answer, so I just don't try. Put me in a silly situation and I'm going to mock you.

"Oh, Scar-rett! You so bad! You so bad! Why you so bad to me, baby? You know I just want to please you, lick you pussy all up, make you squirt, Scar-rett."

Lovely.

I didn't feel even slightly guilty when he revealed his three-inch cock. I'm sure it wasn't often that he managed to exceed expectations with it.

Yoshi sniffed the air like a dog on the hunt. He started at my feet, carefully smelling each toe.

"Next time, Scar-rett, you let your feet get real stinky. I like to smell you, baby."

Sure thing, baby.

I began to get really uncomfortable when he hovered inches over my lady bits, still sniffing.

"Oh yeah, baby. I smell your pussy juices. I want to lick them all up. Why you not let me lick your pussy, baby? I lick it so good for you."

"Because that's against the rules, Yoshi."

I didn't want to be there anymore. He wasn't doing anything that bad and wasn't saying anything worse than I hear from strangers walking down the street on an average day. But it felt dirty. On some level it seemed better that at least I was getting paid, but on another I think that may have actually made it worse.

He sniffed his way up to my chest and hovered over my bra.

"Oh, Scar-rett . . . one day you let me suckle your titties. They look so *nice*."

"Thank you," I said, faking a smile.

He lifted my arms above my head and smelled deeply over each armpit.

"Scar-rett, you showered today, you bad girl."

With no warning, he licked my armpit, so I squirmed away.

"No deodorant next time. It ruin your scent. I like you natural. I want to taste you, Scar-rett."

I had only been using my new name for a matter of days, but suddenly I was sick of hearing it.

He had me roll over, and he flipped my skirt up to reveal my ass. He lightly spanked for a few minutes, but what he was mostly doing would better be described as playing with my ass, making it jiggle. He kept trying to hold the cheeks apart and smell my lady bits through my thong, repeating his filthy comments. When I thought I couldn't take any more, there was a knock at the door and Raven said, "Excuse me . . . this is your five-minute warning."

"Thank you!" I replied with a little more enthusiasm than was really necessary.

The significance of the five-minute warning became apparent when Yoshi stepped back and started to jack off. I was oddly struck by how sweaty his upper lip got. He was leering at me and panting intensely.

"Oh, baby. Oh, yeah, baby."

He was going to ejaculate on the floor like a fucking animal if I didn't do something. I grabbed a hand towel from a stack in the corner and tossed it to him with seconds to spare.

He wiped himself off, dropped the towel on the floor, put his pants back on, tossed $100 on the table, and left without saying another word.

Raven came in and pointed out latex gloves and sanitizer in a metal cabinet in the corner.

"Cleaning equipment over here, Scar-rett."

I smiled and gave her an exaggerated shudder. I put the gloves on and wiped down the table and anything I thought he may have touched. I grabbed the offending towel and Raven directed me to the laundry room, where I dropped it straight into the wash and threw my gloves in the trash.

"We'll wash everything with bleach at the end of the shift," Raven explained.

I kind of wished someone would wash me with bleach as well, though it was brain bleach I needed more than anything. One more session to go. Surely it couldn't be any worse than that.

9. HARVEY

I didn't mention how repulsive I had found my session with Yoshi to Dominic or Raven, who were waiting to talk me through my next session in the dressing room.

"Harvey is going to be your challenging one today," she said as she dipped a boot into what looked like a bucket of mud and started rubbing it in.

"He's into heavy spanking, but he'll know that you're new and that he's supposed to keep it light. Have you ever been spanked before?" Dom asked as though it was the most natural thing in the world to be asking me. Because it was him, I wanted to play it cool, lie, and give him a saucy answer, but I refrained and told the truth.

"Not really. Maybe the occasional slap on the ass during doggie."

"This might be kind of intense for you then, but don't be afraid to speak up. Harvey will push you as far as you'll let him go, so it's up to you to stop it from going too far or you'll get hurt. Tell him if he's getting too hard and keep in mind that you can always use the safe word if you need him to stop."

"What's the safe word?"

"It's *mercy*. Shit, that should've been one of the first things we told you. Sorry about that," he said, giving my shoulders an apologetic rub. From anyone else, I would've taken this as flirting, but he just seemed like a man who was used to touching half-naked women all day and it was part of how he interacted.

"Mercy. Got it. Sorry . . . Raven, why are you doing that to your shoes?"

"I'm about to play with Alex. He's into anything gross. I get my boots filthy and make him lick them clean."

"Right. And he likes that?"

"Loves it." She laughed.

"Focus on Harvey, Scarlett . . . your time for having men groveling at your boots will come."

I wasn't going to deny that it sounded bizarrely appealing.

"So communicate if he's getting too heavy and use the safe word if necessary?"

"And make sure he doesn't sneak any heavy implements into the room with you. It's his favorite move and he'll hit you with something way too heavy when you aren't looking or at the very end when there isn't much you can do about it. He's a great regular to have if you can manage him . . . but he's really fucked some girls up who didn't keep him in line."

"Sounds like a party."

When he arrived, Dom and Raven were both in sessions, so Erin went into the interview with me. She let me do all the talking, but when I said I was a light player, she interrupted, looked at Harvey without the slightest hint of a smile, and said, "Light, Harvey," and held eye contact with him for long enough that it was awkward.

I was grateful when she came back to the implement wall with us and picked out the correct tools for the job since I didn't have a clue. Into our bag went two slightly bendable leather black paddles and a red riding crop. It was disconcerting looking over all of the implements and choosing what someone was going to hit you with. I said this to Erin and she smirked.

"Keep that feeling in mind when you start topping. Most girls think the scene starts when you get to the room, but if you do it right, this is where it really begins. There is power to be had from choosing for them and making them quiver in anticipation or from making them choose the method of their beating."

When Harvey went back up to the desk to pay, she put her hand around my waist, and against my ear said, "Don't let the fucker get the better of you. You've got a spine. Use it."

Erin made me so uncomfortable. When she said things like that I wanted to tell her to fuck off, but she also seemed genuinely concerned, which made my heart race. She had been a bitch to me when I started, but another part of me wanted to admit it was kind of funny. Muddling all of this was her irresistibly appealing androgynous charm. I could still feel where her hand had rested on my hip. And I suspected she knew it.

Harvey looked a lot like my high school principal, which was a little weird since that's exactly what he liked to role-play. He was just under six feet tall and always wore a perfectly ironed white dress shirt and slacks. He had salt-and-pepper hair and wore glasses. He was one of the few clients I can think of who always remained fully clothed and never pleasured himself during a session. In fact, he never said anything overtly sexual or indicated anything was arousing in all of the times I would come to play with him. I think he got off on the head-fuck.

His session was essentially that he was a headmaster whom you had been sent to because you were caught smoking cigarettes at school. He had a mint that he used as his cigarette prop. It was one of the plastic-wrapped ones that you get when you leave a restaurant. I'm fairly sure he had been using the same mint for years. He had me hide the "cigarette" somewhere on my person, then come to his "office" for my punishment.

He always played in the school room, which was an adorable space on the ground floor decorated with all of the features of a classroom: student desks, the teacher's desk at the front, a chalkboard, bookshelves with textbooks, the works.

I entered the classroom in the classic naughty-schoolgirl uniform he had asked me to change into. I had hidden the mint in the waistband of the skirt.

He stood and faced me, leaning on the teacher's desk as I entered.

"Scarlett, you've been caught smoking in the bathroom again. In fact, Mr. Smith tells me that you've hidden a cigarette somewhere on you. Is that true?"

"No, Sir!" I whined. "I'm a good girl, Sir. I would never do anything like that. Mr. Smith just hates me!"

"Scarlett, you're already going to be punished for smoking. Now I'm going to have to add punishments for lying and being disrespectful about a teacher. I'm going to need to search you for this cigarette you've hidden."

He slowly slid his hands up and down my body.

"What's this, Scarlett . . . not wearing a bra, either? We'll need to punish you for that as well. What a naughty girl you are."

"No, Sir! Please, I just forgot today! Please, I won't do it again!"

He had to have found the mint already, but he kept searching for much longer than was necessary before pulling it out and exclaiming, "And how do you explain this, young lady?"

"Ummm . . . Sir . . . I don't know. That's not mine. Mr. Smith must've hidden it there."

He chuckled and shook his head.

"You're in enough trouble as it is. Best stop there. Now you're going to take all of your punishment. We'll go in groups of ten strokes until I think you've been properly punished. You are to count each stroke aloud and thank me after each set of ten. Now bend over the desk and spread your legs. First, we'll start with your warm-up . . . no need to count. Let's just see if we can get that bottom to turn scarlet."

I was anticipating the blow, but still jumped when his bare hand struck my left cheek and his other hand struck immediately on the other side. He alternated sides and moved in circles, finding a rhythm and covering every square inch of my ass and upper thighs with slaps that stung slightly but didn't really hurt. He occasionally threw in a

heavier one that stung deeper. I would come to learn the difference between stingy and thuddy pain. Most people love one and
hate the other. As a Domme, it pays to read which your sub prefers.
Sometimes it makes sense to give them the kind of pain they crave . . .
but other times it's better to give them exactly the kind of pain they
hate because it breaks them down mentally. It all depends what kind
of scene you are doing and what kind of sub you are playing with.

When Harvey had finished my warm-up, I could feel the heat coming off my ass. I couldn't say I had enjoyed it, but it really hadn't been
bad so far either.

He sat in a chair and said, "Now, Scarlett, you're going to take
the next part of your punishment over my knee."

He had me lie over his lap so that I was pressed against him and
trapped in his control. It was a position that gave him all of the power.
I had seen girls list "over-the-knee spanking" on their profiles as
something they enjoyed on the Dungeon Web site and hadn't really
understood what made it special. I was beginning to figure it out.
It was simultaneously humiliating and terribly intimate.

He struck his first blow and I clenched my teeth together, knowing that the tone had shifted. This was no longer a warm-up. He struck
two more times before pausing to say, "You aren't counting. We'll
need to start your punishment over."

"One."

I could feel him chuckling.

"Good girl."

"Two."

By the time we got to ten I was sweating. I thought we were maybe
entering a territory that went beyond light.

He paused and rubbed my backside before saying, "Naughty Scarlett, you were supposed to thank me after each group of ten."

Goddamn it.

"Thank you, Sir!"

"Too late. We'll do that set again."

"One . . ."

This time I didn't forget to thank him. It didn't escape me that I as much as I hated this, I was getting a firsthand education into the mentality of a sub and what impact the Dom's actions can have.

We did two more sets of ten with his bare hands and then he had me bend over the desk again while he got the paddles out. My ass was already tender, so the blows of the paddle stung like a mother-fucker. I didn't know yet that guys like Harvey like it when their subs react. Some of them want the girl to enjoy it and make noises of plea-sure. Others want to hear squeals and grunts of pain to make them feel powerful. Some enjoy tears. I wasn't experienced enough to fake any of those noises. Stoicism was my instinctive reaction, so I didn't make a peep. I would've gone home with far fewer bruises that day if I had swallowed my pride and squealed a few times. In Harvey's eyes, if I wasn't making noise, he could keep going heavier. And in my eyes, the heavier he went, the quieter it made sense for me to be. The advice I had been given in the dressing room to keep him in line didn't even cross my mind. I was simply focused on getting through the rest of the session without crying.

He must have been able to tell from my changing tone of voice as I counted each set that I was somewhere between agony and tears, but was resolutely refusing to break.

He looked at his watch and said, "This is going to be our last set, young lady. I want you to beg me for ten more good ones."

I could think of few things I wanted less, but I complied.

"Please, Sir. Please give me ten more good ones and then I'll be a good girl."

"Okay, Scarlett. Since you've been so good, no need to count these ones. I'll make them quick. You just need to give me a hug to thank me at the end."

I bent over the desk and braced myself. He leaned his forearm on my back to hold me down, which he hadn't done up to that point. He had taken a heavy ruler that was on the wall as decoration down without me seeing. He struck me viciously ten times with it in quick succession with as much force as he could muster and my mind ex-ploded with the pain. I struggled to stand and stop him after the first few blows, but he was ready and held me down for the rest. I felt tears stinging my eyes, but it was over with so quickly that I was still shaking when he let me up and embraced me in a hug. It was then I saw the ruler in his hand, but I was too close to tears to yell at him without breaking down.

"Excuse me . . . your session is over," came the voice from the intercom.

"You were such a good girl. You did so well. You're not a light player at all, Scarlett." He smiled as though this was a wonderful compliment.

I couldn't look him in the eye as he tipped me and left. As he walked out the door he said, "I'll see you next week."

I hastily cleaned up the room, taking deep breaths to compose myself before seeing anyone else. My ass and thighs were on fire, but I tried not to think about it.

I didn't look at Caterina as I passed the desk and walked to the dressing room. Dominic was on the couch having his hands massaged by two pretty subs I hadn't met yet.

He looked up at me expectantly and I thought he was going to ask me how it went, but whatever he saw on my face made him stand up and hug me instead. I didn't think I wanted human contact but was surprised at how good it felt.

"Turn around," he said in a tone that brooked no argument.

He lifted my skirt without asking, and I heard both subs gasp in horror.

"Scarlett, what the fuck? He's actually broken the skin in a few places and you're bleeding. That's not allowed even in a heavy session!"

He turned me back around and forced me to look him in the eye.

"Erin said you only took light leather paddles in there. How did he manage this?"

"Mostly with the paddles and his hands."

He wasn't letting that slide.

"Mostly . . . ?"

"He took a ruler off the wall at the end."

"That son of a bitch! I don't know why he hasn't been banned. Are you okay?"

"Yeah, fine."

"You need to get some arnica on that," said one of the unknown subs.

I knew she was just trying to help, but I was pissed off and hurting and confused about where to direct it.

"I'm fine," I repeated and walked outside to the patio to take a deep breath.

I avoided talking to anyone else, took the $400 I had made that night from Caterina, and started driving home. Amelia looked appalled when I showed her my ass, but thankfully didn't criticize. She just sighed, shook her head, and gave me a hug. We curled up on the couch and watched episodes of *Sex and the City* until I was able to fall asleep. Sometimes your best friend knows just what you need.

Finding reasons to avoid Wes in the following days was not as simple. The fact that I was already too tangled in my lies to see him made me doubt myself even more. I felt like I was already in too deep to be able to tell him. There was a line somewhere that I had willfully ignored as I skipped across it, and now that I was on the other side, I didn't see how I was going to resolve the situation. Part of me wanted to just break up with him and be done with it. That would be the easiest way out, but I just couldn't bring myself to do it. He was my best friend and I cared about him. I wasn't ready to lose him.

Probably should have thought about that before lying to him about becoming a sex worker, ass-hat.

10. DOGGIE DAN

I gave serious thought to never going back to the Dungeon and pretending none of it had ever happened, but not for long. I had been overwhelmed by my second day, but I was determined to stick with it. I had seen some of the less appealing sides of being a sex worker. No matter how you try to glamorize it, you are charging someone money for the use of your body and mind for their sexual gratification. Like all human interaction, this occurred on a spectrum and sometimes it was impossible to tell where a particular client would fall. I could leave a session empowered or utterly humiliated, disgusted or agonizingly turned on. Whether a client was attractive or not was not a good indicator of how it would go.

I was sure there was a light at the end of the tunnel, something worthwhile to be had from persevering. I needed to learn from my experiences subbing so that I could be a better Domme. If there was one thing that had become crystal clear in my mind, it was that I wanted the power I saw in those other women. I wanted to know what it felt like to be the one in control and they all swore that the best way to learn how was through the path I was on, so I resolved to stick with it.

My next shift at the Dungeon was on Sunday, which was nice because I didn't have to make the dramatic switch from one job to the other. I got there a little early for my evening shift and walked in to pandemonium. Five subs and Switches were engaged in an intense round of Twister in the middle of the lobby. Raven, with the spinner in hand, was directing the action. The players were in an assortment of lingerie, costumes, and leather, and were contorted into an impressive mess of positions. When I walked in and set my bag down, Raven waved and held the spinner in front of me. I flicked the black arrow, and before it had even stopped, Raven called out, "Left hand: boob!"

The girls shrieked with laughter and scrambled to find a way to get a hand on someone else's boob.

"Don't blame me," Raven said, giggling, "Scarlett is the perv who spun it. We were having good clean fun until she arrived!"

I had been nervous about coming back in but found myself laughing along and bantering with the group within seconds.

Erin had a long feather on a stick and was using it to tickle the helpless contenders. An exotic-looking blond Domme who I deduced was called Storm was blowing gently into one of the sub's ears to distract her. Erin eventually used her feather to get one of the girls to cave, squealing as she took the whole pile down with her.

"Mistress Erin wins!" shouted Raven. The rules of Twister were apparently a little different around here.

Back in the dressing room, I didn't bother trying to hide the marks on my derriere, which was now an exciting assortment of black and blue with some yellow, green, and purple thrown in for good measure.

"Damn, girl! Someone got you good . . ." said Storm by way of introduction. I caught a hint of a Russian accent that made her icy blond coloring that much more exotic. She had gorgeous high cheekbones and frigid blue eyes that belied her warm smile. She looked like Dominatrix Barbie.

"Harvey," I replied, and she shrugged and nodded as though this sounded about right.

"Here," she said, tossing what looked like a toothpaste tube to me. "Put some arnica on that and it'll help the bruising."

It was the second time I had heard this mystery substance mentioned. Later research would tell me that it was a homeopathic remedy derived from a plant in the sunflower family used to treat inflammation, pain, and bruises. Experience would teach me that it really worked.

I rubbed the cream onto my ridiculous-looking backside and glanced up to see Erin watching me from the doorway. There was nothing sexual about what I was doing, but her watching me made it feel like there was. I finished and let it dry before getting dressed.

Raven appeared in the doorway with Erin and said, "We thought after your last shift that you might want to take it easy today and shadow us in some of our Domme sessions since that's what you want to learn. Erin has Doggie Dan in a little while and then I have Alex again tonight if you want to see what the muddy boots were all about. I think you only have one session booked right now, so we should be able to work around it."

My session was booked with a guy named Ethan, but that was as much as I knew about him. The desk Mistress for the night, a bottle blonde named Viv who was past her prime but still dressed like she was twenty-two, looked at me like I was an idiot wasting her time when I pressed her about what the session would be. I left it alone, but I sincerely hoped he wasn't into spanking.

I had to wait until Erin had completed her interview with Doggie Dan and gone upstairs to their room before joining them. We could shadow a session for the final fifteen minutes. If the extra girl was a client request, it was known as a cameo and came with special pricing. In this case, I was simply there to learn. Viv called back to the dressing room and let me know I could go upstairs.

Erin opened the door with a wink and ushered me inside.

I had been sitting downstairs trying to imagine what someone named Doggie Dan would look like and my imagination was completely wrong. He must have been pushing eighty and had the gray hair and wrinkled skin to show for it. Lots of wrinkled skin. I had never seen a man that old completely naked in person before. He was on all fours with a collar on and Erin was holding the end of his leash.

His tongue was out and he was panting excitedly. When I closed the door behind me, he started to wag his "tail," which meant he wriggled his body in excitement. I couldn't repress a laugh, but played it off as mutual excitement to see him.

"What a cute puppy you have, Mistress Erin!"

She patted him on the head, so I followed her lead and tickled behind his ears. He thumped his left leg in excitement and continued to pant.

"Doggie, why don't we show Scarlett the tricks you've been learning today?"

I sat on a throne on the far side of the room and watched in genuine amazement as Erin took him through an elaborate sequence of tricks. He was fucking agile for his age! She didn't have to correct or reprimand him even once. She just kept repeating, "Who's a good boy? You are such a good dog!"

It was clear that Erin was in absolute control and that he was not only fine with this, but seemed at ease and confident in the knowledge that his Mistress would direct him. At the end of their show, Erin allowed him to kneel behind her and sniff her backside the same way you would expect a dog to. This had an unexpected effect on Dan's man parts: from the wrinkles emerged an obvious erection.

Erin came and joined me on the arm of the throne and Dan lay down on a towel on the floor in front of us. As he manually stimulated himself, Erin told him all about the walks she was going to take him on and the dogs they were going to meet at the park.

"When you get to the park, there will be lots of owners there too. I'm going to walk you over to each of them and make you sniff their butts."

He moaned loudly at this.

"And then with all of us watching, you're going to have to squat down and shit right there in the dirt!"

This was apparently too much. Dan's back arched off the towel and he came in a stream across his stomach. He didn't stop after that, though, he kept arching as though he was having a seizure and shouting grunts for about thirty seconds. I was genuinely concerned that he was having some kind of medical emergency, but Erin didn't react so I just watched it play out.

He caught his breath and gave me a smile that made him look twenty years younger. "Sorry if that alarmed you. Tantric orgasms. You just have to ride out the wave."

I helped Erin to clean up after he left.

"He's an easy session. You have a great ass, so I'm sure when you start Switching he'll want to play with you. Raven can fart on command and that's his favorite, if you fart while he's sniffing your butt. I have no such skills, but we make it work."

I would come to learn that a large percentage of our clients fell into Dan's age category and it made me curious to know their stories. Had they gone their whole lives adhering to a vanilla lifestyle, all the while burying their kinks? At what point did they wake up and decide that they were going to go to a dungeon and live out their fantasies? Did they just reach a certain age when they stopped giving a fuck? Was it after their wives had died? Or was it awareness of their own mortality that drove them to experiment, lest they go to the grave never having really lived out their deepest desires? It would take awhile before I had the confidence and relationships with my clients to be able to ask, and their answers were as wonderfully varied as their fantasies.

Doggie Dan, it turned out, was in his eighties. His marriage to his late wife, Margery, was a classic love story that revolved around World War II. He had been a pilot in the war, and they had eloped in secret before he went off to fight in the South Pacific. He told wild stories of the war and of the tumultuous years that followed. They were only teenagers when they wed, but their love had endured until Margery died in a car accident when she was in her sixties. Dan said he knew he would never love again, but that exploring his fetish had given him a new reason to live. He had been coming to the Dungeon at least once a week like clockwork for over a decade. I always stood in awe of him for having the balls to start exploring at that age. He simply explained that he had lost everything when Margery passed, so he had nothing to lose by doing whatever the hell he wanted in the years he had left. It struck me as sad that in spite of how madly in love they were, he had never felt able to tell her his secret fantasies.

Every time I played with Dan, I was reminded that just because people get older doesn't necessarily mean their libido withers and dies. It is perhaps uncomfortable to think of our grandparents in that light, but I think we unfairly cast older men as "dirty old men" simply for not having the decency to lose all interest in sex because they've passed an arbitrary age. And the idea of a promiscuous older woman is unacceptable to most people. Women of a certain age shouldn't even think about sex lest they be judged. I for one plan to be a dirty old lady.

11. ETHAN

I was apprehensive going into the interview room with my new client Ethan but I insisted I could manage it on my own. I loved that the other girls were being supportive, but I didn't want to get used to using them as a crutch. I needed to figure things out for myself.

I was pleasantly surprised when I met Ethan and discovered that he was a moderately attractive guy of roughly my own age. He seemed like a kid next to all of the other clients I had seen come and go so far. He was fairly tall but carried a little extra weight that I think added to the overall sense that he was just a baby. Oddly, my first impression of him was that he was into magic tricks, which proved to be amusing when he told me that his session revolved around hypnosis.

"I want to try to hypnotize you and then control you. We can try the methods of hypnosis that I've learned, but then I want to role-play that I have a magic necklace that gives me total control over you. I can make you do whatever I want."

"Sounds fun," I told him with a flirty smile. "What kind of stuff would you have me do? Just so we're clear on boundaries before we get into the scene. I'd hate to have to break the moment."

"Mostly silly stuff. Hop on one foot, jog in place, bark like a dog. Then once I've proven that I can make you do whatever I want, maybe get a little more risqué . . . make you touch yourself, stuff like that.

Whatever you'd be comfortable with. You could decide what it means."
He suddenly looked shy.

"I can decide? I thought you were going to have control of me?"
I teased.

"You know what I mean." He smiled. "I'll leave those directions
vague enough that you can do whatever you're comfortable with and
we don't have to do more than that."

"I can make that work. Anything else?"

"That's it really."

"Great. This is going to be fun! Why don't you take care of payment at the desk and I'll grab us a bag for the room?"

I didn't bother taking any toys with us. It sounded like we were
going to mostly be using our imaginations. I grabbed some spare towels and a gaudy fake jewel necklace from the cross-dresser props closet.

We played in the lounge, which reminded me of a Victorian sitting room. It was decorated tastefully with lush furniture and lots of
lace.

Ethan had me lie on a chaise longue, the reason he had selected
the room, and took me through some breathing and relaxation exercises. His voice was soothing and I found myself relaxed and hanging on his every word. He had me sit in peaceful silence for several
moments that felt much longer because of the quiet. Just when I started
to get twitchy, he got serious and talked me through the hypnosis he
was attempting. I really wasn't sure whether he wanted me to fake it
or not since I was pretty positive I would not be entirely under his
control. I wished I had asked him in the interview. But if he wanted
me to fake it, then spelling out that I was going to fake it in the interview might have killed it for him because he would've known I was
faking it . . . so maybe it was better we didn't discuss it. I decided I
would fake it, but not overdo it. I thought seeming pliable and out of
it, but not zombie-hypnotized would be a good middle ground.

He snapped his fingers and I remained motionless.

"Scarlett, I want you to tap your nose with your finger."

Slowly, as though I was doing it in my sleep, I raised my right hand
and touched my nose.

I could hear the smile in his voice as he said, "Good. Now stick your tongue out and pant like a dog."

I complied and kept going until he said, "Stop panting and close your mouth."

I did exactly as he said, which meant my tongue was still sticking out. He laughed and said, "Put your tongue back in your mouth.

"Now that I have you under my control, I want you to open your eyes, take this necklace from me, and put it on."

I did as he said, and as I dropped the necklace around my shoulders, I gave an exaggerated jolt and kept my eyes unfocused and staring into the distance.

"*Good.* Very good. You're under my spell now."

From the way he said it, I pictured him stroking a wizard beard.

The rest of our session wasn't particularly eventful. Under his "control," I barked like a dog, jogged in place, spun in circles, and then essentially gave him a lap dance. I kept it pretty tame, but he seemed to enjoy the session overall. What was remarkable about it is that I found I had enjoyed it too. It was mostly silly and harmless, but it was his fantasy and I was able to let him live it in a way that he had never been able to before. There was an adrenaline rush that came with that knowledge that sent me back from my scene giddy and feeling much better about working at the Dungeon.

When I walked back through the lobby, there were three younger guys huddled together in front of the desk, stealing surreptitious glances at the photos on the wall. One of them was holding a pizza, and Lady Caterina seemed to be ignoring them. I found Raven dumping a bag full of women's clothing into the washing machine and asked her what the deal was.

"Ha! Delivery guys. One of them must have told their buddies about what they saw when they came in here, so this time three of them showed up to take a look. Cat lets them get away with it, but the first time they pull that shit when Viv is at the desk, they're going to feel the wrath!"

12. ALEX

"Alex is the perfect training tool because he's so extreme," explained Raven when she came out to bring me into the room with him. Alex was the youngest of thirteen in a strict Mormon family. He was still part of the church, but had accepted the fact that he needed a release for his thoughts or he was never going to be able to play the part his community expected of him. His mother had run a fastidiously clean household. I suppose with thirteen children, it would have to fall under one extreme or the other. He wasn't sure if it was related to how manic she had been about cleanliness, but Alex was turned on by anything and everything disgusting, along with corporal punishment. He came to the Dungeon, got his fix of gross, and went back to living a quiet existence as a good Mormon. He evidently played in multiple-hour increments, so Raven had been in the session already for about an hour and a half and was letting me shadow for the last half hour.

"He's a masochist and loves all the classic implements and forms of pain: spanking, flogging, caning . . . you name it! He loves CBT—"

"Cognitive behavioral therapy?"

"Cock and ball torture."

"Holy shit."

"Yeah, he's into some heavy, heavy stuff. But the other side of his sessions is that he's turned on by being made to do things that are disgusting. Like the nastiest thing you can think of—within the rules of the Dungeon—and he'll be excited. Spit on the floor and make him lick it up. Lick your boots clean. If you can come up with something none of us have ever thought of before, then you, my dear, are both a monster and a genius!"

"Challenge accepted!"

She opened the door to the cave and it took my eyes a moment to adjust to the darkness. This room would become one of my favorites. Everything about it was pleasingly dark and menacing. It looked like a satanic cult had decorated it. Standing in the center, all of the surroundings were black and red, the colors of secrets and sex.

Alex was naked and on his knees facing the door with a blindfold on, our sacrificial victim. His head jerked in acknowledgment of our presence in the room, but beyond that he remained motionless, hands folded neatly in his lap. Raven gestured for me to stand directly behind him while she paced circles around him, the clicking of her heels on the floor echoing in the silence.

"You're a spoiled slave, Alex. I've brought a gorgeous new Mistress to play with you. I've told her how well-behaved you are, so you better not let me down."

"I won't, Goddess. Thank you, Goddess!"

His voice was soft and wavered slightly. It could have been excitement or nerves.

"Get on all fours, slave. You don't get to see your new Mistress until you've proven you're worthy of her."

Raven smirked and stood next to me, inclining her head toward his genitals in invitation. I looked back at her with confusion, unclear about what she wanted me to do. She grinned. And kicked his dangling balls with considerable force. He groaned and arched his back, but quickly returned to his original posture, presenting the family jewels for more punishment.

Was I actually going to do this?

I had been taught my whole life that you didn't mess with a man's junk. It was unforgivable territory.

Fuck it.

I gave him what I thought was a pretty good kick, barely over-coming the urge to apologize immediately afterward. He hardly flinched, so Raven rolled her eyes and raised an eyebrow at me in chal-lenge.

I tried again and managed a much harder blow. Alex's groan was thrilling. Raven stepped back and gestured with her hand toward him as though to say, he's all yours. Instead of one kick at a time, I got my balance and kicked him over and over this time, not giving him a chance to rest in between. His groans turned to shouts, but he continued to present himself like a good slave.

When I paused he panted, "Mmmm, thank you, Mistress."

I had just kicked a guy in the balls. Fucking hard. And he had thanked me for it.

"Good boy, slave."

Raven lifted his blindfold and we made eye contact for the first time. It was short lived. Raven kicked him in the balls again and said, "That's enough, greedy slave. Get those eyes back on the floor!"

She dragged him by the collar over to what looked like a large black torture table and had him bend over. Upon the table, she had spread out a daunting assortment of implements.

"I thought we could let you experiment a bit since Alex is just a worthless little shit and it really doesn't matter if you fuck up and maim him. In fact, he might please me more if you maimed him. Maybe we'll move left to right . . . we'll start with a good sturdy paddle, then the riding crop, a nice whippy cane, and then if we have time we'll move to electro-play.

"He's already warmed up, so you can jump right in. With the pad-dle, you mostly want to smack him on the fleshy bits of the backside, staying below the peak so you don't hit organs or tailbone. There's a sort of looseness to the wrist that'll let you get the best strokes. Just start playing with it. Like I said, he's worthless, so it doesn't really matter."

I could already see him tensing and knew what effect her words must be having.

I struck him across the ass cheek with the paddle and it made a satisfying *thwack*. I kept smacking, experimenting with softer and heavier blows, learning what angle to hold it at to make different kinds of contact. I found myself naturally bracing his left leg with my own left, and I draped my left arm across his back like I was going to hold him down, but there was no need since he was staying perfectly still. Touching him let me be more in tune with his reactions as I learned to inflict pain, but it also gave me more precision when it came to my blows. I found this even more when I switched to the crop since it has such a small leather surface to flick against the skin, but its long, bendy wand let me crack it with force once I mastered the wrist movement involved. I was glad Raven had established ahead of time that I couldn't really make a mistake because I missed my intended target a few times and managed to hit him partially with the handle and not just the leather head at the end. Each time I did this, Raven would simply laugh and say, "Get him good! Hit him with whatever part of that crop you want!"

I flinched each time I made a mistake, so she could tell that correcting me wasn't going to serve any purpose. It was confidence I needed, and she had enough to share.

When I picked up the rattan cane, she stepped in to coach, swinging it up and down through the air rapidly, making a terrifying whooshing sound. I would come to learn that the unique noises that each implement made were a part of the overall sensory experience. Hearing the cane will send shivers through the sub who is about to be struck with it. Cracking a whip just a few inches shy of the skin can have a devastating effect.

"Favorite punishment of British schoolboys!" she said with glee. "The tricky part to the cane is that it wraps even though it seems like it's rigid and shouldn't. Wrapping is when a flexible or soft implement wraps around the side of your sub when you strike your blow. I suppose you could do it on purpose, but it's something you need to be aware of because by the time it wraps around to that skin, it has flicked with more force than your original intended blow and can break the sensitive skin on the sides or hurt bones like the hips or ribs. The flogger is the easiest to see it with, but the cane can do serious damage in the hands of an amateur who isn't aware of it wrapping. Hear that, slave? Scarlett is going to pop her cane cherry on your ass."

The cane is a long, thin stick, but she explained that it's the tip you want to focus on and aim with to avoid wrapping and to strike a straight blow. She demonstrated a few times and I didn't really understand its power. Alex had barely flinched at anything so far, but each time the cane made contact, he expelled a breath with a hiss. I had just attempted a few erratic blows when the intercom crackled to life and Viv told us we had five minutes remaining.

"We'll continue this later. Lie on your back, slave, and get ready to lick the soles of Scarlett's boots clean as a thank-you."

He practically jumped onto the floor and stuck his tongue out eagerly. I placed my boot over his face and he started licking it with abandon.

"As you lick that, you dirty boy, keep in mind that Scarlett walked through a big pile of shit outside before she came in here, so you're getting dog shit all over your tongue. Was it even dog shit, Scarlett? Or did you have another slave shit and now he's licking human feces off the bottom of your shoe?"

"I had a big, fat slave drop a big one outside and then I ground it into the soles of my shoes. Make sure you get all the little bits that are trapped in the cracks. All of that shit belongs on your tongue, you disgusting little worm."

I was a little surprised to hear what was coming out of my mouth, but Alex was writhing in excitement now and rubbing his dick frantically. Instinct took over and I carefully adjusted my standing foot to be over his balls and pressed down with my toes. This meant I had to lean my other shoe on his face slightly to balance better, but the added pressure excited him more. I crushed his balls even harder and it was too much excitement for him. I didn't think quickly enough and part of his splooge landed on my boot. At first I was appalled, but the answer seemed obvious. I held it over his mouth and said, "You've defiled my boot, slave. Now lick it clean."

After the session had ended and the door closed behind Alex,

Raven tossed me gloves and sanitizer and said, "You, darling, are a natural."

She sent me home with a mountain of implements and the homework assignment that I would try them out during my next few days off. I just didn't know who I was going to try them on. I couldn't exactly see Amelia volunteering. Maybe if I let her try them on me first . . .

13. VANCE

I was still smiling to myself about my crazy shift at the Dungeon by the time I got to work at the jobsite the next morning. I had a secret. Which made me wonder . . . who else here had one too? People who I would have overlooked entirely in the past were suddenly making me look again. So far, the biggest freaks had been the totally normal-looking ones—the quiet, unassuming guys who looked as likely to be coaching a T-ball team as begging me to kick them in the balls.

I wasn't working at the Dungeon again for a few days, so I was looking forward to getting home and experimenting with the toys that Raven had let me borrow. It was all I could do to stay focused on the job I was at and remind myself not to look up BDSM techniques on my work computer.

That afternoon we had a meeting off-site in our downtown L.A. office, and I was in a good enough mood that I had volunteered to drive our on-site team of four up there. I was amused knowing that the implements were tucked safely in my trunk.

If they only knew, I thought smugly.

Rich rode shotgun and directed me to the parking entrance of the Bank of America building in downtown. I stopped at the attendant and rolled the window down.

"We're here for a meeting at our firm. We normally work at the jobsite, so I don't have a parking permit."

"No problem, ma'am. I can give you a visitor pass. I just need to take a look in your trunk."

"In my trunk?" I asked, trying to keep the panic out of my voice. *What kind of parking attendant searches my fucking trunk? This isn't happening.*

I couldn't see a way out, so I popped the trunk and stared straight ahead as he walked behind the car. He was back there for a few minutes and I was just imagining what he was seeing. Had this been covered in his training? What to do if a small white female attempts to enter with a medieval torture chamber in her trunk . . . ? Surely he wouldn't call me out for it?

I played it cool as he came back to the window, but he made no attempt to hide his grin. He handed me a visitor hang tag, looked me straight in the eye, and said, "You have a nice day, ma'am."

"Will do," I replied with a cocked eyebrow and a smile and drove into the parking structure, purposefully avoiding Rich's quizzical glance.

Back at the jobsite the next morning, I was full of initiative after an evening spent beating our living room couch senseless, much to Amelia's amusement. I was a bad bitch just like Raven or any of those other girls. Surely I could handle a little traffic control in a job trailer.

I got to the site early and did some furniture rearranging. I didn't even try to be subtle. I moved my entire reception-sized desk directly in front of the door where before it had been tucked on the other side of the trailer. Walking straight past me was no longer an option. If someone came in the door and took more than two steps, they were going to stub their toes on my desk.

I was pleased when Rich came in and did just that. He was close enough that I could smell the booze leaking from his pores. He glanced from where my desk had been and back, as though slowly processing why he had run into something, and said, "Doing a little feng shui?"

"Just trying something new. Figure if they have to talk to me then they can't just blow by me into your office."

"Whatever works," he said and took his coffee and doughnuts back to his desk.

For our first few visitors, my tactic was effective, but I knew that Vance would be the real test. I didn't have to wait long.

He came into the office a few hours later and I barely hid my glee at his confusion.

"Something I can help you with, Vance?" I asked sweetly when he came to an abrupt halt in front of me.

"Nope. Just here to talk to Rich."

I started to tell him that Rich was in a meeting in his office, but he was already making his way around my desk and had his hand on the door handle before I had the first few syllables out.

Motherfucker.

I sighed and wondered absently what Raven would do. And quickly decided that likely wasn't a road I wanted to go down as it would probably involve the police being called. I would need to find a better way to assert myself.

14. BUSTED WES

One Saturday about a month in to my double life, I was sitting on the bed anxiously waiting for Wes to get dressed and leave so that I could get my Dungeon bag out of the closet and get to work. I didn't dare pull it out while he was there in case he asked questions. As far as he was concerned, I didn't have anything to do that day, so I tried to sit calmly on the bed and feign nonchalance when I was desperate to chuck his pants at him and push him out the door.

When he finally left, I watched his car pull onto the street and then scrambled to get ready. I grabbed my bag from its hiding place and was just about to leave when I heard a buzzing from the bed. My phone was in my hand, so I realized Wes must've left his. I picked it up and glanced at the screen.

Melissa: *You left the used condom on the floor last night and my dog ate it. . . .*

My stomach dropped. I held the phone with a trembling hand and tried to think of an innocent explanation for that sentence, but came up blank. It couldn't have been much more damning. He was supposedly having beers with the guys the night before. Melissa was his ex-girlfriend.

Well, fuck me. Didn't see that one coming.

My first impulse was to call him and rip him to shreds, but since

I was holding his phone, that wasn't an option. I took a deep breath and acknowledged that he was hardly the only guilty party in this relationship. Somehow, this seemed worse, though, more personal. I didn't feel anything for my clients. Did that make it okay? Not really, I admitted reluctantly. It was an absurd situation. I was hiding from him that I was moonlighting as a Dominatrix, but was seething angry that he had slept with someone else. It made me feel inadequate and insecure in a way that I had never felt before—deeply betrayed. It hadn't crossed my mind that he was unsatisfied with our sex life and felt the urge to cheat. I was stunned both at my arrogance and naivety.

My thumb hovered over the unlock screen. When you see your partner unlock their phone hundreds of times, it's hard not to become familiar with the combination. I didn't ever want to be the jealous girlfriend who snooped, but I felt compelled to find out exactly what I was dealing with. I sighed and entered the code, opening the conversation with Melissa. I scrolled up quite a bit, took a deep breath, and started to read. The more little colored messages paraded across the screen, the less my reality made sense. I thought I knew just about everything there was to know about this man after a year together, but I didn't at all. Turns out, my polite, vanilla boyfriend was a super freak. From one conversation, it was apparent that he liked to be peed on, kicked in the balls, and fantasized about being crushed by fat chicks.

I was perplexed. Why hadn't he told me any of this? For the same reason I hadn't told him what I had been up to, I supposed: fear of rejection and judgment.

Everything in our relationship seemed fine, and I suppose fine is exactly what it was. We had fun together and we encouraged each other, but if I was brutally honest with myself, we kept things superficial. There were clearly barriers up between us that I had never considered before. Not only had I not told him about the Dungeon, but I had never talked to him about my family struggles in the past. If our relationship was this superficial, was it worth saving in the face of such betrayal on both sides?

I picked up my work bag and headed out to my car. I was so distracted that I barely noticed I had arrived at the Dungeon. I got dressed and plopped down on a chair next to the reception desk, hoping Lady Caterina would have some wisdom to share. She had seen some shit.

"My boyfriend is cheating on me. And he's kinky and didn't tell me. And I haven't told him I'm working here. Or that I'm kinky too."

Her forehead creased as her eyebrows shot higher and higher.

"Well, that's quite a mess, isn't it? Do you want to break up with him?"

"I feel like I don't have a choice. He fucked some other chick and clearly neither of us thinks we can trust the other. But he's my best friend and I'm not ready for the relationship to be over. I hate this."

"If you think the relationship is going to end, what do you have to lose by experimenting with something a little different? Why don't you confess to what you've been up to, tell him you know what he's been doing, and lay it all on the table? Try a poly, honest relationship and see what happens."

I sat back and considered what she was saying. Could I be in a relationship in which I shared my partner with other women? I apparently already am, I scoffed. Would it feel different if I gave him permission? If I was there to see it? I was surprised to discover that I wasn't fundamentally opposed to the idea. Giving him permission to be with other women in some capacity would probably be just fine with him, but would he be okay with me continuing to see clients? What about when I wanted to be with other people? And then there was the giant elephant in the room: How do you take a vanilla relationship and turn it kinky?

Only one way to find out.

I was waiting at Wes's place when he got home from his lecture. I opened a bottle of wine and told him to have a seat in the living room.

"I have your phone."

"Oh, awesome, I thought I had lost it!"

"I read some of your messages. I know about Melissa."

I tried to keep the reproach from my voice. He started to stutter

and looked scared. I imagined that he was trying to remember exactly what they had texted about and how much I knew. I couldn't
resist letting him suffer for just a second before cutting him off.

"It's okay. I'm not angry. Or I was, but I've thought about it and
calmed down. I don't have any room to talk because I've been keeping secrets too. I haven't been sleeping with someone else, but I've
been working as a Dominatrix at a dungeon for about a month
and I didn't know how to tell you or if you would be okay with it, so
I hid it from you."

I almost laughed as I watched the disbelief, confusion, and shock
work their way across his face. I handed him a glass of wine. I knew
he was about to start asking questions, but I needed to get the rest of
the speech I had been rehearsing out before I lost my nerve.

"So we're both liars. And we're both into some freakier shit than
we've been willing to admit to each other. Here's my proposition: We
start with a clean slate and, going forward, we're completely honest
with each other. On top of that, I think we should try being in an
open relationship. I think we need to talk about exactly what that
means, but I'm willing to give it a try if you are."

He was.

Wes found it thrilling that his girlfriend was secretly a Dominatrix
and he didn't know it. He didn't seem at all bothered about me playing
with clients, and was positively ecstatic at the prospect of me bringing
some of my new friends home to play with us. I pulled up the Web site,
and we drank our wine and looked through the pictures and profiles
of my coworkers. When he initially commented on how attractive
Raven was, I felt the automatic flare of the green dragon of jealousy
stir within me, but it was just that—a trained response. When I really
examined my feelings, I found I wasn't jealous at all. In fact, I agreed
with him. It was a revelation to realize that just because he found
someone else attractive didn't mean he found me any less so. It isn't a
zero-sum game. I would come to learn that in most cases, particularly
for men, attraction to a new woman is a passing whim that generally
fades once they have experienced her or get to know her better. The
emotional connection between us was unshaken by these guest stars.

15. SLAVE WES

A decision had been made. I was in a polyamorous, kinky relationship. Now I just had to figure out what that really meant.

We had preliminarily agreed that our main rule would simply be no sex with other people. In other words, his penis wouldn't enter any foreign vaginas and I wouldn't have any foreign penises in mine. We would keep something sacred to our relationship. We would later need to clarify that my big black cock was exempt from that rule and could fuck whomever I pleased, but we were novices and didn't know where the road would take us yet. Our other rules were absolute honesty and no judgment. I needed a week to plan, but the following weekend, we had decided we would play together as Mistress and slave for the first time.

I had spent the week nervously gathering advice from the girls at work in the hopes that I could channel their badassery and blow Wes's mind right out of the gates. Once we had opened up to each other, I came to learn that he was into a plethora of fetishes. It rounded out to basically CBT, smothering, and anything disgusting: stinky feet in his face, golden showers, sweaty armpits, dirty socks, and farting in his face. He didn't know whether he liked any kind of corporal punishment, but was open to experimentation. It was a big jump to go from thinking he was uninterested in kink to imagining him doing any of those things. Next, I would make the jump to doing them to him. I supposed I had to start somewhere.

On the agreed-upon day, he was supposed to arrive at 5 p.m. From the moment he walked in the door we would be Mistress and slave so that we didn't need to try to flip from "normal" to BDSM. I worked at the Dungeon in the morning, but convinced Caterina to let me leave a little early so that I could be ready. All of the girls knew that today was my big day and wished me luck, calling out last-minute suggestions as I ran out the door.

Raven followed me out and left me with this parting advice: "Remember, you're the Mistress. That means you can't make a mistake. If you fuck something up, it was on purpose."

She slapped my ass encouragingly as I got in the car. Amelia was waiting when I got home to help me prep.

I was already dressed from work, but wanted to have my rope and implements laid out and candles lit before he got there. I wasn't sure the candles I had at home would work properly for wax play, so I needed to test them the way Raven had taught me.

"She said to let some melted wax pool and then pour it on my inner thigh to make sure it isn't too hot," I explained to Amelia while we waited for it to melt. "I don't know what it's made of and different waxes apparently burn at different temperatures."

"What kind did she say to use?" Amelia asked.

I smirked.

"She said the Jesus candles that you can buy at the drugstore work the best . . . the ones in glass jars with religious icons on the side. I think she just likes being sacrilegious. Claims to be attracted to Jesus."

"She's fucking nuts."

"That she is." I laughed.

"Okay, there's wax melted. Pour it on your thigh," she said, offering the candle to me.

"You do it! I'm scared!" I squeaked out, offering my bare thigh and looking away.

She dumped the melted wax, and it landed with a splat on my bare skin. It stung, but didn't burn too badly, so we decided these candles would do. Amelia went to work lighting the rest around the room while I laid out rope, clothespins, and a crop that I had borrowed from Storm.

I was zipping up my boots as the bedroom door opened unexpectedly and in waltzed Wes. He grinned and asked, "Ready for me?"

I looked down at my watch: 4:47. He was early and I wasn't ready. Amelia wasn't supposed to still be in the room when he got here, and I had intended to be in control of the situation from step one. Had he done this on purpose to piss me off, or was he just too excited to wait? He leaned in to kiss me in greeting and I knew I needed to do something quickly to get us back on track. I turned my head, offering him my cheek instead of my lips.

"You haven't earned a kiss yet, slave."

The words sounded awkwardly forced to me, but he smiled in surprise. He stepped back and looked me up and down, admiring the leather minidress I had borrowed from Raven. He had never seen me look like this and seemed to approve of the change. Amelia handed me a bottle of water and hurried out the door. She winked at me as she closed it behind her.

Here we go.

"Strip naked and kneel."

He obeyed and I circled him slowly, getting my thoughts in order as I quickly chugged the bottle of water. I chose a length of rope and took one of his wrists. I managed to make cuffs for both arms and bound them together. It wasn't pretty, but it would hold. I secured his wrists by pulling the rope over the open closet door, so he was now standing spread-eagle against it. His goofy look of expectation made me feel stupid and insecure. I could be in character with my clients because they were strangers, but it felt so unnatural with him.

I took the bag of wooden clothespins and held it up in front of him.

"I told you to arrive at five. You were thirteen minutes early, so you're getting thirteen clothespins as punishment."

"Okay." He laughed skeptically.

I couldn't handle his facial expressions anymore. I didn't have a blindfold, so I pulled a pillowcase over his head. He may have still been able to see through it a bit, but it was mostly for me anyway. Now he was anonymous and I could get into my element. I mused that it also meant he could imagine me as whomever he pleased. I think a healthy imagination in the bedroom is a good thing.

I clipped the first clothespin on to the tip of his right nipple and he flinched and tried to pull away.

"Ow, shit! Are you sure you're doing that right?"

I wasn't.

"Shut the fuck up," I said calmly and kept attaching clothespins to him in a line down both sides of his chest and upper thighs, pinching tiny bits of skin between them. He was squirming but otherwise cooperating. I had one left, and considered where to put it for a moment before clipping it to the very edge of one of his balls. He liked CBT, right?

His breath hissed between his teeth, but he didn't protest.

"Now it's time for your punishment," I said quietly, trailing the crop down the inside of one of his legs.

"What? I thought the clothespins were the punishment."

"They have to come off somehow. . . ."

I whacked the first one I had applied to his nipple with the tip of the crop, and it popped off and hit the floor at our feet.

"Jesus! Fuck!" he screamed.

I worked my way down the rows of pins. Sometimes I hit them off first try. Other times I missed the one I was aiming for and hit a different one, failing to knock either one off. A few times I missed altogether and smacked him with the crop. I just kept thinking of Raven's parting words.

If I fuck up, I did it on purpose.

I was glad he couldn't see me. I was wincing along with him. Where was Scarlett the sadist when I needed her?

When only the pin on his balls remained, he was panting and pulling his legs together to protect himself.

"Spread your legs," I commanded.

"Maybe we should just take that one off," he pleaded, and I found I was amused by his fear.

"Maybe . . ." I said, but I swung the crop down and smacked where the clothespin was attached to his testicle. I hit it squarely, but it didn't come off. I whacked it two more times, and got part of it off, but now it was just hanging at an awkward angle. Wes howled in indignant pain.

"I thought you liked CBT, slave?"

"I thought I did too! Just take it off! Take it off!"

I knew he meant for me to unclip it, but I couldn't resist hitting it one more time. The clip finally flew through the air. Wes relaxed a little, but was flexing his hands and shaking slightly. I glanced at his balls and saw I had drawn blood.

Bleeding nut sac wasn't part of the plan. Whoops. I'm the Mistress. I can't make a mistake, right?

I unhooked the rope from the door and led him to the bed. I retied his wrists above his head, pulled up the pillowcase, and kissed him deeply, grinding against him to get him aroused again.

"Ever tried hot wax, slave?" I asked playfully, wafting the flame along his side so he could feel the heat.

"Mmm, no, Mistress." I could hear the smile in his voice.

"Maybe you'll enjoy it more than your punishment," I teased, brushing against his boner.

I held the jar of the candle aloft and poured its contents over his stomach. His reaction was a little more dramatic than I had expected. He yelled like I had lit him on fire, and then kept yelling, struggling to get his hands free.

"Get it off! Get it off!"

I had poured it over his belly button without thinking, so it had pooled there and overflowed onto his stomach where it started to solidify. He was freaking out so much, I knew I must have either done something wrong or he was a giant pansy. I moved to untie him, but was laughing so hard I lost my balance and fell off the bed, landing in a giggling heap on the floor. Once I freed his hands, he frantically swatted at the still-hot wax, but it was caught in the hair that dusted his stomach, so now he was ripping hair out to get it free.

"Well, that didn't quite go as planned," I said, looking up at him sheepishly.

"No shit!" he replied, but I was relieved to see he was still smiling.

"I swear I tested it on my thigh first to make sure it wouldn't be too hot!"

"Yeah, but then how long did you have it burning before you used it on me?"

"About an hour," I admitted, beginning to realize my mistake. In the jar, it had continued to get hotter, and I had poured a much larger amount on him than I had on myself, so it didn't cool as quickly. I was embarrassed by how terrible I was at being his Mistress, but was determined to soldier on.

"We're not finished yet. Get in the tub," I instructed him. I expected him to argue, but he immediately lay down in the tub and grinned up at me.

I bolstered my confidence by telling myself that I couldn't accidentally maim him any more with a golden shower. I stripped naked while he waited in the tub. I wondered if I could have left my clothes on so that there wasn't this lull, but I didn't want to risk getting pee on leather, so it seemed safest to take everything off. I didn't really know how the mechanics of it were supposed to work. I had envisioned standing in the tub with him, but now that he was in there, I could see that there wouldn't be room for me to do it that way. Instead, I put a foot on the edge of each side of the tub and balanced over him. I felt extraordinarily exposed. He was looking directly up at my lady bits, gazing at them with intense anticipation as he stroked himself. I looked away from him and stared at the tiles intently, willing myself to start the flow he was so eagerly waiting for. I stood for agonizing moments, trying to block out the sound of him panting and wanking. When I finally started to feel the unmistakable pressure, I looked down triumphantly, and squatted a bit so I didn't splash over the side. As soon as I did, we made eye contact. That distracted me completely and I lost the flow without even managing to squeeze a drop out.

I could hear the insecurity in my own forced laughter as it echoed off the tiles. I looked up, took deep breaths, pictured running water, and tried to forget that my boyfriend was underneath me masturbating. Nothing was working. I was now desperate to go, but couldn't seem to get it out. My legs were starting to shake from balancing, and I felt stupid and totally defeated.

He gazed up at me adoringly and asked, "What's the matter, Mistress?"

I fucking suck at this. I can't make it work. I don't know if I can make the switch and be your Mistress.

I silenced the doubts before they came tumbling out of my mouth. The despair was turning to frustration, which gave me an idea. I had been adhering strictly to my plan and nothing was going right.

Fuck the plan.

"Who the hell said something was the matter? Maybe I'm just teasing you because you don't deserve a golden shower yet. In fact, who gave you permission speak?"

I sat down on one side of the tub and considered my next move. He was still stroking, and it pissed me off. It was a reminder that he was still waiting. I channeled it and punched him lightly in the balls. He moaned and sped up his pace. I punched him again, a little harder this time.

He groaned out, "Squeeze them . . ."

I bristled at the command, but went with it. I wrapped my hand around his sac and squeezed.

"Harder!"

I obliged, gripping with almost full strength.

"Harder!"

He was sweating and panting. He moaned deeply as I tightened my grip a little more. It felt like his balls were going to pop. He cried out and came hard all over my hand and arm.

"Holy hell, that was amazing!" he said, and collapsed back with a contented sigh.

"Wasn't sure whether you'd be okay with all of it," I replied. It was as much as I felt I could say. I wanted to apologize for all the things I had fucked up and look for reassurance that I had done okay for our first time, but that wasn't part of the game. I could decompress with the girls later. With him, I needed to be sure of myself.

"If you'd asked, I would've said no, but in the moment, it was one of the hottest things anyone has ever done."

"Well, I'm glad it worked out."

"Me too . . . I can't wait to see what you come up with next!"

It was then that I started to understand one of the difficulties in being a Dominant. You are expected to decide what is going to happen with your partner at all times. That part would be fine. The challenge is in balancing pleasing yourself and pleasing them since they won't necessarily line up perfectly. I was turned on by being in charge, but the idea of peeing on him didn't do anything for me. I was willing to do it because it excited him, though. In that way, Dominants are subservient to the pleasure of their submissives, since they will do things merely to please them. There are some hard-core Dommes out there who say the pleasure of the sub is irrelevant, but I think that's ridiculous. No one is going to play with you if you don't care what they're into. If you're in a loving relationship, then there has to be give and take.

I filled the girls in at our next shift at work, and they laughed and laughed at my mishaps. When things don't quite go to plan, at least it makes for a good story. When we had stopped mimicking Wes writhing in pain as molten wax filled his belly button, I sought more advice on how I could do better.

Storm had noticed something I overlooked, pointing out, "You should give him a safe word next time. Even if you're playing at home and it's no big deal, you should be in the habit of using a safe word."

"Make it something fun that can be your signature as a couple. Dom and his wife always use 'Sasquatch' when someone else plays with them," added Raven.

"I use 'Rasputin,'" said Storm, rolling her *r* beautifully. "That fucker had a fourteen-inch cock."

"How about 'Cuntosaurus Rex'?" Raven suggested.

"Perfect!" I agreed, suddenly remembering something I had been wondering since talking to Wes about what his fetishes were.

"Raven, Erin said you can fart on command for Doggie Dan. I can't believe I'm even saying this, but Wes evidently is into women farting in his face. How would one go about doing that?"

"Totally easy! You're gonna love it!" she exclaimed as though I had asked her for a cookie recipe. "I just fake it and they can never tell the difference."

"You fake farting? Like you make the sound with your mouth or just tell them you did it and they use their imagination?"

"I just queef and they can't tell where the air is coming from," she said matter-of-factly.

I sighed. "I'm just going to keep urban dictionary open when I'm around you from now on."

"Good lord, girl, how prim and proper was your childhood? A queef is a vagina fart. You use your stomach muscles to suck air into your vagina and then expel it, making it sound like your vagina is farting. They can't tell where the air is coming from, and you can make fantastically juicy noises that drive them wild."

She demonstrated, lifting herself up from the couch slightly and then making a cartoonish farting noise. She did it two more times before we were clutching our sides in laughter.

"Your turn!" she said.

I wiggled and squirmed, but couldn't find a combination of muscle movements that would achieve what she was describing. I wasn't the only one struggling. Two other subs had deeply thoughtful looks, and Storm was turning red in the face from the effort, but none of us were emitting any noises from our nether regions.

Storm stopped to catch her breath and squealed, "I'm scared I'm going to pee myself!"

"Lie down flat on your back! It makes it easier to get it the first time."

We continued our efforts lined up in a row on the floor.

"Now, lift your butt up a few inches, and try to push your stomach muscles up and out."

There was a sucking noise as I successfully drove air into the orifice. I started to laugh, which pushed the air back out and made it sound like I was ripping ass. I was inexplicably embarrassed, even though I had done exactly what I was trying to do. Perhaps I was a little more "prim and proper" than I liked to think.

"Nice! You've got it!" cheered Raven. "Now practice it a few more times upright so you can do it while sitting on his face."

Coach Raven turned us all into queefing pros before the afternoon was over. Then she made us all swear never to reveal that we were faking it. The power of the fantasy was in allowing them to believe it was real, and she wouldn't have us ruining it for anyone.

16. SLAVE TRAINER TOM

The weeks flew by and I found a strange rhythm at the Dungeon and the jobsite. I was actually finding my stride faster as a sex worker than a glorified secretary. I had more spanking sessions, another tickling client (who actually found my ticklish spots), and a bizarre variety of other fetishes. I had been a pony and a naughty housewife. Pretended to be dead. Danced around to ABBA in a purple raincoat. Purple was key. I discovered the wonderful world of food fetishes when I got to do a cake-sitting scene. Cake sitting needs little explanation. My client brought huge cakes with colorful frosting and had me collapse down onto them, squishing them with my behind. It was the kind of silly fun you aren't usually permitted to have as an adult. I got to pretend to punish and ultimately stab pool floaties, and my client moaned in delight as the air seeped out of them. I had one regular who brought note cards with him and nervously psyched himself up in the bathroom before each session, and sometimes during the scene when he forgot what was next. After my struggles with Wes, I had a better understanding of the pressures faced by those in charge. Even clients who were paying for the pleasure got nervous without a plan. It must have been intimidating for some of them to play with a professional submissive.

I had shadowed a few more Domme sessions, but had mostly been too busy with my own clients to spend much time in other people's sessions. I had clients who had tried to pay me absurd amounts of money to do a variety of things that broke the rules, always swearing that no one would ever know. Thankfully, I wasn't desperate enough for money to need to consider any of their offers. *I* would know, and there's the rub. I told Erin about one of the offers I had declined and she told me something that resonated with me the rest of the time I worked there: "You could spend that cash on the way home and it wouldn't mean anything. But what you do in that room will stick with you forever."

I played with Harvey twice a week like clockwork, and through a combination of my ass literally toughening up and learning to manage him better, his sessions really weren't that bad. We found an odd balance of him pushing me and me learning to maintain control— topping from the bottom is what it's often called. Once I mastered this skill, I got to be a bit of a sassy submissive. I didn't want to be doing it and felt like I had learned about as much as I could learn being on the receiving end of things. I craved power and control like I had never craved anything. My clients didn't have much more to teach me as a sub. But I still had more to learn than I could have imagined.

I was in the dressing room practicing knots (the finer points of rope bondage—or Shibari—had thus far eluded me and it was going to take a lot of practice before I would be comfortable doing more than a simple wrist bind on a client) when the intercom buzzed that there was a client here to interview subs and Switches. There were six of us available at the time, so we lined up outside the interview room and one at a time walked in and introduced ourselves. I found this to be one of the stranger rituals at the Dungeon. There was no way to know what a client was looking for, so my plan was usually to just walk in with confidence and poise and hope for the best. For the more desperate girls, this could be a frustrating process that led to misplaced jealousy being directed at the girl who was eventually chosen, even though she usually had no more control than they did.

It turned out that this client was a regular named Tom. I found it funny that no matter how creative our clients' sessions were, their fake names were always as generic as they came, especially compared to the exotic names that the girls assumed. We had so many Bobs, Eds, Harrys, and Toms that we always had to add a qualifier so we could distinguish between them: Tickle Ed or, in this case, Slave Trainer Tom. Just once, I wanted a client to walk in and tell me that his name was Thor.

For the last few months, Tom had been playing strictly with a Switch named Lydia. I hadn't interacted with her much, but that was partially because she struck me as catty and I tried my best to avoid drama. Lydia didn't realize that Tom was going to meet the rest of the girls instead of doing their regular session and she was visibly fuming as we made our way down the line of introductions. I found myself not wanting to be chosen simply so I wouldn't end up in the middle of it—which I would come to learn almost always meant you would be picked.

Tom narrowed the field down to Lydia, a sweet black sub named Minx, and me. It was all part of the game for him. I think he liked the idea of us squabbling over him, so he deliberately tried to pit us against one another. He lined us up in the interview room and paced back and forth, as if inspecting different cuts of meat.

"I came here tonight planning to play with Lydia, but I just have to play with Scarlett instead."

The look Lydia gave me on her way out made it clear that she placed the blame for this turn of events squarely on my shoulders.

The motivation behind a client picking a particular girl from the lineup tended to be as varied as their fetishes. It was simply one of the great mysteries of working at a dungeon. I later asked Tom why he had chosen me that night. He said it was because I was wearing a corset that was lacy and reminded him of something they might have worn in *The Tudors*. I had some guys tell me it was just because I was pretty. Others said it was because my eye contact was sharp and challenging. One client told me he had picked me because I was wearing a ponytail and he had never been caned by a girl with a ponytail.

Sometimes it was something they saw in the pictures we had online, or the color our toenails were painted that day. I think women have a hard time understanding the nuances of male attraction.

So Tom had picked me for my *Tudors*-like corset, and now he informed me that he was going to "train me." His fantasy was that he was the head slave trainer for the sultan in a faraway fantasy land. He wore a full costume of flowing robes and a massive turban when we played. It was always fun when a client owned their role-play enough to dress up and be theatrically over the top.

Tom was a bombastic man who claimed he was a big-shot writer for television shows. I was always torn about whether to believe him or not. He was so imaginative and detailed in his fantasies that it seemed plausible that his job involved creativity. He clearly had money to throw around, so it would make sense that he was successful at said job. The fact that he was so creative, though, made me think that he was inventing that profession as part of his fantasies as well and that he was really a repressed accountant or something. We saw a lot of repressed accountants.

That night, we played in the den. He started by dimming the lights and having me strip down to a thong. He then had me stand in the middle of the room perfectly still with my hands above my head while he inspected his new purchase. He walked slowly around me in circles, occasionally brushing his fingertips over the different parts he was inspecting.

"You are a truly remarkable specimen, and I don't say that very often," he commented. I doubted the part about his flattery being infrequent.

"Thank you, Sir," I said with a slight curtsy that he seemed to approve of.

"Really, though, Scarlett, your body is almost perfect. Supple, smooth, just enough definition."

A client earlier in the shift had remarked, "Damn, girl . . . you got man calves!" To each his own, I suppose.

He had been circling me for an uncomfortable amount of time, and I was getting bored, so I giggled this time instead of saying "thank you" to the compliment. I think he was relieved to have had a trigger. Someone who wants to train a slave has to have behavioral issues to correct or there is nothing to teach or punish for.

"I give you a fucking compliment, and you can't even say 'thank you'?" he demanded with over-the-top feigned anger.

"I'm sorry, Sir!"

"Sorry isn't good enough! You need to learn proper respect, you little slut! Get on your hands and knees!"

I did. He grabbed me by the hair and started to lead me around the room. We had established that a little hair pulling was fair game. He walked faster and faster back and forth, and I had to keep up by crawling at his speed or he yanked my hair. He did this for a while, but since I had no problems keeping up, he figured out that he would need to try something different. I could have deliberately slowed down, but I knew exactly how dirty that floor was and didn't really want to spend any more time there than was necessary.

He had me stand up and led me over to the suspension bar toward the back of the room. He tied each of my wrists to the rings on either end of the bar. He now had me stretched up almost on my tiptoes, and he added a blindfold for good measure. This was the first time I had been blindfolded at the Dungeon. It wasn't an unpleasant experience and let me relax and go to my own headspace without worrying about him seeing that I wasn't really paying attention.

"Now, my slave, I'm going to flog you for your insolence!"

Done well, being hit with a flogger feels like a deep tissue massage, but can be wickedly painful if applied for a long period of time. Erin had demonstrated for me what it should feel like, but I quickly learned that Tom was not anywhere near as skilled. Shortly after that, I stopped expecting any of my clients to live up to any of the girls that I worked with. With very rare exceptions, they couldn't hold a candle to the pro Dommes.

Tom's aim was terrible, and he was wrapping horrendously. He had chosen a thick, heavy flogger that no doubt looked impressive and brutal to him. Heavy floggers are indeed capable of heavier blows, but they are also just plain heavy, so they require a significant amount of arm strength from the person wielding them. Tom did not possess that kind of strength, so although he was wrapping, it wasn't doing me any harm because he couldn't throw it hard.

The giggles strike at the strangest times when you work in a dungeon, and this was one of those instances. The more he flogged me, the more ridiculous it all seemed, and the more I giggled. He thought I was deliberately egging him on, so he was trying to throw the flogger harder. The harder he tried, the worse his aim became and the less effective his blows were . . . which just made me giggle more.

When he gave up, untied me, and took the blindfold off, he was red in the face and sweating profusely. This sent me into paroxysms of laughter again. I still can't explain what was so funny, but I couldn't stop laughing.

"You think this is funny, slave?" he screamed, spit flying from his mouth.

"No, Sir," I managed to get out by holding my breath.

"Get on the bench, slave. I'm going to teach you to respect your Master."

Deep breath. Come on. Not funny. Not funny. Not funny.

I crawled up on the spanking horse and straddled it, bending over enticingly and shaking my ass a little. I had managed to stop laughing, but I was still feeling sassy enough to push his buttons.

That was the night I began to understand the way a SAM's mind works. A Smart-ass Masochist (SAM) is a term for one of the most difficult subs to manage as a Domme. Usually, they aren't submissive at all; rather they have mostly dominant tendencies, but are masochists who like to play with Dommes. This means that they will talk back, laugh in your face, and demand more at every turn. Many a Domme gets pissed and in their frustration, gives them exactly what they want. If you can break a SAM this way it can be great, but takes a great deal of energy and usually leaves you both exhausted and potentially unhappy. It is hard to turn back and save face once you have committed to this method, so you better be sure you're prepared to really go there. I would come to learn that like a petulant child, it's best not to give in to them. I would find something they genuinely didn't like: tickling, CBT, nipple torture, paper cuts . . . everyone had something, and do that instead until they were more manageable.

Unfortunately, Tom didn't realize the spiral he had stepped into. He had committed to breaking me, and given that he only had a soft leather paddle, a pair of floggers he couldn't manage, and his hands, he was going to have a tough time with that. I had taken anything that I didn't like or couldn't handle off the table during the interview. It was risky to push a client like this. He could not like it and not play with me again, but I was feeling flippant.

"Let's see whatcha got, then . . . Sir," I said, shaking my ass to make it an inviting target. He was excited by the challenge, and waved the paddle in front of my face menacingly.

"I'm going to make you regret that, slave. I'm going to give you ten good ones with the paddle and then ten good ones with my hand, and I want you to count."

How original.

He was pretty good with a paddle, and ten strokes had my ass stinging, but it wasn't anything I couldn't shake off. I wasn't finished being a smart-ass, though.

"That was good, slave. You took that very well. I think you are starting to learn. It will take many more months of training, but under my careful hand, we will mold you into one of the best slaves in the kingdom. Then I will give you to the sultan as a gift, and reap the rewards. Now ten good ones with my hand."

Smack. "One, Sir."

Smack. "One, Sir."

Smack. "One, Sir."

"Slave . . ." he said menacingly.

"Yes, Sir?" I asked innocently.

"I believe you are at four."

"Oh. I'm so sorry, Sir. I must have forgotten how to count properly."

"We will start back at one for your mistake. Now, ten good ones."

Smack. "One, Sir."

Smack. "One, Sir."

SMACK. "One, Sir."

He caved and started spanking me over and over again, harder and harder. I put my face down, buried it in the towel, and took in the new sensation. He continued spanking frantically for a while, muttering about training me properly for the sultan the whole time. His blows got lighter, and I could only assume that his hand was starting to sting. That idea made the giggles return for an encore.

"Are those tears, slave? Have you learned your lesson, then?"

I tried to keep my face buried to maintain the illusion that I was crying, but he got concerned and walked over to lift my chin. I tried to stop giggling. I really did. But I just couldn't manage it in time. He lifted my face expecting tears of contrition, and instead saw tears of laughter.

I expected never to play with Tom again after that first session, but we played together for months after that. He said he felt alive again playing with me, that I was a challenge the likes of which he hadn't had in some time. We developed a friendship of sorts and I gradually let him "train" me a little more each time we played. I liked him and he had put up with a ridiculous amount of sass from me, so I had no problem fulfilling his fantasy.

There was no doubt that as a sub, I was starting to have a bit of an attitude problem. I was aware of it and tried to keep it to a minimum in my sessions, but I also knew that it came from a place of excitement at the power growing within me. I had discovered a limitless well of confidence and seemed to be drunk from it.

It was in this state that I decided to take a riding crop to the jobsite with me as the solution to my little Vance problem. I waited until I saw him approaching the trailer through the window and laid the crop blatantly on the top of the desk in front of me. At first I thought he was going to miss it and keep walking, but he did a double take and stopped short.

He looked at it. Looked at me. Laughed awkwardly and said, "Why do you have that?"

I noted that he hadn't asked me what it was. I picked it up and ran my left hand down the length of it suggestively and slapped it across my palm when I reached the end.

"I have it in case I need to teach the next person who ignores me and interrupts my project manager some manners."

I let one side of my mouth curl up in a half smirk and arched one eyebrow expectantly.

"Was there something you needed help with, Vance?"

"I just need to talk to Rich. Could you check his calendar and let me know when he'll be available?"

"Please . . ."

"Please."

"Why don't I have him stop by your office in about an hour?"

"That would be great. Thank you."

"You're welcome. Have a great day!"

I never had a problem with Vance being rude again. In fact, even when he had a scheduled appointment, he made a point of stopping at my desk and politely asking how I was or how my day was going before continuing on. He always seemed to take a few seconds to glance around my desk, checking for the crop. Maybe he wasn't sure it had really been there. I could hardly believe I had done it either.

It was a full week before I was scheduled at the Dungeon again, and when I arrived the dressing room was filled with girls I had never seen before. It seemed crazy that so many new people could have started in a week. Maybe I just hadn't worked the same shifts as them. I was about to introduce myself when Lady Viv came bursting in and said, "I'm out of rooms. I need you girls to clear the dressing room so we can use it for a scene."

Everyone scrambled to grab the mess of stuff that was lying around and move it out to the patio. I had never seen the Dungeon this busy or frantic before. Erin walked outside, and I was relieved to finally see a familiar face.

I hugged her in greeting and asked, "What the hell is going on?"

"We've inherited a bunch of new clients and girls after what happened."

Clearly, I was missing something.

"Viv will chew our asses if she catches us talking about it. She banned everyone from gossiping," she said, pulling me into a corner by the Dumpster.

"The owner of the other dungeon by LAX was murdered by a house slave he tried to fire. The house slave came back with a gun, killed the owner and his dog, and burned the building down. The cops found him hiding in the bushes outside."

"Holy shit, that's terrible."

"It is. I never worked there, so I didn't know him, but most of the other girls did. For a few days it was really quiet while everyone absorbed what happened, but girls still gotta make money and guys still gotta get their fix, so life goes on. They're obviously closed now, so we inherited their clients and their girls. It's chaos."

There had always been rumors that the rules had been looser at the other dungeon, that the girls who worked there would do anything for extra cash. When some of our regulars naturally started sampling the new flavors, some of our girls muttered that they were doing extra favors to lure the regulars away. That settled quickly as we got to know one another, and acknowledged that we were all in this together. Extra girls meant extra options to get a shift covered, which was great since the holidays were just around the corner. The owner of the Dungeon had to send a few more Dungeon-wide e-mails out in the weeks that followed about silly shit. She felt the need to remind us to keep the cross-dresser closet and the costume closet separate. She banned us from using the electric toothbrush for tickling sessions because it was a health hazard since it couldn't be cleaned properly. We had to be reminded that nudity wasn't allowed in the lobby and smoking sessions had to happen in rooms that had an open door or window. Other than that things went back to normal. Or as normal as things get working in a dungeon.

I was rattled by what had happened. I hadn't known the owner who was killed or the man who had snapped, so I wasn't grieving.

The very fact that it had happened was what was keeping me up at night. I had been telling myself that I was safe in this world because everyone was rational even if they were into things that would be deemed irrational. Now I had to question the truth behind that belief. I started having recurring nightmares of clients following me home and hurting my friends and family. In the dark of night, I would snuggle closer to Wes and swear I was going to quit working at the Dungeon before something bad happened. But by the light of morning, the fears seemed silly. Was Sissy Harry really going to turn into a homicidal maniac? Could geriatric Doggie Dan hurt someone? I kept telling myself that everything would be fine until I started to believe it again.

17. DOMINIC

Dom and I had become close over the months and as an experienced Master, he could tell what was missing from my training, but he observed quietly for a while before stepping in.

I hadn't yet experienced anything close to sub space. Sub space is the euphoric state that a submissive sometimes enters as a response to extreme stimulus: generally pain, fear, ecstasy, or some combination of these, which forms an intense bond between the Dominant and the submissive. Subs who are in sub space are usually unfocused and unable to make good choices for themselves, so it requires a massive amount of trust between the two players. It has been described to me as being a better high than any drug can offer. At that point, I had heard the term thrown around, but assumed it was something like the adrenaline rush of an exciting session. Dom was about to show me the truth.

I was caught off guard when he approached me on the patio and asked, "Would you like to play with me for a bit in the cell? My first client just no-showed and it doesn't look like you have anyone for a few hours. Cat said if there are any walk-ins, she'll let us know."

"What did you have in mind?" I asked, playfully imitating his German accent.

Why is it so hot to picture him as a Nazi when it's so fucking wrong?

"I thought maybe we could just experiment and have fun with it. Maybe do some sensory deprivation and sensation play. You said you wanted to know what canes and whips felt like. Maybe some flogging. We can keep it as mellow as you want or I can push you a bit and let you see what it's like."

"Sounds great."

"Cool, I'll meet you in there. Just need to grab some stuff."

I waited for him in the cell wondering with more than a little excitement what I had just gotten myself into. He returned quickly and laid a giant fuzzy blanket and a pillow on the raised table.

"Hop up and lie down. I'll get you started with sensory deprivation while I go get the rest of the toys we need. Here's a blindfold and earplugs, but before you put them in, let me lay some ground rules. From here on out, you are to address me as *Sir*. We'll use the old-school traffic light safe-word system. If something is getting to be too much or you are uncomfortable with something I'm doing, use *yellow*. If you want me to stop something I'm doing, use *red*. I'll only use the implements we just talked about. Are you okay with some over-the-knee spanking?"

"Yes."

He raised his eyebrows.

"Yes, Sir."

"Good girl. And bondage?"

"I would love it if you tied me up, Sir."

"We should be clear then. Put those on so you can't see or hear. Lie down. Don't move until I come back."

I did as I was told and lay down on the blanket in silent darkness. The seconds ticked by and felt like minutes until I couldn't have even guessed how long I had been lying there. I had the fleeting thought that he had been called into a session or forgotten about me, but knew that wasn't the case. It was all part of the mind game. He knew perfectly well that I was lying there nervously anticipating his return, obsessing over what he was going to do. I kept convincing myself that I could hear muffled noises and tensed only for nothing to happen. I began to imagine that he was sitting across the room just watching and waiting. He had said not to move and I had to assume he meant it literally, so I had stayed perfectly still. Now the urge to move was warring with my suspicion that he was watching for exactly that.

Dominic had been born in East Berlin before the Wall fell. One of his most vivid childhood memories was the day it happened. I didn't know all of the specifics of what life had been like for him in Germany, but he made reference to poverty and oppression. The West, and specifically America, had represented a mythical place where you were free to express yourself. Once he got here, he discovered that it wasn't the government that held you back, as it had been in East Berlin, so much as the fear of judgment. Everyone was so worried about what everyone else thought of them that they were scared to take advantage of the freedoms that he had once only dreamed of. He was notorious for coaxing people out of their comfort zones in his gentle, but precise German accent.

I took deep breaths and tried to stay present in the moment, but that seemed to heighten my awareness. Or rather my awareness of my lack of awareness. Just as I started to contemplate peeking, another blanket was laid across me that covered me from my toes up to my chin. I jumped at suddenly being touched, but he didn't do anything further for several agonizing moments. Then he must have taken the blanket by the bottom and slowly started to slide it downward over my body. I was still wearing a bra and boy shorts, but with every inch he pulled it down, I felt naked . . . like he was gradually undressing me. By the time the blanket was gone again, it was like every nerve ending was firing on overdrive anticipating the next touch.

Want to heighten even the most straightforward, traditional sex? Deprive one partner of a few of their senses and suddenly a touch that you've felt a thousand times is charged with erotic anticipation.

Dom had put vampire gloves on, which had tiny sharp spikes covering the fingers and palm and soft leather that covered the top side of the hand. He slid the backs of both hands down my body, almost making me purr at finally being touched. Then he flipped to his palms and gently brushed the sharp edges up my thighs and across my ribs, eliciting a shiver. He kept this touching going in a continuous motion, leaving me guessing which sensation would come next and where. I was panting within moments, needing something but not sure what. He removed the gloves and followed the same lines with his bare hands, which felt like heaven. The man knew how to touch a woman. He traced a fingertip between my breasts, up and over my chin, and teased my bottom lip. I caught it between my teeth and sucked it into my mouth. He let me keep the gentle suction going, but pulled the earplugs from my ears and leaned over me, laughing sensuously.

"You're a bad girl, Scarlett. Breaking the rules of the Dungeon by making me penetrate you with my finger."

The way he said "penetrate" made me moan for more. I had gone from a professional in a learning environment to mindless hedonist in seconds.

"Stand up carefully and lock your hands on your wrists behind your back."

I still couldn't see and was a little off-balance, but did as I was told.

I heard what had to be rope hit the floor as he unwound a coil. I stood perfectly still as he pulled the rope over me and knotted it into an elaborate bind. I soon realized that in the hands of a Master like him, rope wasn't just about rendering someone powerless, but about the sensual experience of the fabric sliding across the skin, the feeling of slightly less control as each knot is tied into place. He pulled a length up between my legs and secured it through a knot that was resting between my breasts. As he pulled it tight, I could feel that he had knotted the rope precisely in the spot that it crossed my clit, so now there was pressure against it. If I moved even slightly, the knot rubbed over it, and I gasped at the shocking pleasure of it.

Once he had finished his bind, my wrists were secured behind my back and there was rope crisscrossing the rest of my body in what felt like an elaborate design. Not to mention his naughty knot that I was hyper aware of. He led me to the leather spanking horse by pulling the rope at the front and I straddled and bent over it, finding a rolled up towel to lay my head sideways on, resting my knees on the padded leather supports on the sides. Once I was in this prone position, it would have been almost impossible to get back up without his assistance, so I felt momentary panic. I reminded myself that it was Dom and I trusted him. I could always use the safe word.

He ran his fingertips up the back of my thighs and over my ass and then brought his palms down on each cheek with a loud smack. I jerked in surprise, but he didn't leave me time to anticipate the next blow. He gave me a good warm-up that covered the tops of my thighs and both cheeks. It stung when he hit me, but was quickly replaced by a glowing warmth in that entire area. There was a brief pause during which he must have picked up a cane.

For such an innocent-looking implement, the cane can knock the breath out of you in a flash. There is a sting as it smacks the skin, but the real pain takes an instant to sink it. It's deeper and radiates up through your spine. He was using it like a paintbrush to lay perfectly measured strokes across the back of my thighs and ass. He never struck the same spot twice.

I was breathing heavily and shaking, but managing to hold back my tears. I kept telling myself it was just pain, that I could retreat deeper into the cool, dark place in my mind and detach from it if I needed to. But Dom seemed to know that's exactly what I was doing and found ways to jar my senses and pull me back out to full awareness. He changed to a pair of floggers and I relaxed beneath the sensual rhythm of them across my back and shoulders. I could picture Dom, in his element, swinging them in perfect alternating unison, and the image was extremely erotic. The eroticism became confused with the pain when he started to strike harder and land his blows across my tender ass and thighs. I was still turned on, but I didn't want it anymore. I wanted to stop, but needed to know what came next. I pressed my lips tight to hold back the safe word. As he gently ran his hands down my back, I arched into the touch, begging for more. He roughly took me by the wrists and lifted me up from the spanking horse. I could feel burning bruises forming where his hands had been.

I stood as still as I could where he had placed me, but I still couldn't see and I was unsteady.

"Stand perfectly still or I might miss," he said with quiet menace.

I jumped as a whip cracked inches from my right shoulder.

"I said, 'don't move.' You wouldn't want me to miss and hit the wrong spot."

This time the whip cracked as it brushed my left ass cheek. I screamed in pain and my knees buckled. My instinct was to put my hands out to break my fall, but they were still tied behind me. Dom was there to catch me. He stood me back upright and stepped back again.

The whip cracked inches from my skin three more times. I was trembling. I had felt enough. Just the sound made me want to run screaming from the room.

Whips fucking hurt. Got it. Check. Lesson learned.

"Take a deep breath, Scarlett. You're going to take one more strike from the whip."

I wanted to protest, but I wanted to please him. I didn't want him to think I was a sissy, but I felt like a sissy at the idea of another blow. He paused and stood very still. I hyperventilated in anticipation, not knowing where or when it was going to fall. He didn't even need to hit me and he knew it. He cracked the whip to my left and I screamed and lost my footing once more. This time he let me fall gently to my knees and helped me to balance there as he started untying me. He rapidly slid the ropes back and forth until I was free, his dexterity another display of his control. When I was completely untied, he paused to see whether I would stand or remove the blindfold myself. I didn't. I stayed on my knees awaiting his direction.

"Good girl," he said as he slid the blindfold off my eyes and helped me up. I was simultaneously terrified of him and purring in his arms as he hugged me. It was a head-fuck.

Women read about Christian Grey and lose their minds, but they are reading the fantasies of a woman who I don't believe has ever experienced what it's really like to be controlled by a man like Dom. He was magnetic.

"Thank you, Sir," I said quietly when we were finished. And I meant it.

After I got back to the dressing room, the floodgates opened. I couldn't explain it, but I just started to sob. I didn't know how to handle the depth of what I had experienced. Dom had found a deep, dark place within me—that dishonest place where we hide things from ourselves—and ripped it open. He came to check on me after cleaning the toys and was alarmed to find me in a sobbing heap.

He didn't say a word, but sat on the couch and wrapped me in his arms. The intimacy I felt nestled there was akin to the passion that can ignite out of grief: that need to connect with another human being to feel tethered back to life again. He must've felt the same energy because his fingers stroking my back turned from the reassuring rub of a friend into the caress of a lover. He tilted my head back and gently kissed the tear that had just spilled down my cheek. I wanted to fuck him right there in the dressing room just to feel in control again. Like I belonged in my own skin. Raven spared me the embarrassment of getting fired for doing so by walking in and interrupting.

"What the fuck happened to you? Do I need to castrate someone?"

I didn't know what to say, so Dom answered for me, "Sub space for the first time."

"Oh . . . got it. With whom?"

"Me," he replied.

I managed a laugh through my tears at her look. "But don't castrate him. It was amazing. He was awesome. And I needed to learn. I just . . . I don't . . . didn't know what this could feel like . . . how intense it could be."

"Why don't you come sit outside with me? Dom's clients are here and it looks like you need some more aftercare."

I sat across from her at the table and took a few deep breaths, but tried as I might, the tears kept streaming down my cheeks.

"Why would anyone want to feel like this?"

"It's what they crave. For a sub, it can elicit the same level of emotion that you're feeling, but it's all positive. It's euphoric. A release. A sub yearns to surrender control and go to that place in their heads. The magic you'll discover is that as their Domme, they're throwing that energy at you. You feed off the glazed, dopey, adoring look in their eyes. It's an incredible rush to have someone trust you like that and know that you've taken them there. You might hate some part of what you're feeling right now, but you'd never have really understood the power of it if he hadn't taken you there."

"I know. I get it, I do. I just can't seem to stop crying."

"It can be a lot to process for you tightly wound control freaks. Most of you need it. Feel amazing after it. You just happen to fall in the category of control freaks who aren't turned on by giving up control. Not as common as you might think."

We sat in silence for long moments and I started to feel a little more level and clearheaded, which let me take a good look at Raven. She didn't really look like herself either. I didn't want to pry, but when she let out a shuddering sigh, I couldn't help asking, "Is everything okay with you? Seems like you've got some shit on your mind too."

She looked up at me and for an instant I could see the unmasked pain in her eyes.

"I'm good. Or I'm not good, but I will be. It needed to happen. I got an abortion this morning. Don't really know why I'm so torn up about something I didn't want, but it's hitting me harder than I thought it would."

For a moment, I didn't know what to say. I had never been there. I believe a woman has the right to make decisions about her own body, but given the number of birth control options that are available to us today, I had a hard time understanding how pregnancy could happen accidentally . . . especially to someone as intelligent and scientifically inclined as Raven. I dismissed that line of thinking, though. If the Dungeon was teaching me anything, it was that I had absolutely no place to judge anyone. Instead, I just tried to be there for her.

"That sucks. I'm sorry . . . do you want to talk about it?"

"Not really. I don't know. I never thought I would be this girl. It's not like I don't know how babies are made. I just fucked up one weekend. Or I was fucked up and just didn't think."

"Who's the guy?" I asked and then immediately felt like I had crossed a line.

"He lives in Hawaii. We were down there for a surf trip. He said he loved me and wanted to try to make it work, but there's no way. In what world was that going to work? He doesn't even know I'm a Domme. And I don't need some macho fuck in my life telling me what to do."

"So you did the only thing that made sense."

"Ugh, nothing fuckin' makes sense anymore," she said, and a tear spilled down her cheek.

I got up and hugged her tight, but feeling her shaking with tears started my own waterworks again. Our crying turned to laughter when we realized how silly we must look. But our superficial friendship had become something deeper.

I cried on and off most of the drive home. I didn't want to worry Amelia, and I thought it would be hard for her to understand, so I went straight to my room and crashed for the night.

When I awoke the next day with a clearer head, a line of Ovid came to mind: *Perfer et obdura, dolor hic tibi proderit olim.* Persist and endure. This pain will be useful to you someday.

I stretched and smirked. *Oh, it would be useful . . .*

At the Dungeon, I told Harvey it would be the last time we played together. After playing with Dom, I didn't think there was much more that Harvey could teach me, and I was coming to loathe his sessions. In hindsight, I probably shouldn't have told him until afterward. He told me we were playing for thirty minutes, but when I was in the back grabbing implements, he paid the desk Mistress for forty-five minutes.

By the end of the session, I was usually over it and responding minimally. He desperately wanted me to be a whiny, disrespectful schoolgirl, so since it was our last time, I decided that I would mouth off for the last minute or so of the session just to get him all hot and bothered, but not have to deal with his retaliation. I kept an eye on my watch, and as the end of the session was upon us, started to act like a bitch.

"You're a pathetic excuse for a headmaster, and a filthy old man," I said in my brattiest voice. I further prodded, "You hit like a sissy!

Maybe you should be a headmistress next time, so that I don't have to pretend you're a man. Maybe people will respect you more if you just give up and become a girl! You'd have to be a lesbian, though, because everyone knows you're a big pervert! We all talk about it in the locker room, and we laugh at you when you're not there!"

I planted that one to make him think later. Did she really mean it? Were all of the subs laughing at me in the dressing room? He looked stunned. I had never mouthed off before in all of our sessions. Then he got a look of grim satisfaction. I'm sure in his mind I was egging him on, looking for a harder spanking. I was going to enjoy watching that look fade to dismay when Lady Viv called the session in five, four, three, two . . .

Nothing.

The son of a bitch grinned.

I realized something was off when she didn't call, but initially thought maybe my watch was off. For the next six minutes, I took one of the hardest spankings of my life. I could have told him to back off, but my pride got the better of me. I simply took it as a challenge to accept whatever he could dish out in total silence. He was layering bruises on top of what Dom had already done the day before. I eventually had had enough and broke character to stop him.

"I think maybe the intercom isn't working. We're past time."

"I changed my mind and paid for forty-five."

"Harvey! We agreed to thirty."

He lifted his hands and shrugged innocently.

The wily bastard got me one last time.

Later that week, Viv handed me a postcard when I arrived at the Dungeon. It was from the Paris hotel in Vegas. Curious, I flipped it over. It read:

"I'm in Paris. The one in Vegas. The bathrooms here say Homme and Femme.

Missing you, Harvey"

It was such a bizarre gesture. He was obviously thinking about me, but didn't quite know what to say. It's not as though he knew any-thing about me or we had anything in common. I was surprised at my reaction, but it made me kind of sad. I had never given any thought to who Harvey was outside of the Dungeon, and it suddenly occurred to me that he must be lonely. And then I sat down and felt a little less bad when I remembered what he had done to my ass with his devi-ous ways.

18. COLIN

I had been working at the Dungeon for four months and had managed not to see very much of my mom at the jobsite since she had been all over the country handling other projects. It was now Halloween, her birthday, and there would be no avoiding her. Amelia, Colin, and I were going to the house she had rented nearby for her annual costume birthday party. Amelia and I were then going to find a way to separate from Colin so that we could meet Wes at a vampire-themed fetish party in downtown L.A. where the girls from the Dungeon would be performing. Not wanting to alarm my family, I had toned down my vampire costume for my mom's party and was almost entirely covered by a flowing dress and cloak. Underneath, however, was a costume suitable for a Dominatrix vampire: a miniskirt with a slit up to my hip bone and the corset that had ensnared Slave Trainer Tom.

My mom's Halloween birthday has always suited her. When she was little, the other children were told that the fairies had brought them, but my grandma told her that she had been brought by the witches. With her jet-black hair and electric-blue eyes, she definitely has a witchy look about her.

Since my family is from Scotland, when we were growing up my mom insisted that we adhere to Scottish traditions on holidays. That meant that Halloween was all about "guising" rather than trick-or-treating. The tradition follows the pagan holiday of Samhain, the eve on which the veil between the spirit world and our world is at its thinnest and the spirits can walk among us. The idea behind guising was to dress the children up so they could disguise themselves among the spirits and go door to door getting protection from the members of the community. My mother compromised and gave out candy rather than protection spells, but where we come from you don't just get candy for showing up, you have to do a "party piece" to earn your reward. This generally means singing a song, doing a dance, telling a story, reciting a poem, or showing off a talent. As a child, I dreaded this part as I don't have any talent as a dancer and people think I'm mimicking a dying animal when I attempt to sing. It was also mortifying when she would force my initially confused American friends to perform for their candy, but she eventually developed a reputation as the crazy Scottish lady and they delighted in her eccentricities. The other Halloween tradition we had to do every year was dooking for apples. No one has ever given me a satisfactory explanation for this tradition in which you dunk your head in a bucket of water that also contains apples and have to try to grab one with your teeth. As a fully made-up twenty-three-year-old, I felt I should be exempt from dooking that year, but one look at my mom told me that resistance was futile.

I got down on my knees, held my hands behind my back, and made a good show of attempting to gouge one of the apples, while putting as little of my face in the water as I could. I wasn't really trying, so I choked when I accidentally stabbed one with my fangs, flailing and knocking the bucket, splashing water all over myself.

"Jenny's the next one to get married!" shouted my mother, clapping her hands.

I had forgotten that part of the tradition. Strangely enough, of the guests in attendance that night, I *would* be the next to wed . . . but we don't want any spoilers just yet, now do we?

I carefully pulled the apple off my teeth and shook my head with a smile.

"Best of luck with that dream, Mum. That whole marriage thing makes absolutely no sense to me."

"Nonsense. You just haven't dated the right guy yet!" she said with a pointed look at Colin, who thankfully was too distracted taking a shot to notice her meddling.

I rolled my eyes and blushed the same color as the apple. I was now a moist, disgruntled vampire, so I found the laundry room to throw my cloak and dress in the dryer.

I had been standing in there for a few minutes, enjoying the gentle hum of the dryer, when Colin came bursting through the door.

"Hey! I wondered where you had gone. . . ." He trailed off, taking in the fact that I was definitely not wearing the same costume I had been before. I was suddenly hyper aware of my breasts heaving with every breath over the top of the corset. I saw the exact instant that he noticed the livid bruises that covered my upper thighs. At least he couldn't see my ass. Unfortunately, there's no mistaking the bruises from a cane as anything other than having been smacked with a stick-like object. A series of lined, fading bruises worked their way up my thighs in impressively consistent increments. I had admired Dom's handiwork earlier, but now wished the bruises weren't so distinct so that I could claim to have just fallen on my ass or slipped on the stairs or something.

"What the fuck, Jenny?"

"Please just leave it, Colin. It's not what it looks like."

Did I really just try using that line?

"Not what it looks like? It looks like someone fucking hit you."

If an earthquake could happen right now, that would be really helpful. No idea how to get out of this one.

"It's complicated and none of your business. I was a consenting adult."

We were treading in uncomfortable territory here. I didn't want to explain my BDSM proclivities to Colin, but I also didn't want him making a scene in front of my mom so that I would need to have this conversation with her too. Colin grabbed my arm and held it out in front of me revealing the handprint bruise around one of my wrists.

"Yeah. That looks consensual. Why do you let guys treat you like this?"

"Let go. You're drunk and you're hurting me. No one did anything wrong. Just let it go. You're not my boyfriend, and you're certainly not my dad. Drop it."

"Why don't—"

"I said drop it!"

He glared daggers at me, but shut his big mouth. I felt bad since his heart was in the right place. He saw something out of context and, given my track record, it wasn't an unrealistic leap for him to be concerned. But there wasn't much I could do about it. I sure as shit wasn't telling him the truth and couldn't come up with a plausible lie, so I was just going to have to accept him being upset. I adored him like a teddy bear big brother and for the first time had to contemplate the reality of how the people who mattered to me would feel if they knew what I was doing. It was an unpleasant thought.

I grabbed my clothes from the dryer and threw them back on even though they were still a bit damp.

"Everything okay?" my mom asked, looking to where Colin had been standing.

"Yeah, no big deal."

"Are you sleeping with him?"

"Mother!"

"It's a fair question. He looks at you with puppy-dog eyes."

"Definitely not. We're just friends. Good friends. And I'd like to keep it that way, so don't go making it awkward! And I have a fucking boyfriend, thank you very much."

Who I'm now in a polyamorous relationship with . . .

"I'm not sure Colin would know what to do with you anyway."

"Moving on . . ."

"How's work going? Is Rich managing okay?"

"Everything's fine."

"And how about your extracurricular activities?"

I hesitated and looked at her skeptically, not sure whether she was fishing or knew something.

"C'mon, as if I don't know what you're up to. You can't keep secrets from me. Rich let it slip that you've got volunteer work a few
days a week, so you work earlier. It's no big deal. I don't know why
you wouldn't just tell me."

"I guess it didn't really seem important?"

"Are you really just volunteering or is there something else going
on?"

"Hate to disappoint, but nothing scandalous going on here!"

"I wasn't saying there was," she said defensively. "Just want to make
sure everything is okay with you. We haven't been talking as much
lately."

"Everything is great. Just been really busy."

I was sweating by the time Amelia and I escaped and were driving to the party. The guilt monster inside of me was rearing its ugly
head and there was nothing I could do to assuage it. I hated lying.
I had to acknowledge that I would potentially be lying to some of
the people in my life indefinitely. Certainly as long as I worked at the
Dungeon, but even after that I was beginning to understand that
there were some things I was never going to be able to share.

19. SIR LIAM

Amelia seemed nervous in the car on the way to the fetish party and I wondered if I had made a mistake bringing her. It was my first public play party too, so I was already faking a level of confidence that I didn't really have without needing to bolster hers. It was too late to worry about it, though. We parked and met Wes on our walk over to the club. I squared my shoulders as we approached the entrance, knowing that I needed to have enough confidence for all three of us. We bypassed the line that wound around the building, and I addressed the guy at the front who was holding a clipboard.

"I'm Scarlett. From the Dungeon. I should be on the list of performers. These are my guests."

He looked me up and down before flipping a few pages on his list and waving us in. It was thrilling to be part of the list at an event like this. I walked into the club feeling like the Queen of the Damned. Amelia looked like a deer in the headlights. Wes was a kid in a candy shop.

There were no bullshit, half-assed costumes here. Everyone was an over-the-top mixture of terrifying and sexy. The sinister electronic music was so loud I could feel it vibrating in my chest. The club space was absolutely massive and I wondered how we were going to find my friends in all this madness. Go-go dancers twisted sinuously on platforms and cages around the dance floor and I found myself mesmerized by their erotic movements. A hand grabbed my shoulder and I turned to find Dominic looking devastatingly handsome in a tailcoat and vest. He took me by the hand and gestured toward a door in the far back corner. I grabbed Amelia's hand so I didn't lose her, and the three of us made our way quite easily through the crowd that parted before Dom. We went through the door into an almost pitch-black hallway, and then emerged onto a huge outdoor patio that was also filled with people, but the music wasn't nearly as loud.

It looked like we had walked out into the midst of a vampire bondage orgy. Immediately outside the door, a girl was tied to a chair and being fingered by a huge black Dominant wearing black latex gloves up to his elbows and a black leather butcher's apron. He nodded acknowledgment to Dominic as we walked past, barely reacting to his sub reaching a screaming climax. His eyes drifted over to Amelia and did a leisurely survey of her female form. She didn't even notice because she was so distracted by the debauchery that surrounded us. Dungeon rules clearly didn't apply as we had just witnessed, but there seemed to be some rules. Nipples were covered and it wasn't as though the people around us were having full-blown sex . . . but still there was a different vibe than I had experienced before. The air was rife with arousal and mischief. This wasn't about a controlled one-sided exchange of experience for money like it was at work. This was about experiencing hedonism with wild abandon.

Dom led us to the side of a stage and showed us where we could put our coats and bags.

I looked up on the stage and saw that Raven had a sub from work named Minx tied to a spanking horse and was paddling her ass to the frantic beat of the drums. A crowd had gathered to watch and it was obvious that Raven thrived on the attention. Dom brought my gaze back to the floor and said, "Scarlett, I'd like you to meet my lovely wife, Vanessa, and our good friend Sir Liam."

Vanessa was a pretty woman with dark curly hair and kind eyes. I instantly liked her. She squeezed me in a tight hug and said, "I'm so happy to finally meet you! Dom always talks about you!"

I didn't have a chance to formulate a good response to this because Sir Liam had taken my hand and kissed my knuckles in a formal greeting. I was mesmerized by him and couldn't have said why. I have always been attracted to very tall men and he was barely my height and slight of build. He had long blond hair and a goatee, but it was his eyes that drew me in. They were rimmed in smudged black eyeliner, but their blue depths seemed so open and unguarded that it made me self-conscious.

"Pleased to meet you," I responded to both of them and introduced Amelia and Wes, whom I had embarrassingly forgotten now that we were outside. The next few moments were a blurred rush of hugs from friends and introductions to new and fascinating-looking people. This was the first time Wes had seen any of my coworkers in person. He kept giving me looks of amazement and approval as he met each new girl. I could tell how eager he was to instigate something, but I was too nervous to ask anyone to play with us yet.

When the madness had calmed a bit, Dom pulled me to one side and said, "You should play with Liam. He does fire play. It'll blow your mind."

I wasn't entirely sure what fire play meant, but it sounded intriguing. I was hesitant about subbing for anyone, though, particularly in front of a crowd. I wasn't sure how I felt about Wes seeing me in that role either. He knew in theory what I did for my clients, but I felt that it might shatter his image of me as his Mistress to see me submit to another man. I voiced this concern to Dom.

"Nothing really subby necessary. I could tie you up just to give it a bit of flair and then he can do his fire thing. Nothing corporal, no protocol."

Vanessa chimed in, "You *have* to try fire. And Sir Liam is amazing at it."

"Okay. Do you think he'd be down to play with me?"

They both laughed. "Fuck yes, love. Look at you right now."

Before I had time to get nervous, I was stripping out of my skirt next to the stage and putting on a pair of Vanessa's boy shorts. I took my corset off and she helped me to apply electrical tape in two *X*'s to cover my nipples. I had never seen this before, but within months would be carrying electrical tape with me at all times. You know, just in case I needed to whip my tits out in public. We left my thigh-high boots on and pulled my hair back, lest it get singed. I suddenly wished I hadn't brought Amelia because I was worried about her judging me, but to her credit, she didn't say a word as she helped me to balance in my heels as I stripped off and she folded my clothes into a neat pile. She just smiled at me with wide eyes and shook her head as though she couldn't quite believe what I was about to do. Neither could I.

Liam, I would come to learn, was a well-respected Dominant within the community who happened to be living with cystic fibrosis. His disease explained his smaller stature and his wiry build. His fetishes primarily revolved around piercing, ritual scarification, and tattoos. In light of his condition, I found this fascinating. On some base level, he seemed to be trying to leave his mark. Already in his early thirties, he was unlikely to live another decade. He had to know that, in all likelihood, the marks that he left on the people in his life would outlast his time on this Earth. There was something incredibly poignant about that thought.

Dom and Liam explained to me what we would do once we were on stage. Dom would take the lead with tying me up while Liam got his fire implements ready. Fire play, they explained, worked by brushing a stick dipped in flammable fluid across the surface of an area of skin and then lighting it with another stick that was on fire. The fluid would briefly flame up, but as long as he quickly swiped over it with his hand, my skin wasn't at risk of burning. It sounded straightforward enough.

Once we were up on stage, I was a little insecure at how naked I was in front of such a big crowd, but it was easy to get caught in the moment. A Puscifer song hammered through the speakers. Maynard James Keenan's seductive voice combined with the hypnotic beat were enticing me to join the rest of the sybarites and surrender to my baser desires.

Dom tied me spread-eagled to the Saint Andrew's cross on stage while Liam lined up his tools on a small table. He fiddled with fluid for a moment and then approached me with two tools in hand. One stick was on fire and the other was covered in fluid. He looked me in the eye and asked, "You ready?"

I laughed nervously and replied, "Let's do this."

He swiped the fluid stick down my thigh, leaving it glistening. I could feel my heart pounding over the music as he drew the flame closer to me. He started with it in front of my face and slowly moved it down my body. I could feel its warmth against my skin and shivered in anticipation of him reaching my thigh. When he did, the fluid ignited and flared up for a brief second before he wiped it out with his hand. It was electric to the senses. All of the information being fed to my brain was screaming that I had just been on fire, but the logical part of me knew that my skin hadn't actually burned. It didn't mark the skin, but left it tingling deliciously as a reminder of where the wicked flame had been. Now that he had let me feel it once and reassured me, he started to find a rhythm with the flame, crisscrossing all of the exposed skin on my body. I twitched every time he touched the flame to me, but it quickly turned from twitching to writhing at the glorious sensory experience of it. Liam was captivating. The crowd looked almost as entranced as I was. I wondered whether they could possibly be as painfully aroused as I was too.

It was over too soon for my liking, but my skin was beginning to sting, so he couldn't keep doing it in the same places without burning me. While Dom untied me, Liam took a damp cloth and wiped the remaining traces of fluid from me. I didn't bother to hide how badly I wanted him. I stared him down with fuck-me eyes and moaned at his touch. Ever the gentleman, he kissed me on the cheek and whispered in my ear, "You were incredible."

To which I could only reply, "No, *you* were incredible. That was amazing. Thank you."

Looking back on it, I'm fairly sure he put me in sub space, but I was too excited about it to even notice. I felt high as I rejoined Amelia and Vanessa on the side of the stage and they helped me to dress.

"That was fucking hot!" I exclaimed to them. "I'm going to have blue balls for the rest of the night!"

Raven appeared as though that was her cue, and yelled over the music, "Blue balls? No blue balls allowed! Wanna get off? We were about to play with one of my subbie boys in the bathroom. Come on . . . he can take care of you!"

She said it matter-of-factly. Oh, you need an orgasm? No big deal. I have one waiting for you in the bathroom. I didn't really know what that meant, but went along for the ride. I couldn't find Wes. I assumed he was at the bar, but thought he would be fine until I got back. Amelia came with me, and Raven led us into a medium-size bathroom with two stalls and a counter with two sinks. There were six or seven women already in there and an attractive male sub wiping the counter down. He had short salt-and-pepper hair and a five o'clock shadow that highlighted his strong jaw and cheekbones. He was naked and looked totally unselfconscious about it, but then he didn't have anything to be insecure about. Raven introduced us.

"This is my subbie. He doesn't really need a name, so we just call him Boy. Boy, this is Mistress Scarlett."

"Pleased to meet you, Mistress," he said, making brief eye contact before bowing his head. That fleeting look was enough to know that there was a spark of mutual attraction between us.

Raven continued, "Boy, Mistress Scarlett says she has blue balls from fire play on stage. Your job is to get her off while we do whatever we want to you. Clear?"

"Yes, Goddess."

She turned to me and asked, "Are you okay with him going down on you? He's skilled with his tongue, this one."

If I'd taken any time at all to think, there's no way I would have done it: let a perfect stranger go down on me in a bathroom at a club with an audience? Not a fucking chance, for reasons innumerable. I must've still been riding a high from the fire and feeling a little reckless, though, because I said, "Fuck yes!" and hopped up on the counter.

I hadn't noticed Erin in the room, but she appeared in front of me and, without saying a word, reached under my skirt and slid my panties down and over my boots. I watched as she tucked them in the pocket of her trench coat and wondered if I would be getting them back. The thought was titillating. As was the realization that if Raven was right about her sub, I was about to get off with Erin watching.

I looked up and saw Amelia's back as she left the bathroom and the door closed behind her. I thought she was probably freaked out and possibly offended by my behavior, but going after her didn't seem reasonable. I had told her what would likely be going on here tonight and she had agreed to come. Maybe she just didn't need to see me doing it.

This is the part where I'm supposed to tell you that I submitted to my inner wild child and rode the thrill of the moment to a mind-bending climax. But to my dismay, it didn't work like that. Raven was right: Boy not only knew where my clit was but what he was supposed to do with it. Mechanics, however, are only part of the battle. I couldn't get out of my own head long enough to let go. My thoughts were suddenly racing out of control and I wanted to stop but I didn't want to look lame in front of my new friends. They were all watching me expectantly and I found myself faking pleasure. I had started this journey to avoid this very thing and now I felt more pressured to fake it than ever before. How did it come to this?

At my first throaty moan, Raven said, "Right? I told you he had a talented tongue! Let's see if he can keep it up when he's distracted!"

Two of the other girls took that as their cue and started spanking him hard. He flinched, but didn't break his rhythm.

It seemed unreasonably soon to pretend to come no matter how good he was, but I really didn't want to be the center of attention anymore and was starting to freak out, so I threw my head back and made the sounds of what I hoped was a convincing orgasm.

"Good, Boy," she said. "Now you can have your reward!"

I looked up to see Raven approaching him wearing a big pink strap-on. I had never seen someone get fucked with a strap-on before and was riveted as he bent over in front of her. I was still on the counter, so Boy's head naturally fell in my lap. He looked up at me with adoring eyes and said, "Thank you for letting me please you, Mistress."

I stroked his head and replied, "Well done, Boy. That felt amazing!"

I didn't have a clear view of what Raven was doing, but it was obvious when she lined up her cock and pushed it slowly forward into Boy. He expelled his breath and I couldn't tell whether he liked it or not. I tilted my head and saw how hard he was and at least deduced that he must not hate it. The girls went back to spanking him. Storm reached under him and stroked his hard dick. Raven grinned at me and asked, "Scarlett, wanna practice some CBT? You can punch him in the balls if you want. He likes that . . . don't you, Boy?"

"Yes, Goddess!" he groaned as she thrust harder.

He lifted his head and stood partially upright to give me access. I slid my hand under Storm's and grabbed his sack as hard as I could, eliciting another groan. I let go to make a fist and swung upward to punch him hard in the balls. He bent his knees slightly to absorb the impact, but locked eyes with me, daring me to do it again. I did. Repeatedly. I alternated hands, punching him harder and harder right in the balls and it was thrilling. As a woman, it's a forbidden act to ever punch a man in the junk unless you are in imminent danger of being assaulted by said man. Everything about this was taboo and erotically charged. Raven, Storm, and I found ourselves moving in time to the drumbeat that was vibrating through the room. Boy maintained eye contact with me, but begged Raven, "Goddess, may I please come?"

She handed Storm a plastic cup and said, "Into the cup like a good Boy!"

He came into the cup and then Storm presented him with it and said, "Looks like Boy has his drink! Anyone else need one? I'm heading to the bar!"

I straightened my skirt and jumped down from the counter, following the crowd out of the bathroom. I felt disoriented and confused as I made my way back outside to find Amelia. I was worried she would be upset, but when I eventually found her, she was draped over Liam's lap getting a spanking. She was facing away so she didn't see me. I didn't want her to get self-conscious because I was suddenly there, so I melted back into the crowd.

Looks like someone else has a kinky side she wants to explore!

The rest of the night was a blur of voyeurism and exhibitionism. I felt isolated and disjointed, like I knew I was trying too hard to be cool but couldn't seem to stop. At the same time, I felt obligated to facilitate a scene for Wes with some of my girls, or I knew he would be disappointed. I asked Raven for assistance.

"Want to beat my sub's balls?"

"Abso-fuckin-lutely! He's a cutie. And I'm always in for beating balls. Storm, wanna help me?"

"Sure!" she replied, setting her drink on the side of the stage.

"Do you need to tell him, or can we just accost him?" Raven asked.

"He's all yours. He likes it pretty heavy, but I'll step in if I think it's getting to be too much."

I melted back into the crowd, watching as they approached an unsuspecting Wes. Raven didn't waste any time, seizing a grip on his balls and saying something in his ear. I found myself smiling at the grin that lit his face. In her boots, Raven was nearly as tall as him, so she got behind him and wrapped him in a headlock. Storm kicked his legs apart so that they were spread in a wide stance. She booted him in the balls much harder than I had ever done. I heard him grunt, but he looked up at her with fire in his eyes. She moved in closer and started punching his balls over and over without letting up. His groans got louder until he was yelling at each punch, but he knew he could use a safe word and wasn't, so I let them continue.

Raven and Storm switched places, and Raven nailed him so hard with her first kick that he dropped to the ground. He was too heavy for Storm to hold up, so she let him pant on all fours for a minute. I thought maybe it was time for me to stop them, but I trusted these women not to take things too far. They were pros. When Wes looked back up, Storm stood behind him and held his arms behind his back. He was still in a wide stance, but was now on his knees with nowhere to go. By the time Raven was finished with him, he was definitely in sub space. And he fucking loved it. His eyes were glazed over, and he couldn't seem to stop grinning. He wasn't normally one for PDA, but suddenly he couldn't keep his hands off me. He was adoring, attentive, and grateful for the rest of the night.

Thoughts and adrenaline swirled through my head as I laid it down on the pillow and tried to sleep afterward. It had been such a positive experience for Wes, and only seemed to make our relationship better . . . so that was a good thing.

Erin had definitely kept my panties. What the fuck did that mean?

Amelia had a kinky side. Who knew?

I had done fire play. And let someone's sub go down on me. And punched a stranger in the balls. And seen some seriously crazy shit.

Yet somehow, in spite of all the madness of the night, my mind kept returning to the same image of Raven thrusting her strap-on into Boy for the first time. I wanted to do that. As my hand slid slowly down under the sheets, Raven was no longer part of the image. It was all me.

20. LADY CATERINA

I was shy of six months of experience at the Dungeon, but I desperately wanted to be able to start Switching and had been training hard toward that end. I was a sponge who probably drove the rest of the staff nuts trying to learn more. Everyone had different strengths and tricks for each scenario and I wanted to know them all.

My rope work was still weak, but I could do the most useful binds and a simple harness. Clients usually didn't want anything too elaborate anyway because it took too much time to tie and untie. I had focused on utilitarian knots that I could use efficiently in a session.

A visiting German Domme had taught me the basics of CBT bondage, which I found much more interesting than traditional Shibari. A bind around the cock and balls can serve as anything from a pleasant cock ring that keeps the blood from leaving the penis and intensifies sensation in a most pleasurable way. *Or* it can be a gloriously sadistic means to better torture male genitalia. Weights can be hung from the balls and kicked. It was incredible how quickly I went from being nervous and uncomfortable with CBT to reveling in it. Who knew a shoelace could be so versatile?

I had a basic working knowledge of all of the common implements from paddles to whips to the Violet Wand (an electro-play toy). I knew the difference between a buggy whip, a signal whip, and a bullwhip, and I had experienced the indescribable thrill of cracking a single tail for the first time. I could swing floggers in the double Florentine style. I had learned the different varieties of gags, blindfolds, spanking techniques, and verbal humiliation. There were dozens of little gems of knowledge planted in my mind. I knew there was a sweet spot on the upper thigh just before the cheek starts that stings like a motherfucker when struck. There were voices in my head now that I couldn't silence. Sometimes at my vanilla job, they would whisper of suspicions about people, of instincts about what people wanted to do behind closed doors.

I had decided that it was time to undergo my Switch test so that I could start taking a greater variety of clients. Lady Caterina would be administering the test and I was going to use Minx as my test bottom.

I liked Minx. As one of the few black girls who worked at the Dungeon, she had to put up with a lot of shit from the clients. Guys constantly wanted to play out the most appalling racist fantasies with her—a slave and master on an antebellum plantation, pimp and hooker, or some variation of an African native. She always took it in stride. The rest of us were usually more offended than she was. She didn't see any of it as being any worse than home invasion or schoolgirl fantasies. In her eyes, people couldn't help that they were into it, and this was supposed to be a safe space to explore the things that other people were offended by. The one time she drew the line was when a guy named Hal wanted to pretend she was being gang-raped by an African village who performed genital mutilation on her. I'm not even sure how he envisioned playing that one out, but it seemed like a reasonable place to put her foot down.

Cat had Raven watch the desk and she met Minx and me in the cell for my exam.

"Okay, Scar, we can either go through this one skill test at a time or I can tell you everything you need to cover and you can just build it all into a scene that I observe."

"I would prefer to do a scene for your amusement, Lady Caterina."

I would usually just have called her Cat, but I had a feeling she would be meticulous in testing me, so I stuck to protocol. My suspicions were confirmed when she smirked and scribbled something on her clipboard.

"Great. I don't think we need to do everything since I already know you're proficient at most of the basics. So why don't you restrain your sub and then give her a good light to medium hand spanking. You can decide the rest of the scene, but I'd like to see you use a medium paddle, light flogger, heavy nipple torture, face slapping, and verbal humiliation. We'll condense it to fifteen minutes including your prep time. Sound good?"

"Yes, Mistress."

Fifteen minutes wasn't very long to throw together something decent, so I immediately went into go mode. I had moved to race toward the hallway to collect everything I needed when I paused and turned back to Minx. I knew Cat had cleared everything with her already, but if this was supposed to mimic a real session, I would need to run through limits and a safe word.

"Kneel, slut," I commanded. She dropped gracefully before me and bowed her head in submission.

"Our session will include light to medium impact play, heavy nipple torture, face slapping, and humiliation while you are tied up. Your safe word will be 'shenanigans.' Are you comfortable with all of that?"

"Yes, Mistress," she said with confidence but didn't raise her eyes.

"Marvelous."

I walked quickly but calmly from the room and started pulling implements from the walls. Two medium lengths of nylon rope would get the job done. I picked a sturdy leather paddle that I had been on the receiving end of a number of times. I wasn't as sure about nipple clamps, but I pulled a set from a hook that didn't look too frightening and hoped they would still qualify as heavy. I walked quickly to the dressing room and grabbed my own floggers from my bag. I wouldn't necessarily have used them in a session with a client, but I knew I could control them better than any that belonged to the Dungeon.

I paused for just a moment outside the door to the cell to take a deep breath and make sure I had a plan of action that would hit every-thing in the allotted time.

The next twelve minutes blew by, but I managed to successfully cover everything Cat had listed and felt that I had nailed it. My flog-ging had been outstanding. My verbal humiliation was colorful and on point. Minx's derriere was an even, glowing red across both cheeks. My wrist bind hadn't taken too long and I didn't get myself tangled. I had never tried face slapping before, so my slaps were probably a little on the sissy side, but I knew I hadn't done anything unsafe. I was confident that I had passed with flying colors.

Cat finished scribbling notes on a clipboard and looked up with a smile.

"Good job, Scar. I'll let the Webmistress know that you'll be send-ing her your new pictures and profile so she can move you over to Switch. You did a nice job on most of that, but I just want to go over a few things that I think you could improve on now that you'll be able to take Domme sessions."

She dropped her clipboard in the corner and approached Minx. She circled her slowly. Gone was Cat the bubbly, matronly desk Mis-tress. In her place was Lady Caterina. I was about to catch a glimpse of how spectacular she must have been in her prime.

She stopped behind Minx and wrapped her arms around her to pull her back with one hand and take her by the throat with the other. Minx smiled with surprise.

Her lips were against Minx's ear, as she said, "You think this is funny, you worthless little cum Dumpster."

The quiet menace in her tone wiped the smile from Minx's face. The actual words she said were irrelevant. She could've asked about the weather and it would've been clear that Minx's existence was insignificant.

"No, Mistress," Minx replied on cue.

I sensed the violence in the air a fraction of a second before she exploded, spinning Minx around and striking her across the cheek with a stinging blow. Minx's head whipped to the side.

"That wasn't a question. I didn't give you permission to speak."

"I'm sorry, Mis—"

This time Caterina backhanded her with a crack.

I knew that part of what she was trying to show me can't really be explained. I had been checking boxes in my mind, constantly thinking about mechanics and the next steps. I was playing at being in charge. She was the real deal. I was stiff and clearly forcing it. She fucking owned it.

Point taken.

She wasn't trying to make me insecure. She was pushing me to be better and I loved her for it.

Caterina went through the mechanics of face slapping and nipple torture, showing me how I could do it more effectively. I learned that the more force is concentrated on a smaller area closer to the tip of the nipple, the more painful it is. She taught me exactly where on the face to strike with which part of my hand. But the real lesson I walked away with was that it wasn't enough to simply go through the motions. I needed to *become* Mistress Scarlett. For now, I was officially a Switch and that was enough to open a whole new world of possibilities.

I convinced Cat to have a drink with me after work to celebrate and to thank her for all of her guidance. It gave me the opportunity to ask her something I had been wondering for a while.

"How the fuck do you deal with the constant stream of obnoxious randos on the phone and at the desk? Where do you get the patience?"

"I try to live my life by the saying: 'Everyone you meet is fighting a battle you know nothing about, so be kind.'"

It was a more profound response than I had expected, and it stuck with me.

21. THE DOC

I had passed my first real test at the Dungeon with flying colors, but it would be a few more months before I got an opportunity to prove myself in the vanilla world. Rich had been heading for an inevitable rock bottom for months, and I'm ashamed to admit that I had shown little interest in helping him. I didn't know him well enough to feel comfortable prying, but it was also convenient for hiding the fact that I was moonlighting as a sex worker. The more of a shit show he was, the less he paid attention to my comings and goings, and that made it much easier to get to the Dungeon on time. The days that my mom visited the jobsite were brutal and stressful when I was trying to get out the door but didn't want to tell her why. My volunteer work lie was starting to sound pretty sketchy and I could tell that she was beginning to doubt me. I didn't think for a second she suspected anything close to the truth, but I really didn't need her prying.

On my way in to the jobsite one morning, I passed Denny's and saw Rich's car. I initially dismissed his presence there as normal and assumed I would see him in the trailer after he had grabbed his breakfast, but some instinct made me turn around and park next to him. Closer inspection revealed that Rich was passed out drunk in the driver's seat and the engine was still running. At least he was breathing. No story that I could come up with in my head had a good explanation for this outcome. I opened the driver's side door, turned the engine off, and shook him by the shoulder. I didn't envy him in the least when he opened his bloodshot eyes and tried to make sense of his surroundings.

"Morning, Jen," he croaked out.

"Morning, sunshine. Want to grab some breakfast and tell me what's going on here?"

"Sure thing."

I had to give him an arm to stop him from stumbling on the way across the parking lot. I let him fall into a heap on one side of a booth and slid across the other side. I knew better than to engage him without coffee, so I signaled the waitress and let him get some caffeine in his system.

"Went to the bar after work last night and must've had a few too many. Was going to drive home, but decided I should eat something and sober up a little first. Made it to the parking lot, but must've passed out before coming in. At least I don't think I came in here."

"For fuck's sake, Rich, driving blackout drunk is not okay. You could've killed someone. You're not in high school. You know better."

Shit, I sound like my mother.

He winced and looked like a puppy who had just been kicked. Rich ordered food and we sat in silence while he continued to medicate with coffee. I wanted to ask if he'd checked his blood pressure recently, but knew the answer and left it alone. I didn't know that much about heart attacks, but he didn't look like he was in imminent danger of dying, so it didn't seem constructive to keep prodding him. I also wondered whether his wife knew where he was, but didn't want to dive too deep into his business.

"She kicked me out," he said as though reading my mind. "Said I need to get my act together. That she wasn't putting up with me anymore."

"I'm sorry."

Given that the guy was rarely sober, I couldn't say I blamed the poor woman.

"I just don't know how I ended up here."

"Well, it looks like you at least managed to drive without hitting anything."

"No, I mean *here*," he said with a vague sweep of his hand. "I'm an old man doing a job that bores me going home to a sexless marriage with no excitement on the horizon between here and the grave. I drink to feel better," he finished in a mumble.

"How's that workin' out for you?"

"Not so good."

"I can't do anything about most of that. What I can do is cover your meetings for the day. You can't go in like this and we can't reschedule with that many surgeons—it took me weeks to get them booked and I'll be damned if I'm going through that again for your sorry ass. You go check in to the extended stay down the street and take the day to sober up. To be clear, that does not mean take the day off and go on another bender. Clear your head and maybe some of the other stuff will start to look more manageable."

It either spoke to his faith in me or how drunk he still was that he didn't question my ability to take over his meetings for the day.

"Thanks, Jenny. Really. Thank you. And your mom doesn't hear about this?"

"Lorna has no need to know. It'll be fine."

As though I wasn't already keeping enough secrets from her . . . what was one more?

Once I got to the trailer and looked over the schedule for the day, I had a moment of utter panic at the magnitude of what I had just taken on. We had a full schedule of equipment validation meetings. These were discussions with each clinical specialty that was going into the new hospital to review the equipment that was slated to be purchased for their area and confirm whether it met their needs. It may not sound that complicated, but there were several things that made these meetings challenging. The first was that while it was impossible to be an expert on every piece of equipment that went into a new hospital, there was an assumption that the person running the meetings (now me) had at least a basic working knowledge of the specialty and the equipment required. I knew that cardiac surgeons were heart surgeons. That would get me through the first meeting, right? Speaking of cardiologists, the second challenge was the people involved. So many of the docs and nurses were the nicest people I have ever encountered and they were only too happy to give their input. A number of them, on the other hand, felt they were above having to deal with mere mortals and that the precise equipment that they wanted should just appear in the new hospital. The knowledge that the mere mortal they were wasting their time with knew fuck-all about their equipment would have understandably made their heads explode.

I sat and took a few deep breaths and considered canceling all of them. That would be the safest choice even if it would piss the client off monumentally and land Rich in a pile of shit. It was also the pussy choice. For months, I had been sick of my role as Betty Bimbo and wanted a chance to step up. This was it. I just needed to bullshit my way through a few meetings.

I got to the conference room where our first meeting was being held and sorted the paperwork we would be reviewing into piles in front of me. I had frantically Googled most of the equipment and made little notes for myself of questions to ask that I hoped would prevent me from making an ass of myself. I had called as many of the vendors as I could reach on short notice and had them give me a rundown on their equipment and what would need to be determined to properly order it. Salespeople are always happy to tell you as much about what they sell as you're willing to listen to. I knew I just needed to get the framework today, and could work through the specifics afterward to make sure I didn't get anything wrong.

Eventually, the surgeon, a few of his nurses, and some of the hospital administrators filed into the room and sat looking at me expectantly.

"Good morning. I'm Jenny from Hunter Associates and I'm going to be reviewing your equipment list for the new hospital with you. The idea is to have a purchase-ready list when we leave this meeting

so that when the time comes, we can start buying the equipment and
have it here on time for each of your timeline milestones."

"I just don't understand what I'm doing here," came the curt reply from the surgeon.

*How many men are going to tell me that today? If he starts talking about
his sexless marriage as well, I give up.*

"I'm sorry. Did I not explain that well enough? Let me try to be
more clear. . . ."

"No, you explained it fine. I just don't understand why *I'm* here.
When they built the Staples Center, did they sit Kobe Bryant down
and ask him how to build it? No, they didn't. They didn't need to ask
Kobe what materials to use for the court, so why am I here?"

*This motherfucker just compared himself to Kobe Bryant. Clearly no ego
here.*

It was in that moment that I realized that managing clients at this
job would require basically the same things as managing clients at
my *other* job . . . patience, a whole lot of confidence, and a massive pair
of balls. I didn't need a degree in each specialty. I just needed Scarlett.

I smiled politely.

"I completely understand your concern. Fortunately, we won't be
asking you what materials to use in the ORs or how to build the building today. We'll only be dealing with the actual pieces of equipment
that you touch on a daily basis. Kobe may not have been asked how
to build the Staples Center, but I bet he wanted to give some input
on what shoes he would be wearing. We just want to extend you that
same courtesy so that you get exactly what you need to do your procedures."

I saw the tiniest hint of smiles on his nurses' faces and knew
that had been the right answer.

Fascinatingly, as the meeting went on, I began to perceive
that his reservations about being asked his opinion on the equipment stemmed less from arrogance and more from being insecure
about how oblivious he really was. He may have been using these
instruments on a daily basis but hadn't the slightest clue who
made them, what model they were, what accessories they needed,

or what options he may want. This was not a man who was used to not having the answers and it made him extremely uncomfortable. Once I understood this, it was much easier to proceed without ruffling any more of his feathers. I worked with his nurses to fill in the gaps in his knowledge, while still gleaning the essential pieces of information from him. I even found a way to trim some unnecessary equipment and make room in the budget for an instrument that he had been trying to get approval to purchase for three years. He was positively glowing when I told him I would walk it through the approval process myself, and let him know when it was signed off.

As the group filed out of the room at the end of the meeting, they were happy and making jokes, clearly confident that I had their equipment needs for the new space under control. They trusted me. They would never know it, but I had fallen back on the principles of BDSM to earn that trust. I had assessed what my sub needed and given it to him with a steady hand and confident consistency. Dr. Ego had surrendered to me as his Dominant—and I think he liked it.

One meeting down, four to go.

The rest were straightforward. I listened attentively, made notes when I didn't have the answer, and persuaded each group that their needs would be met. I was going to have to bust my ass to figure out how, but it would be worth it to honor their trust.

In the weeks that followed, Rich continued to go downhill, and I continued to gain confidence and take on a bigger role. People started coming to me for answers instead of waiting for him and I was surprised to realize that I actually had them to give. The clinical staff had a calling. They were saving children's lives every day when they went to work. I look at it now through slightly more mature eyes, and know that the surgeon I met with that day was entitled to his ego.

22. JONATHAN

I was brimming with excitement to start Switching. I checked the appointment book and noticed that my first client was a foot guy. I would come to have many wonderful foot clients, but I'll always remember my first. Foot fetishes are fascinating because for something that seems so simple, there is a surprisingly diverse array of sub fetishes that fall within this larger category. Just to name a few, foot people can be into stinky feet, clean feet, perfectly manicured feet, toes that are painted, feet on which the second toe is longer than the big toe, feet with bunions, feet in stockings, toes tearing through stockings, toes that are covered in a substance (often food related), feet that are smashing a squishy object (also often food related), feet in sandals, feet in high heels, feet with a high heel dangling from the toes, the arch of the foot specifically, feet pushing the pedal of a car, feet smooshing the person's face, feet penetrating a vagina (or any other orifice for that matter), feet popping bubble wrap, feet stepping in mud . . . you get the picture. The most creative foot session I ever encountered was a client who wanted to do "foot dentistry." He liked to pretend he was doing painful and unpleasant dental procedures, but on the toes. He came fully equipped with dental tools and a whole treatment plan. He liked to play with girls who were terrified of the dentist. I never figured out why part of the eroticism for him was that the procedures were being done on toes, but am happy to report that after extensive fillings and root canals, my toes are now cavity free.

I personally don't find feet erotic, but neither am I disgusted by them. I am, however, in the minority of American women when it comes to foot maintenance. I got a pedicure exactly one time and failed to see the point of it. I have, on a whim, painted my toenails from time to time, but they are generally just neatly trimmed and toenail-colored. As a distance runner, I feel I have worked hard to build up the callouses and scars that adorn my feet, earned them with miles and blisters, so it seemed counterproductive to want to get rid of them and have soft, vulnerable feet once more. This was my mindset when I walked into work, a proud new Switch, and discovered that my first client of the day was a foot guy.

Not having had such a client yet, I consulted with Storm in the dressing room about what I should do to be prepared.

"Unless he specified otherwise, I would just wear heels and assume your normal pedicure is fine. You can't really do anything special without knowing."

"Right. My normal pedicure . . ."

I was suddenly embarrassed to let her see my feet, but she wasn't going to judge any more harshly than some guy who was paying to interact with them, so I took a deep breath and asked what she thought.

"They're not that bad," she said, taking an uncomfortably close look. "I'd just throw some nail polish on if you have time and it'll be fine. If you don't care what color, you can use this one."

She handed me a dark burgundy polish, which I quickly started to apply with an unpracticed hand. I kept getting it on the skin, but wiped off my mistakes so that the end product looked pretty good.

The whole time I was painting my nails, Storm was lying massaging her boobs. They were fairly new implants, a gift from one of her lovers who was an executive of some sort. Storm had started as a stripper, but found she made significantly more as a high-end escort. She had been doing it for a few years, and now only went on "dates" with a handful of regulars. She took a few weeks off from the Dungeon at a time to go on exotic vacations with her clients, coming home with bags full of new clothes, accessories, and jewelry. She usually brought a pile of stuff into the dressing room that she didn't want to keep and offered it up for grabs.

I thought I had enough time to apply another coat, which I had just finished doing when Caterina appeared at the dressing room door and said, "Scar, your client is here."

I tried not to look too panicked, but as soon as she left I started frantically blowing on my toes, hoping to get them to dry faster. I could keep him waiting for a few minutes, but didn't think I could wait long enough for them to properly dry. I couldn't walk to the front on bare feet or they would get filthy, but if I put shoes on it was going to mangle the wet polish. Storm saw me freaking out and chucked me a pair of open-toed wedges that were too big and didn't match what I was wearing, but I was past caring.

Her parting advice as I stood up carefully to leave was, "Just stall as long as you can in the interview or it's still going to be wet when he touches it."

I found my new client Jonathan already seated in the interview room smiling pleasantly with a cup of coffee in his hand when I walked in. He rose, introduced himself, and said, "Shall we? I've already taken care of payment and Lady Caterina says the lounge should suit us best."

"Why don't we have a seat and discuss our session first? Make sure we've laid down all of the necessary guidelines and safe words . . ."

Safe words for a foot session? What is coming out of my mouth? Whatever. He's not paying you for your brain. Keep stalling!

He looked taken aback, but returned to the couch and plastered his polite smile back in place.

"I think you'll find my session is quite straightforward and shouldn't require any kind of safe word. I just want to worship your lovely feet and make them feel as good as possible. Assuming you approve, I would like to massage, pamper, and kiss them."

"Well, that sounds nice. Did you have a specific type of massage in mind?"

"A specific type?" He was beginning to look a little concerned.

"Not that it matters. Some clients just have specific types that they practice and I thought maybe you would need certain equipment to take with us," I finished lamely.

"No, nothing specific. I'd just like to do whatever pleases you, Mistress . . . whatever makes your feet feel incredible."

I was just going to have to go for it and hope for the best. If I kept talking he was going to bail. I could already see the doubt forming in his mind. And my brain cells were rapidly killing themselves listening to what my mouth was expelling.

"Well, it sounds like we're all set, then. I'll just get us some towels and blankets and we can head to the lounge."

"Marvelous," he said with obvious relief.

Once we were in the room, I reclined on a Victorian chair and Jonathan lay on a blanket on the floor at my feet. My polish felt mostly dry to the touch, but I could only stare with trepidation as he brought my toes to his mouth. I wondered what wet nail polish tastes like and pictured it smeared all over his face. I was thus distracted and not thinking about the fact that this was the very first time someone had sucked my toes. The initial contact tickled and I wasn't prepared for it, so I nearly jerked my foot and kicked poor Jonathan in the face. But then he kept going and, damn, it felt *good*. Who knew that the warm, wet contact of a mouth on such neglected body parts could be so gloriously erotic? As he rubbed his thumbs up the arch of my foot at the same time as his tongue glided across each toe, I couldn't help groaning and sinking lower in the chair. I didn't really care whether he was eating nail polish anymore as long as he kept going.

It is in such moments that I become aware of just how tightly I cling to control and order. I like to always be prepared, know what I'm getting myself into. I hate surprises because I like to know that my reaction will be appropriate. I don't relax completely around other people. But fuck if this relative stranger hadn't reduced me to a puddle simply through touch. There is such power in the purely sensory experience but we usually don't stop running our minds and our mouths long enough to appreciate it. By the time the hour was up, I had concluded that I should be the one paying him for his services.

His glazed-over, blissed-out expression led me to believe that he enjoyed it as thoroughly as I had.

The next time I had a foot session booked in my schedule, I made a point of going to get a pedicure the day before. I arrived at the Dungeon confident in the state of my now immaculately manicured feet. I couldn't stop staring at my perfect red toenails. I began to understand why women like to get their nails done. It made me feel flirty and very feminine.

I breezed past the desk on my way to the dressing room, and Viv called after me, "Are you ready for Randall?"

"Absolutely." I whirled back with a smile and pointed to my toes. "Got a manicure yesterday, so I'm ready to go!"

She rolled her eyes.

"Randall likes stinky, dirty feet. You better figure out how to make that happen in the next hour or he's going to cancel."

Of course he does. How the fuck was I supposed to know that?

"Next time, do you think you could make a note about that instead of just writing 'feet' in the appointment book? Since I'm a new Switch, I don't know the regulars yet, so a little guidance would help me a lot."

"Not my problem."

She turned her back and answered the ringing phone. I had been dismissed.

I went in search of help once again.

I found Dom on the patio, but wasn't hopeful he would know what to do. It didn't really seem like his forte. I popped my head in the dressing room and was relieved to find Raven making faces at her laptop. She spread her legs and offered a crotch shot to the camera. She licked her finger, and I could see where things were heading, so I cleared my throat and asked quietly, "Are you Skyping a client? I don't want to interrupt. . . ."

"No, I'm on Chatroulette. I sometimes tease guys on there when I get bored. I get them all hot and bothered and then click Next and there's nothing they can do to get back to me!" she said with undisguised glee.

"What the hell is . . . never mind. Hey, question for you: Any idea how I can make my feet stinky in the next hour? I have Randall, and was apparently supposed to intuit from his name that he wants stinky feet."

"Oh yeah . . . he likes 'em nasty. The stinkier and dirtier the better. You don't have smelly flats?"

I didn't bother answering, just stared at her blankly.

"You're gonna want to make some smelly flats for emergencies like this. Pick a pair of old flats and start wearing them barefoot, especially when it's hot out. They'll get really smelly, then if you're in a pinch, you can just walk around in them for an hour and your feet will magically stink. Just triple freezer bag them in your work bag or they'll make everything else in there stink. Oh, and you'll have to refresh them occasionally if you go awhile without wearing them or they'll stop smelling as bad."

She unzipped several bags and tossed me a pair of shoes. I sniffed them without thinking.

"Fuck, Raven! That's disgusting!"

"*Right?*" she responded with genuine pride.

"If you don't want to borrow them, I'll happily take Randall for you. He's super easy and it's dead tonight."

I hesitated, contemplating.

Fuck it.

"Thanks, but I've got it. I'll bring these back before my scene."

I spent the next hour pacing in Raven's smelly flats, which was surprisingly effective. For the last few minutes before Randall's appointment, I stomped around in the dirt behind the patio, covering my feet in dust and mud. I looked down at the finished product, only able to see flashes of red through the grime. My feet were disgusting. Mission accomplished.

23. ELEVATOR

With my new Switch status, I was enjoying work at the Dungeon much more than at the hospital. Every shift seemed to have some kind of new thrill that I could enjoy because now I was the one in control. People in the real world felt boring and closed off compared to the madness that was revealed within those walls. I was doing well at my vanilla job, but I was starting to make excuses to leave early to take more clients at the Dungeon and was picking up extra shifts for special clients. Rich paid no attention to where I was as long as my work was completed, and even if it had been slipping, he had no room to talk. I got away with it until my mom showed up on-site one afternoon for meetings that I didn't know about and found me absent.

She called to find out where I was. I answered it in the dressing room, signaling to the girls around me to be quiet.

"Hey, how's it going?"

"Good. Where are you? I'm in the trailer and you're not here."

"Oh, I had to leave early," I stalled while I tried to think what to tell her that she wouldn't call bullshit on.

Naturally, at that very moment, Raven emerged from the cell walking her client on all fours wearing nothing but a leash.

"Bad dog! You are a bad, *bad* dog! Time for your shock therapy!"

"Where the hell are you?"

"I'm at . . . the vet. Amelia's dog is really sick and she had to go to work, so I'm at the vet with it."

"I didn't know Amelia had a dog."

Damn it, why does she have to pay attention?

"She just got one."

Fuck. Remind me to tell Amelia that from now on as far as my mom is concerned, she has a dog. Or had one and something happened to it.

"Okay. I don't think it was good for you to leave work early and no one here knew where you had gone."

Before she could continue, I jumped in with what I thought she wanted to hear.

"I know. I'm really sorry. It just came up and Amelia just sounded so worried, so I dropped everything and drove up here. You know she would've done the same for me."

"If it was that much of an emergency, I don't know why Amelia couldn't have missed work instead of you. But that's between the two of you. Next time make sure someone here knows that you've left."

"Will do."

Viv popped her head in the dressing room door, but I frantically gestured that I was on the phone and she took the hint. She looked meaningfully toward the lobby instead of yelling that my cock-and-ball-torture client was waiting. That might've been a little tough to explain away.

"Hey, Mom, the vet is ready for me, so I really need to go. I can call you when I leave here if you want?"

"No, it's okay. I'll just see you on-site tomorrow."

Note to self: reschedule my early client tomorrow. This guy better be worth the bullshit I just had to spew.

He was.

My client ended up being a guy who was really into having his balls beaten, but was concerned about the long-term impact on the health of his man parts. He had managed to get his doctor to agree to do an ultrasound and a semen analysis the day after a heavy CBT session to see whether there was any noticeable impact. I would've loved to have been a fly on the wall for that conversation.

I got to do my worst to his balls . . . in the name of science.

It turned out there was some bruising (that's right, gents . . . let that one sink in for a second: bruising on your balls!), but the ultrasound showed a minuscule amount of scar tissue despite decades of abuse, and it wasn't impacting function at all. His sperm count was higher than normal. Evidently, man parts are more resilient than we give them credit for.

I always gave Wes a full download of what I had done with my clients when I got home. Sometimes, he was just fascinated by the crazy shit I saw, but with clients like this one, telling him about it was foreplay. He never once got jealous about what I did with my clients.

I showed up early to the jobsite the next day ready to stay late if necessary in order to appease my mom. I needed to check out the seismic anchorage that had been completed on some of my equipment, so I took her with me over to the new hospital instead of just hanging out in the job trailer.

I was basically always the only girl on the construction site, and despite the reputation that construction workers have for being lewd, I was never once catcalled on that job. In fact, permit me to digress for a moment and say that the construction industry as a whole is full of some of the most wonderful, family-oriented people I have ever met.

I was proud of what I considered "our" building and how much I had learned in such a short amount of time. The hospital was coming to life and I was a part of making that happen. It felt good to see the surprise on my mom's face as I was able to walk her through the building and explain our progress and what the next steps would be. It was also nice for her to see the guys on-site acknowledging me by name and with mutual respect. I was part of the team and I wanted her to see that.

We had recently switched from an exterior man lift to the service elevator and it was always packed going in both directions. Somehow we were alone on our ride back down to the first floor, but the instant the doors opened, guys came flooding in without giving us a chance to exit. We were packed in at the very back before I had time to even think about squeezing my way out. I was mortified that everyone had treated us like we weren't even there. I had a split second to make a decision and two options from what I could tell: We could embarrassingly have to go for another ride until some space cleared and then get back off at the first floor . . . or I could make a scene. I didn't seem to know how to be meek anymore. Scarlett wouldn't allow it.

"Out. Everyone get back *out* right now!"

There was a pause as an elevator full of burly dudes contemplated whether this tiny woman was serious. My mom glanced at me with surprise. A few of them laughed, but the door stayed open.

"You heard me. I'm completely serious. Get. The. Fuck. Out."

It didn't occur to me that they wouldn't obey, which would have been mortifying. Sure enough, one by one they started to pile back out and then stood in front of the elevator staring at me like I might be about to light one of them on fire.

"*Gentlemen*," I emphasized as I too stepped off, "let's try that again, shall we? I know your mamas taught you better manners than that. We let people get off the elevator before getting on. Now . . . everyone is off, so you may carry on."

They cracked up and I heard a mama joke being hurled as the doors closed. I only got away with it because I was an attractive young female. I fully acknowledge that had any one of those descriptors been its opposite, I would've been branded a bitch or worse. Instead, I had earned myself a reputation as "the redhead."

24. TA-DA TED

Unfortunately, my reputation as a semi-unstable ginger didn't do much for me off the building site and in the conference room, where the real torture occurred. Meetings piled on top of each other and sometimes it felt like the meeting was simply about setting up another meeting with no real purpose except to make people feel important. Prior to usurping responsibility from Rich, it was easy to just announce I needed to leave and get out the door on time to make it to the Dungeon. Now that I had to deal with my own meetings, it was becoming more and more challenging to find ways to leave early. On that particular day, I knew I had a client booked at 5:00, so with traffic factored in, I needed to be on the road by 3:30 to make it on time. Which was in ten minutes. And these fuckers were off topic again.

Taking a deep breath, I glanced up and surveyed the room. Eight men and two women, including me, circled the conference room table, which was strewn with enough paperwork and drawings to be considered an act of environmental terrorism. We were scheduled to have been finished twenty minutes ago, but no one else seemed to have anywhere better to be, so on it dragged.

"The table in that special procedure room needs to have stirrups so that it can be shared with the women's clinic on Thursdays," I interjected in an attempt to get us back on topic.

"You hear that, Victor? Make sure it has stirrups so that they can do the 'special procedures' in that room," chimed Patricia with a shriek of laughter and a melodramatic wink.

The room erupted in laughter and I knew I had lost them once more. I felt like slamming my forehead on the table. Instead I took another deep breath and looked at my watch again.

"*Oh*, what are you saying, Patricia? Does somebody do horsey things in private? Do you have a special costume?"

More laughter.

I had to keep my eyes cast down to prevent them from rolling out of my head.

How naughty. How terribly scandalous you all are!

I tried a different approach with, "Well, on that note, I think I'll excuse myself and we can go through the rest of this at next week's meeting."

I knew they were going to think that I was offended by their suggestive remarks, but that was fine. This Dominatrix had a client to get to and couldn't care less if her coworkers thought she was a prude.

I was only about ten minutes late by the time I got to work, but was incredibly wound up from sitting in traffic and stressing about the time. It didn't help that my client Ted was already in the waiting room when I walked in, so I had to introduce myself in business attire before running back to change. He seemed shy, but nice enough. He had mentioned that his scene was sort of based on fantasy wrestling, so I knew I needed to put something on that I could move in.

Dom popped his head into the dressing room, so I stopped getting ready long enough to give him a hug.

"I haven't seen you since Halloween! I heard you're now officially a Switch—congrats!" he said with genuine excitement.

"Thanks, love!"

"Hey, I'm about to do an interrogation scene with some dude and I need a girl to double with me. Wanna play the bad cop to my *very* bad cop?"

"I've been dying to do a double with you, but I'm already late for my guy up front and we're playing for two hours. I'm guessing that won't work?"

He shook his head. "Next time. Or you know you could just come home with me one of these days and we can play there. My wife has the hots for you. You and I can top her together if you don't want to sub."

I was caught off guard by the offer, but had to admit it sounded appealing.

"Let's do it. I gotta run, but we can talk more about it later!"

In our interview, Ted described that he liked to do a session that had elements of fantasy wrestling, but was more about the aftermath of being conquered by a woman instead of the actual experience of someone defeating him. He liked to simulate the headspace that came after having his ass beat, that helpless feeling of despair. I was excited to play with him. What little I had gotten to try of fantasy wrestling had been fun and empowering, and this was a new and novel way of looking at that genre.

He allowed me to pick where we would play, so I selected the Dita Von Teese room. I wasn't entirely sure how he wanted the session to go, but I was beginning to trust my instincts. I went to start some music, but when I hit play, he softly spoke up.

"Goddess, would it bother you if we didn't have music?"

I had a strong preference for music over silence to get in my own headspace, but he was so polite about it that I didn't bat an eyelid and hit Stop.

The Dita Von Teese room is one of the smallest rooms at the Dungeon to play in. It is brightly lit, with a bookshelf on one side, opposing mirrors on the other two, and a couch against the fourth. Framed pictures of Dita, the burlesque dancer, adorn the yellow walls. Clients rarely want to play in this room. Size is one factor, but I believe they avoid it because it is a distinctly feminine space.

Ted lay down in the middle of the room fully clothed in his gray sweatpants and white T-shirt. I had to strain to hear his next soft request.

"Goddess, would you mind taking your shoes off? I have a bit of a foot and stocking fetish as well, so feel free to rub your stockinged feet across my cheeks and mouth if you'd like," he finished sheepishly.

"Not a problem," I replied and unbuckled my platform heels, tossing them to one side.

No complaints here.

Without warning, he sprawled out across the floor as though he had just been thrown there by a conquering Wonder Woman. I watched in amazement as a change overcame him. His breathing quickened and his eyes glazed over with a mix of fear and awe. They were pleading with me, but I hadn't yet determined what for. He lifted a hand, as though with great pain and exertion, and beckoned me closer. I walked toward him slowly, feeding on the energy he was throwing off in waves. As his posture morphed, so did mine. I felt my spine straighten and my chin raise. Of their own accord, my shoulders shot back and a small smile crept onto my face. This was why I was a Domme.

"Will you stand with your foot on my chest like you just conquered me?"

I obliged, standing on his right side, planting my left foot firmly over his heart, keeping the other on the carpet.

"Now will you flex your muscles? I need to see how strong you are, Goddess," he added with a sob of desperation as his voice trailed off.

I lifted both arms, flexing my biceps menacingly, and contracted my quads to show off the muscle that was arguably unfeminine. He whimpered and sighed deeply, the fear settling further into his eyes. He was going to a very real place in his head, and I was excited to take him even deeper. If the bulge in his old-man sweatpants was any indication, he was rather enjoying his helplessness beneath my feet.

"I don't like very much talking or orders, but will you just say: 'I'm the winner! I beat you! Ta-da!' Just repeat that . . . and maybe change poses to flex differently? Oh, and when you need a break, you can rub your feet on me." A glimmer of excitement flitted across his eyes, and then he slipped once more into his state of utter defeat, letting his head flop back to the ground and roll to one side.

I now had the full terms of the scene. My mind simultaneously registered how simple this was going to be, and how slowly these two hours were going to pass. Dita and I were going to be well acquainted by the end of this.

After only a few minutes in that stance, my arms started to shake, so I changed position to flex my arms down in front of my body, and changed legs, brushing my stockinged foot across Ted's lips.

Once I had a foot planted on his chest, I broke the silence suddenly by shouting, "I'm the winner!"

Ted shook like a frightened puppy.

"I beat you!" I said in my most menacing Domme voice, glaring down triumphantly at my pathetic conquest.

"*Ta-da!*" . . . Now I felt ridiculous. It was all I could do not to laugh. *Ta-da? Really? Who the fuck says* ta-da *past the age of four?*

I decided I would need to skip that one next time to keep a straight face. The last thing I needed was to start giggling and not be able to stop ten minutes in to a two-hour session.

I allowed the silence to hang in the air, but tried a variety of threatening faces, punctuating eyebrow raises by pushing more weight down with my foot. It was becoming increasingly difficult to stay engaged as the minutes ticked by, but Ted was staring up at me with the eye contact classic to subs. Single-minded intensity focused on you is an amazing feeling, but not when you're doing nothing but glaring and flexing for long periods of time. I was struggling to maintain eye contact, flex, and keep my balance, while simultaneously waging an inner battle not to look at the time. I know how that fractures the intensity of the moment, and nothing says, "Are we done yet?" like glancing at your watch. I liked Ted and didn't want to ruin this for him.

By roughly the twenty-second time of repeating, "I'm the winner! I beat you!" I was feeling pretty silly and was ready for a break. I couldn't keep my quads flexed any longer. I walked around to stand with a foot on either side of Ted's head, my toes touching his shoulders. I took this repositioning as my opportunity to steal a glance at the time. Seventeen minutes down, an hour and forty-three minutes to go.

Fuck.

I took my time, sensually rubbing my feet across Ted's facial features, watching him relax and close his eyes. This was a break for him too. He reached up and took my foot with both hands, and I allowed it. Ted looked like he wanted to snuggle into my stockings and make a nest. I alternated between feet since I was once again standing on one leg, and knew I would be back to flexing shortly. I got caught up in the sensations too, feeling the difference in the way the stocking glided over his forehead, but caught slightly on the stubble on his chin. I could feel his eyelashes tickle my big toe, and his pulse beating into the arch of my foot when I reached his throat.

I was surprised when he broke the silent, sensual reverie with a barely audible, "Goddess?"

"Yes, slave?"

"Don't forget to say 'Ta-da' . . ."

Fuck.

I took this as my cue that he was ready for me to go back to some Wonder Woman post-throw-down flexing. I had only managed to kill eight more minutes, but I was refreshed and focused enough to keep a straight face. I resumed my position at his right side and forcefully stomped my right foot on his chest, leaning closer to his face to shout, "I'm the winner!"

I watched him sink back into sub space as his eyes glazed over.

"I beat you!" I screamed with a flex of my biceps.

Deep breath. You can do this. You can do this. Not funny. Not funny. Not funny.

"*Ta-da!*" I shouted even louder, trying to practice saying it with some kind of emphasis that I could buy into. I didn't laugh, but I was willing to bet that I wouldn't get through a hundred more repetitions without losing it. *One at a time,* I told myself. *Just get through one at a time.*

An hour and twenty-three minutes later, I realized that I had given up all pretense of caring without even noticing. All of my major muscle groups were trembling when I tried to flex them. I had run out of mental games to play to stop myself from playing Guess the Time, and the fact that Dom's intensely serious session was taking place next door was making it that much harder to take myself seriously. If I could hear them conducting their interrogation, they could certainly hear my every "Ta-da." The idea that it was distracting them made it excruciatingly difficult not to laugh.

I felt guilty and decided I had to snap myself back into it.

In studies regarding the nature of happiness, there is a well-tested theory that the way we rate and remember an experience is an average of the peak of the experience in terms of its emotional charge and the end of the experience. Thankfully, in my line of work, the peak of the session tends to coincide with the end of the session (if ya know what I mean). I was still confident I could blow Ted's mind if I just gave him my focus back for the remaining twelve minutes of the session. I decided I would spend five and a half minutes soothing him and reconnecting by going back to sensual foot rubbing on his face. I rested my muscles by perching on the stool behind me and leaning both feet on his face at once. This let me find a rhythm by making slow circles around his features, pointedly ignoring the voice in my head that was screaming at me to force my foot in his mouth and make him deep throat it.

Not this session, penetration pervert. I don't care how bored you are.

I put both feet over his eyes to check my watch. Twenty seconds to go. I took a deep breath, rolled my neck and shoulders, and let Wonder Woman come back to the forefront of my mind.

When I lifted my feet and assumed the position once more, I locked eyes with Ted and sensed that he knew I was back. I glowered down at him, and struck a bodybuilder pose with my arms in the air. I looked deeper into his eyes, and without showing the slightest reaction with my features said, "I beat you. I'm. The. Winner." It took a conscious effort not to thump my chest after each word. His sweatpants bulge had returned, and he was shaking again. His whole body was moving, hips thrusting to that rhythm as old as time.

Deep breath. You can do this. Not funny. Not funny. Not funny.

"*Ta-da!*" I screamed to the ceiling.

Next door, I heard Dom start to giggle hysterically, and I lost it. Laughter tore through my chest, and there was nothing I could do to stop it. I laughed loudly, with an edge of hysteria, but still managed to make it sound triumphant.

Still laughing maniacally and feeling like I was starting to mentally slip, I desperately repeated the three magic phrases twice, in quick succession. Tears rolled down Ted's cheeks. His breathing was labored with sobs. I hesitated, but his dick was still hard and he was humping the air, so I kept going.

"I'm the winner."

He shuddered and sobbed.

"I beat you," I yelled, still laughing like a mad woman.

"*Ta-da!*"

He groaned while crying and thrashing his head. I was concerned until I looked down and realized that Ted had just come in his pants without any manual stimulation whatsoever.

Where the fuck did he just go in his mind?

I handed him a towel, but he was still way too out of it to care that he had just come all over his trousers and was going to have to leave like that. He scrubbed his face with his hands, and steadied himself with a deep breath. His eyes filled with tears again as he looked at me and said, "Goddess, that was incredible. No one has ever laughed at me like that."

I let him kiss my feet, and stroked his head gently, suddenly very glad we had at least a minute or two for aftercare. I hadn't anticipated that I would need to worry about it for such a simple session, but he was in no state to drive. He was showing all the telltale signs of having been deep in sub space. He chattered away while he tried his best to clean off his pants, babbling excitedly about the session and about how happy and relaxed he was. The quiet, subdued Ted I had met was no longer in the room with us. This Ted was ebullient. I thought he was going to skip to his car. I felt incredible that I had been able to evoke that kind of reaction from another person and honored he had shared that piece of himself with me.

I walked back to the dressing room with a shit-eating grin on my face, feeling about ready to skip myself. I opened the door and was greeted by a chorus of, "I beat you! I'm the winner! Ta-da!" We were all laughing hysterically. Dominic and Storm were clinging to each other trying to explain how difficult I had made their scene. Darling Ted had given us all a good laugh that day, and for many more to come.

25. ELEANOR

Rich came in to work one morning with a huge smile on his face, looking younger and more refreshed than I had ever seen him. The source of such a transformation could only be trouble.

He hummed and danced while filling his coffee cup, saying with a grin as he passed my desk, "Mornin', Jen!"

"Morning . . ." I replied skeptically, giving him the side-eye. I followed him to his office trying to figure out what his deal was.

"Okay, I give up," I said. "I don't smell booze on you and your pupils aren't dilated, so I'm ruling out substance-induced happiness for now. You didn't win the lottery or you wouldn't be here."

He cocked his head with a guilty smirk and shrugged.

"Could it be that Mr. Rich got proper laid?" I said in a pathetic excuse for an Asian accent.

"The Young Grasshopper is correct."

I gasped and nudged him in the ribs. "Am I also correct in assuming that this didn't occur at home? Who is she?"

"Right again. God, Jen, I'm a new man. I'd forgotten what this was like. She's young enough to be my daughter, but for some reason is into a wrinkled old dude like me. And, God, she's wild. It's like anything goes. She calls me 'daddy' and lets me turn her over my knee. And her ass . . . God, her ass when I spank it is like poetry."

"Well, then . . . I guess I should be scolding you, but your marriage is none of my business. It's good to see you happy."

He kept whistling as he booted his computer up. I rolled my eyes playfully and went back to my desk.

Vance appeared at the door carrying a child that I assumed was his daughter. The smile on his face as he looked at the girl made it obvious that this little girl was the light of his life. She had platinum blond hair that fell in ringlets to her shoulders. Freckles dotted her cheeks, and her long eyelashes gave her an angelic look.

"Jenny, I'd like you to meet my daughter, Evie. Evie, this is Jenny."

Evie reached out her hand in my direction, and looked up without making eye contact. I took her hand as I connected the dots. She was blind. Vance had a blind little girl. As we talked about Evie, a number of puzzle pieces fell into place. Vance was always the first out the door so that he could get home to his family. He was impatient to the point of being disrespectful because his priorities were elsewhere, and when we slowed him down it kept him away from this little girl.

Everyone is fighting a battle that I know nothing about? Now I knew what Vance's battle was. I looked at him through new eyes, seeing the loving father who must struggle in ways that I could only imagine. I felt like a dick for thinking that he had been an asshole.

As he carried Evie back out of the trailer, I mumbled to myself, "He could still be a little more polite about it."

That evening, Storm, Raven, and I had just returned to the dressing room after a triple trampling scene. I had definitely been the odd girl out. The gentleman was visiting from Switzerland (he brought us all a box of Swiss chocolates), so he had picked us based on our profiles online. He had properly assessed that Storm and Raven were both around six feet tall and had ample curves, ideal for a man who wants to be crushed under their feminine weight. I was about six inches shorter and forty pounds lighter than either of them, but I had done my best to look heavy and use my strong muscles to compensate. Our

Swiss friend wanted us to crush him under gym mats and take turns walking on him, which had been delightfully fun. It was like a kinky jungle gym. He also said some CBT would be fine, but once we got in the room and he undressed, we were appalled to discover that his man parts smelled like a construction site porta potty. He was uncircumcised, but I didn't think that was the reason since I'm partial to the uncut penis and had never encountered an issue like this before. His dick fucking reeked, so none of us would go near it with anything but our shoes. At the end of the session, he complimented us thoroughly, but expressed disappointment that we didn't interact more with his genitals. Except he pronounced genitals in his accent with a hard *g* as in *garbage*. We were still giggling about it and mimicking his pronunciation as we settled on the couch with our laptops in the dressing room.

"Fuck," groaned Raven. "I have so many papers to grade. It's like the one thing in my life I don't like doing that I can't have a slave for. I love lab work and lecturing, but grading is the worst."

"I was sure you were going to lecture our Swiss friend about personal hygiene for his stinky gen-eetals!" I told her.

"I almost did, but he was so sweet I just couldn't do it."

"What? Raven's got a soft spot for the little Swiss man and his stinky gen-eetals? I never thought I would see the day. Poor guy is never going to know now why women won't go near his junk."

She smacked me with a pillow.

My Web browser had opened to the Yahoo homepage as I prepared for some mindless surfing of the Interwebs. The first headline that caught my eye was about a murder suicide in the town in Texas where I grew up. Appalled, I clicked on it. That click was another delineating moment in my life. The day I started at the Dungeon, I knew I would forever be different. This time, I was unaware that I had just clicked the link that would drop a bomb on my life.

The headline read, "Man finds wife, son shot to death." The man was my father. The wife was my stepmom who had torn my family apart. The son was the seven-year-old half brother I would never get to know. Crime news is reported like entertainment, and most of us are guilty of indulging in a little sensationalism from time to time. I can't properly describe what the moment feels like when you realize that the people in the story aren't distant strangers, but your family.

I closed my laptop and dropped it on the table next to me, as though getting it away from me would make the story less true. I had a moment of confusion, and then it all exploded in my mind at once: They were dead. She killed him. She killed herself. He was seven. My dad came home from work and found them dead in the living room.

My entire body was shaking from the shock, and I was sucking in the deepest breaths I could manage trying to regain control. Control of what? I didn't know.

Raven and Storm thought I was trying to be funny, and then they realized something was legitimately wrong with me. They couldn't understand what had gone that wrong in the space of a few seconds.

"Scarlett, are you okay? You need to breathe, honey!" Raven said, trying to take my hand.

I jumped up from the couch. I didn't want human contact.

I stood there and stared at my own chalk-white face in the mirror trying to understand how this could be reality when it felt so distorted and wrong. In the movies, moments like this are depicted with warped sound and visuals, but in real life what is warped is that the world keeps moving as though nothing has happened. From one second to the next, everything is the same and yet nothing can ever be the same again.

My phone was ringing on the couch, but I didn't care. Raven looked at it and said, "It's your mom. Maybe you should talk to her."

I stared at her blankly and continued to shake.

She handed me the phone, and I answered it and held it to my ear automatically. I didn't want to hear her say it, so I preempted her by saying, "I just saw."

"Oh, God, sweetheart, I'm so sorry. Are you okay? Where are you?"

I could hear the tears in her voice, and didn't think I could talk to her without crying. And if I cried I wasn't sure I would ever stop.

"I'm okay. I don't really want to talk right now. I just want to go home."

"Okay. Where are you, though? Are you with Wes? You don't sound like you should be driving."

"I'll be fine. I just want to go. I love you. I'm fine. I just don't want to talk."

I hung up the phone and grabbed my work bag. Raven and Storm were staring at me as if I might explode, and they weren't sure how to approach me. In so many ways, I felt close to them, but in this there was a void too big to fill. I needed someone who knew the history but who wasn't personally affected by it. I couldn't be around anyone who was as raw as me. I knew my family would take care of one another, but I wanted space. I just needed Wes.

"Can you tell Cat that I needed to leave? I'll e-mail and explain later."

I got to my car and felt the flood of tears that I had been holding back start to burn my eyes, but I didn't give in to it. It was an abyss I refused to step into.

I called Wes, looking to be steadied.

"Hey!" he answered, mid-laugh, obviously with someone in the background.

"Umm . . . hey . . ." I responded, hearing my voice crack.

"What's up, pookie bear?"

He couldn't hear in my tone that something was wrong, and that pissed me off. I heard him laugh again, and concluded that he was stoned. I blurted out what had happened anyway, needing him to snap out of it and be there for me.

There was a long pause, followed by more giggling and, "Who did what?"

I hung up.

It wasn't worth trying to explain it to him. I told myself that it wasn't his fault that he had been high when I called, but I couldn't shake how angry I was that I needed him and he was useless. Angry wasn't good, but angry I could work with. It was a feeling I could control better than mindless grief.

I kept breathing deeply and started the engine. Driving gave me something else to focus on. My gas light was on, so I eventually pulled into a gas station, but I kept pulling up on the wrong side of the pump. I must have pulled to the wrong side six or seven times before I eventually got it right. The shock was having more of an impact than I was willing to credit. I acknowledged that I probably shouldn't be driving, but just wanted to get home.

When I got there Amelia was waiting with the front door open. I could only assume my mom had called her. She gave me the hug I didn't know I needed and we made it to the living room. I don't remember much about the hours that followed. She let me babble about it all and if she thought it was strange that I was eerily calm, she didn't comment. I didn't cry. I stopped hyperventilating. But by the time I went to bed that night, my whole body was still shaking with repressed emotion.

26. SPANKSGIVING

Thanksgiving arrived too quickly on the heels of tragedy and I still wasn't ready to spend that much time with family. Deep down, I think I knew I was burying my head in the sand, but I was convinced that if I could compartmentalize it for long enough, it wouldn't hurt so much, and I could just move on. Turns out repressed feelings don't fade. They fester.

I told my mom we were spending Thanksgiving with Wes's family but really made plans to spend "Spanksgiving" at Raven's house with a big group from the scene. The holidays are a surprisingly busy time at the Dungeon. It seemed to be a combination of lonely guys who didn't really have family and guys who had too much of their families. By the time Thursday rolled around, we were all exhausted from fulfilling everyone else's fantasies and ready to blow off some steam fulfilling our own.

Like a traditional Thanksgiving, there was an abundance of food at Raven's because everyone had brought a few favorite dishes. We shared dinner, drinks, and laughs like a normal family—if your family openly discusses the merits of using kitchen utensils for cock and ball torture, tentacle fetishes, and the distractingly awkward squeaky noises the girls always make in Japanese bondage porn.

When other families were gathering around their tables to play board games, we were gathering around a huge pile of tarps for a giant sploshing scene. Sploshing falls within the wet and messy (WAM) category of fetishes. It is an attraction to throwing and smashing food items on another person, usually covering them in a creamy, sugary mess. We were basically going to have a sexy food fight. Everyone had brought extra cream pies, cupcakes, and whipped cream, which we laid out around the tarps at the ready.

We were all naked or very close to naked. Wes, never one to be shy, had stripped everything off, but I had elected to leave my underwear on in the hopes that it would keep frosting out of my lady bits, which didn't sound particularly pleasant. Wes and Boy were the only men present in a small crowd of women. Their grins indicated that they liked their odds.

Raven stood in the center of the tarps, pie in hand, and said, "On my signal!"

She smashed the pie in Boy's face, and mayhem ensued. I raced to grab a can of whipped cream, but before I could get the cap off, Storm was standing in front of me with two cupcakes. I was pretty sure I knew what she was going to do with them. We giggled as she smashed one on each of my boobs. It felt so silly and wrong, but was naughty and hot at the same time. She smeared the frosting all over my chest and stomach, and I retaliated by spraying her utterly perfect fake breasts with a whipped cream bikini. I turned to show off my handiwork to Wes, but found him occupied. My boyfriend was wrapped in the arms of Raven's friend Gwen. Her body was pressed against him. His tongue was in her mouth. Until then, I hadn't witnessed such an intimate moment between Wes and another woman. I paused to consider how it made me feel. It was thrillingly erotic and not the least bit threatening. If anything, it strengthened our bond because we each appreciated that the other allowed us to experiment. It also reminded us that we were in a relationship because there was more to it than just sex.

I relaxed a little and enjoyed some good messy fun. I was self-consciously aware that I was participating the least of anyone, mostly keeping things light and silly long after the others had gotten hot and heavy. For the moment, I was happy observing without having to put anything on the line.

All of the women eventually ganged up on Wes and Boy. They sprayed whipped cream targets onto Wes's balls and took turns kicking them. I got nervous when they formed a line and walked across his body, finally smearing the frosting on his face with their feet before stepping off him and rejoining the line again. He loved being crushed under heavy women, particularly if they smashed his face under their feet. Everyone here knew what they were doing with trampling, so I trusted they were conscious of where it was safe to step. But he was slippery from all the icing, so I was worried that someone would slip and rupture an organ or break one of his ribs. I didn't want to put a stop to the fun, so I stood next to him and took the hand of each woman who walked across his length to help them balance. I learned that part of my role as his Mistress would be babysitting to make sure things never went too far. He would always push for more, so I needed to know when to steer things in another direction to keep him safe.

When all of the dessert was exhausted, we stood in a mess of epic proportions. I hadn't really thought through how we were going to clean up. We went two at a time into the shower, which took forever because we had to keep unclogging cake bits from the drain. I also suspect that Wes and I weren't the first couple to get dirtier before getting clean.

It was certainly a unique way to celebrate Thanksgiving. I think things would have gone much better between the Pilgrims and the Native Americans in the long run if they had started things our way.

It felt like I had reached a new level of comfort in my open relationship with Wes. People seem to think that being in an open relationship must be easier because you can do whatever you want, but it is much, much harder. In a monogamous relationship, maybe you have to wonder what else is out there or fight off temptation, but it's mostly about staying centered and learning to shut out the distractions in favor of what you have committed to. For an open relationship to work it requires constant communication that, no matter how uncomfortable, is always necessary. One of the hardest things for us to accept was that it didn't matter how silly we thought our partner was being, it was imperative to listen to what they were saying. Even if I thought his concern was ridiculous, if it was what he was feeling, then it mattered and needed to be worked through.

One of our biggest issues was something I would never have anticipated. He got bored of the guest stars in our relationship almost immediately, finding that the fantasy was usually better than the reality. Once he got to know the women we were playing with better, he wasn't as attracted to them. They always started on a pedestal as the stars of his fantasy, but slowly came down to reality once they revealed their individual quirks and flaws. He tired of them, often after one scene, but they usually wanted to play with us again. They were my friends, so I wasn't going to tell them that he was bored of them and no longer interested. I had to coerce him into playing with them again by threatening that he wasn't going to be allowed to play with my friends anymore. He basically had his pick of the Dungeon, and in a way it turned him into a spoiled child who only wanted the next new toy until it was given to him.

27. MOLLY

The AVN awards in Vegas are essentially the porn Oscars with a multiday porn convention attached. That year, most of us weren't attending the ceremony or the awards but were there for the fetish after-party. It was one of the biggest and most exclusive fetish events in the world every year, and almost everyone in our group was a featured guest. Most of the women I worked with were trying to make a name for themselves, so they promoted their brand at every event. I, on the other hand, was trying my best to do the opposite and draw as little attention to myself as possible.

Wes was devastated that he couldn't go because of school, but I was excited to take a trip with the girls. Eight of us from the Dungeon were sharing a room after concluding that sleep wasn't particularly high on our agendas. We really just needed somewhere to get dressed and to dump our shit.

Eight Dominatrices getting ready in one small hotel room must have been a sight to behold. I had brought a red latex miniskirt with me, but couldn't seem to find a suitable top to wear with it. I tried corsets and bras and an assortment of options from the other girls' bags, but nothing seemed to look right with it. I appealed to Raven for help and she looked me up and down before her face lit with a grin.

"Hang on. We'll use bondage tape!"

I wasn't following her yet, but stood patiently while she grabbed a roll of bondage tape from her bag and unrolled some of it.

"We'll make suspenders!"

Holy hell. The woman wanted me to go in public wearing nothing but a two-inch strip of tape over my ta-tas.

"I got it," said Erin, taking the tape from Raven to let her put her boots on.

"You have really nice tits," she said as she covered one of them with a strip of tape.

"Thanks . . . you too," I replied, and she smirked her Erin smirk that made her dimples appear.

Once the tape was in place, I was surprised at how sexy I felt wearing nothing but suspenders and a latex skirt. A quick walk through the casino and we would be at the party anyway. I squared my shoulders and got ready to rock it.

We were about to leave when Minx pulled a sandwich bag full of tiny pills from her purse and shouted, "Who wants Molly?"

She grabbed a fistful and handed them out. I took one from her, but wasn't sure how I felt about it. I hadn't done much experimenting with drugs. Sure, I had gone through a high school phase of smoking weed and tried coke once at a frat party, but I hated it. The idea of being out of control terrified me. But a little voice in my head was whispering that *when in Rome . . .*

"I've never done Molly before. Is it going to make me feel fucked up?"

"Not at all," answered Minx. "It's like being drunk or high but with a clear head. Like everything is just better and more intense, but you aren't all fucked up."

I shrugged and knocked it back with a swig of gin.

Making it across the casino floor was more challenging than I had anticipated. We drew every eye in our vicinity, and within moments had drawn a crowd of drunk guys who were blocking our path and aggressively taking pictures. I had a flash of what it would be like to be famous and simultaneously loved and hated it. The attention was a rush, but the crowd around us felt like it was on the brink of clubbing us and dragging us back to their caves. At one point I got culled from the main group and found myself surrounded and alone. The whip I was carrying was a comforting weight in my hand. I wondered if the guys around me realized how lethal its bite was.

We made it to the VIP elevator without major incident and giggled together in the tightly packed space. It felt like we were building to something big with every floor we passed.

After breezing past security at the door, we walked into the suite and I was overwhelmed by the level of debauchery that surrounded us just from the first glance. This was no client session or public play party. It was my first experience of a no-holds-barred private fetish party . . . and it was wilder than I could have imagined.

Glancing in any direction, I could see a panoply of sexual fantasies being played out. A transgender woman was on her knees just inside the door with a line of guys in front of her, hard penises at the ready. The man she was servicing came in her mouth with a grunt, at which point she simply swallowed, looked up, and said, "Next," to the next gentleman in line. People were fucking in every corner of the room, with various levels of participation from the people around them. A naked chick was dancing on a stripper pole while pleasuring herself with a massive dildo. A large Asian Domme took what appeared to be her slave by the collar and dragged him across the room shouting, "I'm gonna make you eat my shit!"

That was the exact instant that the MDMA started to kick in and I freaked out. I suddenly couldn't handle the thought of being on drugs in this setting, didn't want everything to be "more intense." It was fucking intense enough with my wits about me. I wasn't sure exactly what I was feeling, but it was a woozy, off-kilter sort of sensation that was creeping its way up my spine and I was terrified that it was going to get worse.

Raven sighed, grinned lazily, and said, ". . . and I'm on the train. Who's rolling with me?" as she started to make her way through the party.

I was trying not to hyperventilate and play it cool, but it wasn't working. I wanted to go home. I wanted Amelia there with me.

I thought maybe if I could just find somewhere quiet to hide out for a few minutes, I could get myself back under control and be okay. Maybe I could text Amelia and it would all seem funny and not quite as terrifying. I went in search of a bathroom. I swore everyone was looking at me and all of them knew that I was losing control. They probably *were* all looking but because I was a half-naked hot chick who had just joined the party. Out of control was the name of the game for everyone else.

I found a bathroom and waited my turn in line, taking deep breaths. I locked the door behind me and leaned both hands on the sink, looking at myself in the mirror. I still looked like me. Maybe a little pale, but not as fucked up as I felt. I ran some cool water over my wrists and sighed at how nice it felt. Maybe I could do this. It was going to be okay.

The shower curtain slid back abruptly revealing a naked guy giving a very naked chick an enema.

"Care to join us, gorgeous?"

I must've jumped like a cartoon character. I had always been suspicious of closed shower curtains at parties and now I knew why!

I bolted out the door and full-blown panic set in. I needed to get the fuck out of there. I needed a clear head.

Why the fuck did I do drugs? Fuck. Fuck. Fuck!

Erin had obviously been looking for me and found me leaning against a wall hyperventilating. She lifted my chin, looked me in the eye, and kissed me.

And it was everything I had imagined it would be. Her lips pressed against mine were impossibly soft and sensual. The world around me exploded into a kaleidoscope of sensation and, in an instant, I loved the way I was feeling. Wanted to feel more, feel *everything*. I moaned as Erin slid her tongue into my mouth and deepened our kiss. I tried to lace my hands around her neck to feel more of her, but she pinned my wrists firmly above my head and made it absolutely clear who was in control. Not me. And that was just fine as far as I was concerned. For the first time in my entire life, I let go. I surrendered to the gods of hedonism.

Erin kept kissing me, stroking her fingers across my neck and down my exposed chest with her free hand, making me shiver. Her lips followed the same trail, starting behind my ear and working her way down. She nibbled my neck and then sucked on it hard enough that somewhere in the blissful fog of my mind I knew it would leave a mark, but I didn't care. I needed more and she seemed to understand that having ignited this wildness in me, she was now responsible for fueling the fire. Had she been any man I had been with up to that point and most I have met since, we probably would've just fucked right there up against that wall in a quick explosion of drug-fueled lust. But she wasn't having that. We both knew that what existed between us had been building for months and there was greater satisfaction to be had from drawing it out. Her kisses were leisurely. I thought my knees were going to buckle. I had never been so wet before, so desperate to know what comes next.

I had forgotten where I was when our reverie was broken by Raven shouting, "Lesbians!" and screaming with laughter.

Erin released me from our embrace and we laughed along with Raven. I impulsively hugged her and said, "I love everyone!"

"Aw, and everyone loves you too, hun. Glad you're enjoying your first roll. I'm gathering the girls for a golden shower party. Boy just got here and we're going to pee on him!"

"Okay!" I shouted with glee and the three of us practically danced hand in hand to the massive shower suite.

It was a glass room big enough to fit about a dozen people comfortably and there was at least twice that number crowded around the glass watching. Boy was standing just inside. He hugged me in greeting and I kissed him deeply in response. He was initially startled, but he pulled me closer and returned the embrace. Gods, it felt good to kiss people, to connect through lips and tongue and touch. The subtle differences between kissing a woman and a man were amplified by the drugs. I could feel his rough beard against my skin and his big hands on the small of my back. His kiss was harder, but less possessive. Strong, but not consuming like Erin's. I eventually pulled back and said, "I'm on Molly. And I love everyone!"

"You're adorable."

I turned to find Erin, suddenly worried that she would be angry or jealous that I had kissed someone else, but she nodded at me reassuringly. Jealousy had no place here.

Boy stripped naked and lay down on the shower floor, while the rest of us who were participating stripped off shoes and, in some cases, all clothing. Boy was already rock hard thanks to the line of smoking-hot women who were appraising him with open lust, about to fulfill one of his fantasies.

I had tried a few more times to give Wes a golden shower without any success. The more times I failed, the more embarrassed I got that I just couldn't do it no matter how badly I needed to go. It crossed my mind that I was almost certainly going to get stage fright and not be able to do it here in front of this many people. I acknowledged the thought, but it didn't worry me. The way I was feeling, nothing worried me.

I watched as one woman after another entered the shower room, stood over Boy, and voided her bladder. Some of them covered him all over and others aimed more precisely and made him drink it. When it was my turn, I walked across the wet tiles until I reached him, completely unfazed by the fact that it was a puddle of other people's urine. He looked up at me with such intensely pleading eyes. I rolled my latex skirt up, unselfconsciously revealing my lady bits to a crowd of strangers. I straddled his head and squatted slightly, willing myself to release the stream he yearned for. But nothing came. I smiled sheepishly back at the girls and continued to stand there, exposed and straining to go. The crowd clearly assumed I was toying with Boy, teasing him since all of the others had given him what he wanted without a second's hesitation and without receiving anything in return. This wasn't necessarily a problem, but he was a submissive who was deeply eager to please and I knew it would only add to his pleasure if he was allowed to give as well as receive. I slowly lowered myself until I was kneeling over his face.

He groaned loudly and said, "Oh, Goddess, may I please?"

I didn't bother answering him, but lowered just a bit until I felt his wet, warm mouth on me. His clever tongue found my clit and my mind exploded with new sensations. I rewarded him by stroking his hard dick. His hips started bucking under me, but his tongue maintained a steady rhythm. I lifted slightly, closing my eyes to drown everything else out. I guided his hand down to take over for mine. I knew I could do this but needed to focus. It felt like he was getting close to coming, so I released my bladder without warning directly into his mouth. He moaned like a man dying of thirst who had just been given a drink, frantically lapping at all I had to give him. It only took seconds for him to come and the crowd shouted their approval, reminding me that we had an audience.

I couldn't stop grinning.

I turned the shower controls at random until most of the heads were blasting hot water and let Boy rinse off. Standing under the spray of hot water, I could only revel in how amazing it felt. I was nearly oblivious to the fact that I was still dressed, but thankfully water doesn't do latex any harm. I would normally have been worried about messing my hair up after taking the time to do it, but instead I was just amazed by the sensation of the water cascading through it and across my skin.

Erin dried me off with a towel and I practically purred at the terry softness. We made our way through the party, and this time I felt like I was plugged in to the pulsing energy of the place, like I belonged. The scenes we encountered were thrilling instead of terrifying. I watched blood cupping and needle play with detached fascination. We jumped in on a CBT scene and then managed to get seven girls smothering the same male sub. We did spanking and hair pulling and sensory play that blew my mind as much to perform as it did to receive. Everything felt *amazing*. We were constantly touching and kissing, unselfconscious and free.

I'm not really sure how, but we ended up in a very large bubble bath that was heaven to my drug-enhanced nerve endings. There was an unspoken understanding that it was a girls-only space, which was good because with eight or nine of us in the tub, there was no room for anyone else. Like something out of a lesbian fantasy porno, hands started roaming under the bubbles until everyone seemed to be simultaneously giving and receiving pleasure without much thought to what belonged to whom.

Erin and I broke off from the group and I lost myself in her kisses. I wanted more. Deeper. Something . . .

Someone produced a strap-on and I managed to put the harness on under the water. Erin lay back and her look was pure challenge.

"Fuck me."

It was a command. Erin was offering what I wanted but made it clear she was still in control. Which was good since I was a mindless slave to my senses. I learned that night as I thrust into someone for the first time that I have a serious penetration fetish.

I also learned that as good as MDMA feels, it renders me incapable of orgasm. We tried in a Sisyphean effort until the water was cold and we were physically spent. Erin had no such issues. I couldn't seem to wipe the smug grin off my face from the number of times I had made her come.

We dried off, dressed, and gathered our girls as we headed for the exit of the suite. The party was still raging, but had taken on a more lethargic tone. By some miracle, we reassembled our complete group and added Sir Liam, who had just finished fucking Minx, to our posse as we made our way out.

I had no idea what time it was or how long we had been in the tub, but when we emerged from the casino and joined the taxi line, the sun was high in the sky and people were going about their days. A group of female tourists joined the line behind us and began discussing us with undisguised disgust.

"Do you see what she's wearing?" I heard one mutter with a Southern twang.

"Do you think they're hookers just leaving a party?"

"Think that guy is their pimp?" asked another, looking pointedly at Liam.

I grinned at Erin. I was still coming down from the drugs and the exhilaration.

"Sir," I called to Liam in an exaggerated whine, "Mistress Erin gave me a hickey!"

I pointed to the mark I knew was on my neck and pouted at him. Liam played along.

"Mistress Erin, you know marks aren't allowed. We'll have to come up with a punishment for you back at the room!"

His use of the singular *room* was not lost on our audience. Their faces were priceless.

Erin's dark eyes glittered with mischief as she opened the car door and said, "Sounds like a good time to me."

We made it back to the room and sprawled across the two beds in a giant cuddle puddle as we all recovered from such a wild night and came down from the drugs.

When I got home, I was nervous to tell Wes everything, but I knew that for this to work, there needed to be total transparency. He was turned on by most of my tales of what I had seen. He was curiously unconcerned about what had happened with Erin. There was a dramatic distinction for him between me being with other men and other women. In his mind, things I did with other women were just for show or silly fun. It didn't occur to him that there was an emotional connection there as well that was more of a threat to our relationship than another man would be. Men mostly just seem to worry about other penises without realizing that it's women's hearts that run away with them.

28. VANESSA

The next party I attended was a gathering of my college friends, but I brought Dom and Vanessa along for shits and giggles. I had work at the jobsite the next morning, but planned to leave the party early enough that it wouldn't be a big deal. It was a typical college party with kegs, drinking games, and socializing, but somehow it felt different. It was really me who had changed. I couldn't put my finger on the differences between a party with my vanilla friends and with my kinky friends—besides the obvious that no one was publicly committing perverse sexual acts at the former. It was more than that. My college friends hadn't figured out who they were yet. They all still carried around a barrier of insecurity that would protect them from standing out too much from the herd.

After a few drinks, I eventually relaxed back into old routines. I still knew how to be Jenny. I just felt less and less comfortable in her skin.

We were standing around outside when a particularly obnoxious girl, Leslie, came running over to us waving her phone triumphantly.

"Oh, my God, Jenny! Is this you?"

A glance at her screen told me she had found the Dungeon Web site. My stomach dropped. My close friends knew by now what I had been up to, and I wasn't ashamed of what I was doing. But I didn't exactly need it publicized out of context to my entire friend group either.

Leslie had managed to attract the attention of everyone outside by the time she started drunkenly yelling my profile aloud.

"As a sub, I have discovered how much I especially enjoy role-play and tickling. Ropes thrill me. I love the challenge of leaving my comfort zone to yield as your little slave. I'm always looking for adventure . . . think you're up to the task?"

My initial plan was to act like I didn't give a fuck, knowing that the more I protested, the more interesting the story became. But it was interesting enough without me saying a word. And she just kept going.

"As your Dominant, I enjoy role-play, spanking, flogging, and a variety of other delightful instruments. Feminization, puppy play, and humiliation amuse me endlessly. I relish anything corporal. I absolutely love to have my dainty size-seven feet worshipped."

I could hear the key phrases being spread around us like wildfire and tried to just shrug it off.

"Well, Leslie, thank you for that dramatic reading!"

"So, *Scarlett*, do guys, like, pay you to spank that ass?" she shrieked and tried to spank me.

I could've kissed Dom when he jumped in with, "Did you see my profile on there too, Leslie?"

This was just too much for her drunken mind to handle. She stared at him for a moment and then said, "No way! You too?"

He was all charm as he took the phone from her and navigated away from my page to his. The interpretation on Leslie's face was clear: if the tall, gorgeous, foreign dude is doing it too, then maybe it's okay. He had bought me the distraction I needed to quietly disappear indoors to compose myself. I couldn't change what people were saying about me, but I could face them with my chin up.

Unfortunately, Colin had caught Leslie's performance as well and followed me inside. He cornered me and demanded to know, "Is that where all the bruises came from? Guys are paying to beat you?"

Technically, it was Dom and not a client who had caused those particular bruises, but the last thing I needed was Colin barreling outside to pick a fight with him.

"Yes."

He looked like I had slapped him. I think he honestly believed there must be another explanation, but my admission had torn through that last shred of hope.

"Jenny, why do you get yourself into this shit? You're better than this."

"You know nothing about it. Who are you to stand there and judge me?"

"I love you."

Okay. Didn't see that one coming. What the fuck?

"You don't love me, Colin. You just—"

"Fuck you, Jenny. How the hell would you know? Just let me help you. We can get you out of this—"

"Fuck *you*, Colin. I'm not some helpless fucking prostitute who needs to be rescued from her big bad pimp and a life on the streets! I love what I do. I don't care if you judge me for it."

"Fine! Go be a fucking whore."

I didn't stick around to hear what else he would say. I was so fired up, I hurried back outside and impulsively kissed Vanessa. And then Dom. And then Vanessa again. From the smiles on their faces, they knew what I was playing at.

"You guys wanna get out of here?" I asked with a sly look.

They didn't miss a beat. Vanessa responded with, "Your place or ours?"

"Yours."

The three of us set our beers down and walked out hand in hand. I couldn't help glancing over my shoulder as we reached the gate, and I wished I hadn't. Colin looked utterly devastated. And suddenly I felt like a bitch. And a little bit like the whore they all thought I was.

Fuck it.

I couldn't be the girl he wanted. I still regret hurting him like that, but I'm sure it let him move on much quicker than trying to be gentle with him.

When we got back to Dom and Vanessa's place, they stripped the bed and put a shower curtain down and then remade it with a different set of sheets.

"You ever tried baby oil?" she asked with a gleam in her eye.

"Nope."

Now that I was there, I was nervous. This was my first really intimate threesome with another couple without Wes there. Wes was friendly with Dom, but they didn't have any interest in playing with each other, so he had agreed it would be fine if I flew solo on this one. During the drive down, we had laid the ground rules that Dom and I wouldn't have any actual intercourse, but toys and touching were fair game. Evidently, we were going to play with baby oil, something that technically fell within the bounds of a WAM (wet and messy) fetish, but was a different approach from what we had done at Thanksgiving. What that translated to was the three of us dousing ourselves in baby oil and then writhing around on the bed in a sinuous mess of limbs and bodies. Mouths were out of the equation, so it became all about touch. The mixture of Dom's strength and Vanessa's softness was intriguing.

I had continued drinking at their place to soothe my nerves, so by the time we were actually playing, I was hammered and let my guard down. In the clouded back of my mind, I acknowledged that one of these days I was going to need to let go without substances, but for now I needed whatever help I could get.

After my intense sub-space experience with Dom at the Dungeon, I had expected a similar encounter this time. It was quite the opposite. His dominant nature would always shine through, but at home it was more playful and relaxed. He didn't need to prove anything here.

When we were finished and the three of us were lying in a breathless heap, it was obvious I was too drunk to drive home. We remade the bed and showered and I snuggled between the two of them.

We quietly exchanged stories of clients and lovers. Apparently a popular request for Dom was to play out a cuckold fantasy. Men wanted to imagine him fucking their wives. *Their wives probably wouldn't mind*, I thought. I told them that my newest regular was an entertainment attorney who wore stockings and women's panties under his suit every single day. As far as clients went, it wasn't particularly shocking, but to them it seemed bizarre to have to hide like that. Dom and Vanessa were 24/7 Dominant and submissive, and they didn't care who knew. I think I passed out midway through telling them about my client who wants to be my sperm slave, trapped in a dungeon and milked for his seed.

I woke in a blind panic. I was an hour late for work and had barely had much more sleep than that. I had rinsed off the night before, but was pretty sure I still had baby oil in my hair and my eye makeup was smeared in dark circles under my eyes. I parked in the structure next to the site and took a deep breath. It was going to be a rough morning.

I made it through my morning meetings and crawled back into my truck at lunch to take a nap.

How the fuck do people party and still have real jobs?

I woke up at five as people around me were starting their engines to drive home for the day. I could only shake my head. I didn't bother going back in to the trailer to admit what had happened. I just started my engine and began the drive up to the Dungeon to start my next shift.

29. FRANK AND CINDY

The previous year, I had started at the Dungeon just a little too late to attend KinkyCon, one of the BDSM conventions that takes place in L.A. every year, but this year I was expected to participate. All of the girls were encouraged to attend at least one of the days to man the Dungeon's booth in shifts. During down time, we could attend the various talks and workshops that were offered. I wasn't quite ready to be teaching a workshop, but a number of our Dommes were also there as instructors.

You know that convention you've probably attended for whatever industry you happen to be a part of? It was exactly like that. The main convention floor was filled with booths representing toy makers, video distributors, independent Dominas, furniture makers, clothing companies, and the like. Most of them were giving away freebies, so girls were filling bags with tiny cheap toys and free porn as they made their way around the floor. Our booth was offering demonstrations and performances at the discretion of whoever was in charge at the time. Our subs weren't allowed to wander on their own lest one of the pervert attendees (and I use pervert affectionately) prey on them, so they were informally assigned to the Dommes and Switches in attendance, and followed us around like little ducklings.

I had reviewed the class schedule, and there were a few that I wanted to attend. The first was a strap-on workshop, which I had somehow persuaded Amelia to attend with me. Later in the afternoon, some maniac was offering a waterboarding demo that looked too ridiculous to miss. Wes had a legal clinic in the morning, but he was going to be there in time to join me for the afternoon workshop.

I signed Amelia in to the convention as a submissive of the Dungeon so that she didn't have to pay the convention fees, which meant that I got to choose the name on her badge. Under her smiling picture, her name read "Cunty McSquirt."

I made sure I got to the strap-on class early, with Amelia and three Dungeon submissives in tow, so that we could get good seats in the front row. I may have neglected to mention to Amelia that there would be a live demo.

The front tables were set up with harnesses, an assortment of dildos, and a white board, but the instructors weren't there yet. The room slowly filled with a wide assortment of people until there were only a scattered handful of empty seats and the air was buzzing with quiet conversation. Amelia was fidgeting next to me, not daring to lift her eyes from the convention program I had given her, though I doubted she was really reading it. I was turned around in my seat, freely checking out the rest of the crowd. I acknowledged the people I knew with a conspiratorial smile and a wave, and challenged those I didn't with eye contact to see if there was anyone interesting. A few people piqued my interest, so I made a mental note to keep an eye out for them at the play party later that evening.

A middle-aged couple entered the room and walked straight to the front, instantly commanding the attention of all present. His hair was entirely white, and his weather-beaten skin made me think of him as an old cowboy. She was well past her prime as well, but still had sex appeal, and she knew it.

"Good morning!" said the man in a voice that reached the very back of the room. Clearly they weren't going to need microphones.

"I'm Cindy, and this is my husband, Frank," added the woman.

"A little bit about us . . ." continued Frank. "We've been married for thirty-eight years and in an open marriage for most of that. We've been handcrafting leather strap-on harnesses and teaching these workshops for about ten years. We're not going to make this a sales pitch, but if y'all are interested in our goods, we have a booth out on the floor, and would love to talk more with you after the class."

They spent about the first half hour reviewing the basics of strap-on use, most of which I knew, but some seemed like good advice. They talked about the best ways to clean both the harness and the dildo between uses, ways to give your partner a good warm-up before drilling them, different sizes and styles of strap-ons, ingredients in lube that could damage your equipment, how to signal to a prospective partner that you were "packing" a strap-on, and overall strategies for avoiding jealousy in an open relationship. I was riveted.

Frank reached his arms over his head in a stretch and said, "Now, we know you're all here to see the live demo, so why don't we get moving with that?"

Quiet murmuring followed this pronouncement. I didn't look at Amelia, but I felt her sit a little straighter. She was a champ, and rolled with this new development to what I'm sure was already a lot to process.

Cindy added, "We've got a male and a female demo bottom who've been kind enough to volunteer today."

She gestured to the back of the room, and two people clad in black robes made their way sheepishly to the front. The man was slight of build, in his thirties, and looked so timid I was surprised he would volunteer to stand in front of a crowd, far less get fucked. I concluded that it must be part of the fetish for him. Perhaps he was into some variation of public humiliation or forced exposure. The female demo bottom was in her early twenties, but her full figure gave her a cherubic look that made her seem even younger.

I expected introductions, but with no further ado, Male sub dropped his robe, revealing his naked, wiry frame and surprisingly hairy backside. Cindy covered the table with butcher paper and patted it for him to hop up. I had to stifle a giggle, not at his nudity, but at the sudden realization that the table they were about to do the deed on belonged to the convention hotel. It was going to be used next for a book signing, academic conference, or tech convention . . . and the people who sat at it would have no idea.

Male sub climbed on the table, assuming the position on all fours, while Cindy pulled a strap-on over her jeans. I should have been turned on. I was totally into this kind of thing, but there was such a lack of sexual chemistry between Cindy and Male sub that it was like a black hole at the front of the room. Frank gave a running commentary of what Cindy was up to as she mounted Male sub and thrust away. The room was silent with fascination, so we could hear the squelching noises as she added more lubrication. Male sub was obviously flaccid, and offered no sound or change of expression that indicated he was even aware that he was being penetrated. It was awkward, and Cindy and Frank seemed to know it.

"Well, I think that's enough of that!" Cindy laughed and clapped Male sub on the shoulder as she dismounted the table. She wrapped him in his robe as he stepped back down on the ground.

Frank said, "Let's have a round of applause for our brave demo bottom!"

It was touching to hear the enthusiasm of the crowd for what had been a pretty lame demonstration. They cheered and applauded as though Male sub deserved an Oscar for his performance. Instead of judging him, everyone was acknowledging the balls it took to go in front of a crowded room naked and let a woman fuck you.

"Now, sweetheart, you ready for your turn?" Frank asked Female sub, patting her on the rear.

She grinned eagerly and nodded. Cindy had changed harnesses and laid fresh paper on the table, so they were ready to go. Female sub dropped her robe on a chair to cheers from the crowd. She was round in all the wrong places and flat in all the places that should have had curves. She was proof that no matter what shape the female form takes, it can still be beautiful. Both women climbed up on the table, but this time Frank stepped in to assist with the warm-up. This demo already had a different tone. Frank and Cindy stroked and kissed Female sub until she was moaning and begging incoherently.

"What was that?" Frank teased.

Cindy added, "We couldn't understand you over all that moaning, sweetheart."

"Please fuck me!" someone in the back of the room helpfully translated.

Frank chuckled and nodded to Cindy who moved behind Female sub and adjusted her strap-on. After a few minutes of fiddling back there, Cindy grabbed the bottle of lube and rubbed it all over her cock. She continued fumbling until there was some uncomfortable laughter from the audience. Perhaps we were headed for another awkward demo after all.

Female sub looked back at Cindy and said, "Sometimes it's easier to just put it in my ass!"

The crowd roared with laughter. Amelia and I looked at each other, and the same question that was on my mind was mirrored back at me in her bewildered expression.

What the hell does she have going on down there that would make it easier to put it in her ass?

Cindy finally slid forward with a satisfied smile. Female sub began moaning again as Cindy hammered into her from behind. I expected Frank to jump back in on the action, but to my surprise, he started to take his clothes off instead.

Are we in for some double-penetration action? Everyone loves a little DP. . . .

We were indeed heading for some DP, but not the traditional kind. Because double penetration can be traditional, right?

I should have been focused where the action was, but instead I was distracted by Frank affixing a harness to his right thigh, just above the knee, which left a dildo jutting comically out from his leg. He sat down naked on a chair, and as he continued watching the show the ladies were putting on, his own penis slowly rose to join the erect dildo, so that he had two protrusions. Cindy whispered something in Female sub's ear, and they both climbed down from the table.

"Now, sometimes," Frank boomed out, "you want to fuck a pretty little thing like this, but you've promised your Queen that your biodick belongs to her that night. Limitations of being a man, right? Once you blow that load, your bio-dick ain't any good to anyone. Now the way you solve this problem is to use a rubber dick. There's no shame in it. Doesn't make you any less of a man. Come here, sweetheart." He gestured to Female sub, who jiggled her way alluringly over to him. She straddled his leg and lowered herself onto the dildo that was attached to his thigh. I could feel the tension in the audience as we collectively wondered if he would struggle the way Cindy had to get it in, but it seemed that she had opened the way. Frank's rubber dick slid right in. Female sub bounced up and down on it to her pleasure. Frank threw the audience a grin, and they began to applaud. But the show wasn't over yet.

Cindy rapidly stripped naked, stunning me with how absolutely unselfconscious she was. Her body showed the signs of age and bearing children, but her confidence made her the sexiest woman in the room. The look Frank and Cindy shared positively smoldered. The man had a girl in her twenties busily humping on his leg, but his eyes made it clear that his Queen would always come first.

Damn, I want that! Wait, don't I have that? Doesn't Wes make me feel that way?

I didn't like the answer to that question. I wasn't sure that he did.

I dismissed the thought and focused on the present where Cindy was swinging a leg over Frank's to face Female sub. The women were now face-to-face, kissing and touching as Frank fucked both of them simultaneously in one hell of a grand finale. It was quite a feat, and the audience showed their appreciation.

Cunty McSquirt and I were suitably impressed.

She and I wandered the booths on the convention floor for a few hours before she had to leave to get to work. I bought a set of three rattan canes and was considering buying a pair of lightweight black floggers that would be easy for me to swing without my arms getting tired. I wanted to know how they felt, but the guy who was running the booth had been annoyingly eager to show me, so instead I had Cunty try her unpracticed hand at them. I demonstrated how to make a figure eight with her wrist, and she patiently mimicked me. Then, I stripped off my corset top and stood in my bra with my shoulders rounded to give her a nice, wide target. She started by just brushing my back with each up and down sweep, but once she got the hang of it, she flicked me hard on the downstrokes. She was clearly holding back, so there wasn't that much power in the blows, but it was enough that I could feel that the floggers were neat and stingy. Not my favorite sensation to receive, but they would work well if I was administering them. I paid for my new toys, and we moved on.

We watched for a few minutes as an independent Domme with scary-huge fake tits gave a demo on how to turn waxing into corporal punishment. She was straddling a naked man who was lying facedown on a massage table. She spread the wax in a line over his hairy back and covered it with a wax strip. Instead of quickly ripping the strip off and removing the hair in one stroke, though, she pulled slowly, stretching his skin and excruciatingly ripping each hair out one at a time. He howled and bucked beneath her, but she was a heavy woman, so he wasn't going anywhere. When she explained that she would next be tweezing the hair from his balls, Amelia nodded her head to signal it was time to move on. She was a sport, but watching a man have his balls tweezed was asking a bit much of anyone.

People watching at the conventions was always fun. During the day, industry professionals who were doing demos or trying to pick up new clients were dressed in their latex and leather finest. However, most attendees were in casual jeans and T-shirts until the play parties in the evenings when everyone dressed to impress. Some people were warm and friendly, but others, mostly pro Dommes, put on airs of being aloof and superior. It has to be intimidating to be an outsider trying to break into the scene, particularly as a single man.

I thought the scene was wonderful in many ways because it connected like-minded people and provided a safe space for alternative sexual practices. What I found difficult about it was that in many ways it was simply a matter of exchanging one set of boxes and labels for another. Maybe those boxes and labels were a little roomier and more flexible, but they could be unnecessarily confining all the same. There was an emphasis placed on titles and roles that was intimidating to newcomers who weren't sure of their place in the spectrum, and I felt that it prevented old-timers from trying something new. So you like someone else having some sort of power over you? Cool. Are you a sub? Or do you want to be someone's slave? Are you a bottom? Or simply a masochist? The distinctions between each were subtle, and in some cases relevant and helpful, but sometimes I just wanted to scream at the people around me to loosen the fuck up and not worry about it so much. The expectations for dress were sometimes infuriating as well. It is possible to be into kinky shit and not feel the need to be decked out in latex and leather. Sometimes sky-high plat-form heels simply aren't practical, but a Domme didn't wear flats.

My feet were killing me from walking all over the convention in said heels, so I was hoping we would run into one of my regular foot guys so I could get a massage. The only clients I saw were Doggie Dan and Harvey. I carefully avoided Harvey, but I gave Dan a warm hug and introduced him to Amelia just before she had to leave.

When Wes eventually met me at the Dungeon booth, he was dev-astated he had missed the epic strap-on class. We had no idea that the next demo we attended would manage to top it.

30. DARYL

Wes was late, so we had to quickly make our way to the largest of the convention rooms where they were holding the waterboarding demo. I made a mental note to have someone punish him at the play party later. I was sure we could find an appealing Domme from out of town to assist me with it.

Waterboarding had been in the news at that time as an example of torture that some wanted the American government to use on suspected terrorists. Many felt it was crossing a line. I didn't have a stance on it, but was intrigued that someone would demonstrate at a fetish convention what the news had deemed cruel and unusual.

By the time we got to the room that was designated in the convention program, it was almost full, but we found two empty seats toward the front just before the instructor stood up on stage and everyone went silent.

"Good afternoon, my fellow freaks! I'm Daryl, and this is my live waterboarding demonstration."

Daryl was sporting a high and tight with dark green fatigues and combat boots. He was built like a brick shithouse. He paced across the stage as he explained the mechanics of waterboarding and its effects on the human mind.

"The goal"—he paused and smiled—"is to make your subject think they are drowning. You tilt them back on the table so that their head is lower than their feet, cover their face with a towel, and pour water over their nose and mouth. The subject's brain will tell them that they are drowning. They will experience what it is like to die by drowning without actually dying. For this reason, it is imperative that they be properly restrained. They will fight for their lives."

He let that hang in the air, and waved to a girl who was standing off to the side of the stage. I assumed she was his demo bottom, but she wasn't who I had expected to volunteer to be waterboarded. She was a teeny little blonde who probably weighed a hundred pounds soaking wet. She was wearing an adorable polka-dot bikini with her hair tied back in a high ponytail. She looked nervous but resolved.

Daryl introduced her. "This is Heidi. Heidi contacted me when I posted that I was looking for a volunteer to be waterboarded. We have discussed in detail what will happen today. She has consented. Due to the extreme nature of waterboarding, there is not a safe word. We keep going until I decide to stop. . . . Give these folks an idea of why you would want to volunteer for something like this. I'll get us set up. We'll do the demo and then we'll do a little interview with you and give the audience a chance to ask you questions about your experience."

Heidi shifted her weight back and forth between her feet anxiously, but sounded confident as she explained, "I know I'm probably crazy, but I couldn't pass up the opportunity to try something this intense. I like breath play, choking . . . that kind of stuff, so this seems like the furthest I can take that. I wanted to do it with someone who knew what they were doing . . . so yeah."

Daryl wheeled over a couple of carts with five of the big water-cooler five-gallon jugs on each. It seemed like a lot of water for such a little girl. Heidi lay down on the table. Her legs were raised up, and her head was over an inflatable baby pool to catch the water. Daryl began tying her limbs to O-rings on each corner of the table. As he worked with the rope, he explained, "She's going to jerk and fight, so you have to know what you're doing with bondage."

His tone suggested that he did. I hadn't been able to put my finger on what I didn't like about him, but decided that must be it: he was fucking arrogant and I didn't know yet whether he could back it up. I was fucking arrogant too, but I tried not to walk around swinging my dick at people.

Once he had secured Heidi's limbs to the table, he gave her a thumbs-up, and she nodded. Daryl then placed a black hand towel over her face. When he squatted to lift one of the jugs of water, I realized I was holding my breath and felt like the whole room was doing the same. I could see Heidi's rib cage rising and falling rapidly as she anticipated which breath would be the last before the deluge.

Daryl drew out the tension by looking out at us and saying, "You should all know that I am a certified EMT, and we won't need it today, but I do know CPR."

With no further ado, he started to pour water over the towel that covered Heidi's face. She was still at first.

"They always start by holding their breath, but you know the exact moment they run out of air."

As though on cue, Heidi started to thump one of her feet and thrash her head from side to side, but there was no escaping the continuous stream of water that was cascading from the bottle. He wasn't even halfway through the first of five jugs yet. Heidi was frantic now. All of her limbs were jerking violently against her bonds and her back was arching as though she was possessed. It was alarming to watch. My instinct was to put a stop to it, but Daryl just chuckled calmly as he emptied the first jug. He lifted the towel from her face, and she sputtered and coughed before gulping frantic breaths of air. She expelled each breath in huge shuddering sobs. The audience was utterly silent and still. We had come here excited at the prospect of a novel form of entertainment, but what we were watching felt wrong, even to this gathering of sick fucks.

Heidi was still gasping for air when Daryl threw the wet towel back over her face and picked up a second jug. Heidi panicked immediately. I didn't think it was possible, but as he dumped the next jug of water onto her face, she reacted even more violently than the first time, thrashing and jerking against her bonds. Daryl just kept pouring a steady stream that seemed to go on forever.

Just as I thought I couldn't bear to sit and watch any longer, Heidi wrenched one of her legs free of its bond and swung it down and over her head. She kicked Daryl so hard in the chest that he flew backward and crashed into the cart that still held three jugs of water, knocking them over and spilling them all over himself. The audience exploded with cheers and laughter. We had all apparently felt the same way about the two people on stage, so to see her break free of his most excellent bondage was satisfying. To watch tiny Heidi kick swaggering Daryl onto his ass was an image that I will always cherish. She was a fighter.

Heidi didn't know yet what she had done because the towel was still covering her face. She was drawing ragged breaths through the wet towel, still thrashing her head from side to side. Daryl was winded, but trying to get back up and compose himself, so he was in no shape to assist her. An older woman from the front row jumped up and pulled the towel off of her face, and two guys started untying her. By the time she was free, a soaking wet Daryl had resumed control of the stage, and sat next to Heidi on the table. He had given her a towel to wrap around her shoulders, but he had used it first. She perched clutching the edges of the towel and rocking as she sobbed inconsolably. She didn't look like she was even aware that she was on a stage in front of people anymore.

Daryl turned to her and instructed, "Tell these folks what that felt like."

He had to be fucking joking. The poor girl needed a hug, not an interview. We all sat quietly as she continued to cry. It looked like she was going to say something at one point, but she just shook her head before dropping it and giving in to the tears once more. She had been brave to give it a try, perhaps foolish, but brave nonetheless. I didn't know about anyone else, but I certainly wasn't judging her for her reaction. In a strange way, I envied the release she would get from just letting it out.

Daryl stood and paced the stage again as he said, "We'll give Heidi a few moments to compose herself. People say that they have night-mares for years after experiencing waterboarding. Some say it is the most terrifying thing you can experience."

"Have you ever tried it?" someone shouted from a few rows behind us.

I smirked. It was the exact question that had been on my mind. He seemed so dismissive of Heidi's emotional reaction as though she was being a silly little girl, but I suspected he had never had the balls to try it himself. In my experience, female Dommes are much more willing to sub first before attempting something on their partners, while male Doms are more likely to just assume they know how it feels.

"I have not. I do not see a need"—he was interrupted by murmur-ing in the audience—"but . . . I did almost drown during a training exercise once, so I am aware of what happens."

Almost drowning versus allowing someone to tie you down and psychologically torture you seemed a little different to me.

He redeemed himself slightly when he said, "How about a round of applause for Heidi?"

The audience gave her a standing ovation.

"Now," Daryl shouted, clapping his hands together, "any more vol-unteers?"

It was his finale. A forced admission from the audience that none of them would be willing to do it either—that he had a scary BDSM skill that trumped all others. I turned in my seat to see what would happen, assuming that there's always one.

Half the fucking room raised their hands.

And they were completely serious. Daryl didn't know how to handle it when they lined up at the edge of the stage expectantly. He muttered about not having time to tie everyone down and not hav-ing enough water left . . . so the audience usurped the stage from him. Someone appeared at the back with more carts of water, and the line began to form a very civilized, efficient system. The first person lay down on the table, while the next three in line held him down. The fourth in line poured just enough water for the recipient to start to struggle too violently to hold . . . and then they all switched positions and started again. It was polite group torture. It took over twenty minutes to get through the whole line of people. They clearly weren't experiencing the same intensity that Heidi had, but just enough to have an inkling of what it was all about. As each person finished their turn, they hugged Heidi and sat with her until she was surrounded by love and encouragement. Daryl wasn't giving her the aftercare that she needed, but the community takes care of its own.

These are my people, I acknowledged with a smile.

31. RICH HR

After spending three full days at KinkyCon, it was a culture shock to return to my vanilla workplace on Monday morning. When Rich didn't show up at the trailer, I got worried that he was passed out in a ditch somewhere. Or in jail. Or possibly missing a few organs in Tijuana. I initially avoided drawing attention to his absence lest I get him in trouble, but when it reached lunch and he still wasn't there, I gave in and asked the others in the trailer if they had heard from him.

"Yeah, he's in the L.A. office for the rest of the week," was the response.

Patricia explained further, "He's having a sit-down with HR to talk about the complaint that was filed. HR didn't call you yet? They should be calling you at some point today since you were involved."

"Me? Weird."

I was involved in an HR complaint? What the hell did that mean? It didn't sound like I was the one in trouble, but it also didn't sound like something I wanted to be affiliated with.

Thankfully I didn't have to stress for long before Ralph from HR called me to discuss the "incident" in question. He explained that a complaint had been made against Rich and that since I was the other person involved, he needed to get a statement from me.

"Now this may be a little embarrassing to talk about, but I want you to know that if anything like this ever happens again that you can come to us. That's what we're here for."

"Um, okay. Thanks."

"We've already confirmed the story with Rich, so this is really just a formality. There's no need to feel like you're telling on him or anything. The incident in question occurred last Monday at approximately ten a.m. in the trailer at the hospital project. Another employee overheard Rich discussing inappropriate sexual matters with you and felt that you did not want to be a participant in the conversation. Rich is your superior on-site, so this could be interpreted as a form of sexual harassment."

Well, this isn't awkward at all.

He continued, "Specifically, it seems that he was relating an incident in which he spanked a younger woman. Could you give us your version of these events?"

Awkward. I can't tell him I was cool with it without looking terrible, but I don't want to throw Rich under the bus either. Who the fuck even reported it?

"Sure . . . I guess it happened the way you've described. He maybe shouldn't have been talking about those things in the trailer where anyone could overhear, but I didn't necessarily feel harassed by it and certainly wouldn't have called you to complain about it."

"So he was talking about spanking and . . . other things?"

"Yep."

"Okay. Well regardless of whether you were offended by it, that is inappropriate workplace behavior and we will be filing an incident report and getting him appropriate counseling before he can return to the jobsite. The complaint will remain anonymous and shouldn't be discussed any further in the office. If anything like this happens again, I hope you'll feel that you can come forward to help prevent a type of culture where this is allowed."

"Yeah. Will do."

"Okay, thanks for your help in getting this cleared up."

"No problem. Bye."

Poor guy. I hoped his wife hadn't also found out for both of their sakes.

When he returned to the trailer, we went to lunch so we wouldn't be overheard. He confirmed that his wife didn't know, but said that he was thinking about telling her.

"Is that your way of trying to end your marriage?" I asked. "Because it's a pretty shitty way of doing it."

"I don't know what I want anymore. I want to feel like I did when we first got together. I want to do the things I was doing when I cheated, but how do you initiate something like that after fifteen years of polite missionary?"

"Worst she's going to do is call you a pervert and run screaming to a divorce lawyer. It sounds like that's where you're headed if you don't do anything, so it seems to me you don't have anything to lose."

He nodded slowly, saying, "That's one way of looking at it."

"Another is that she's probably just as fucking bored. I'm so sick of men not giving women enough credit. They're usually just as interested in spicing things up, but instead of giving them a chance, guys take the easy way out and cheat."

"Easy, tiger . . . You're right. I'll give it a shot. But if she cuts my dick off for suggesting it, that's on your conscience."

"I can live with that."

32. "OLIVER"

When I moved to L.A., I learned that people who haven't lived here have a misguided assumption that the place is crawling with celebrities. Friends from where I grew up in Texas asked incessantly whether I had met anyone famous. They were always disappointed to hear that, shockingly, I hadn't. Just imagine, in a city of 18.5 million, I didn't regularly run into their favorite actors. It would have upset them that much more to hear that I was so out of tune with pop culture that I could have been running into them all day long without ever realizing it. I didn't think anyone famous would come in to the Dungeon since there would be a risk that one of us would out them, but also since they had the money to hire someone to play with them privately where they could make their own rules. I heard the occasional story of it happening, but the "celebrity" in question was always a D-lister who was probably hoping we *would* out them just to generate some press.

I walked into the interview room one afternoon and was stunned to discover that my client was a mega famous actor. Ignorant to pop culture or not, there was no mistaking him. My first thought was, "My mom is going to be so excited when I tell her!"

And then I came back to reality and accepted that I wouldn't be telling anyone about this—well, maybe Amelia!

Despite how close we are becoming, darling reader, I won't be telling you his name. But I promise you know it. For now, let's just call him Oliver.

I hesitated for an instant when I saw who he was and then mentally kicked myself back into Scarlett mode. Scarlett wouldn't give a fuck how famous he was. She was here to do a job. I squared my shoulders, introduced myself, and joined him on the couch.

Almost as distracting as his fame was the fact that he was wearing sunglasses, and didn't seem like he was planning to take them off anytime soon. It was so dark in the interview room that it was a little hard to see to begin with. With shades on, I couldn't figure out how he could even make out my features. He couldn't possibly think that I wouldn't recognize him because of the sunglasses, could he?

Wearing sunglasses indoors was just the beginning of the douche baggery that he brought to the table. He was chewing gum open-mouthed, and the smacking noise it was making made me want to smack him. He was also being impossibly vague about what he wanted to do. I had been in enough interviews now to know that it could be difficult for clients to open up, but he wouldn't give me *anything* to work with. Our conversation went a little something like:

"So what is it that you're interested in doing today?"

"You choose."

He went back to smacking his gum and not making eye contact. Raven told me that once when a client said something like that to her, she chose to tie all of his toes apart and give him paper cuts between each of them. I was fairly sure that wasn't what Oliver had in mind.

"Well, I'd be happy to guide the scene if you could give me some idea of what you're into."

"I want you to dominate me."

Smack. Smack. Smack went the gum.

"Okay, great. That's a good start. I can work with that. So is it corporal punishment you're looking for? Bondage? Maybe humiliation?"

"Whatever you usually do."

Is he here to research a part and has no idea what to ask for? Is he embarrassed to tell me? Or is he just being a pain in the ass?

Without knowing what was the issue, I wanted to avoid continuously going in a circle with him. Admittedly, with any other client I would have pushed to set some more definite boundaries to make sure our expectations were aligned, but I really wanted to play with this guy, so I tried to compromise and just get us in a room.

"We don't really have a 'usual' here, but I'll tell you what we can do . . . I'll grab some generic rope and implements. We can play for at least an hour so we have time to experiment, and let's see if we can figure out what you're into."

He agreed, so I grabbed a random assortment of implements and bondage equipment and we headed up to the cave.

As soon as I locked the door and started the session, he grabbed me by the shoulders and tried to kiss me. I, like most women and I'm sure a few men, had fantasized about kissing him, but in that moment it wasn't happening. He either thought he had come to a brothel or was deliberately trying to piss me off. Either way, I needed to set the boundary.

"Hey. No. Let's slow down. Take a seat on the bench and we'll get started."

I went and took a crop from the bag to give me a moment to think . . . and so I had something to hit him with if he got fresh again. I sat down next to him on the bench, close enough to be flirty, and planned on trying to find a direction to take things when I felt his hand on the back of my head pushing me down toward his dick in the universal man move for "put it in your mouth."

I ducked under his arm and slapped his hand with the crop.

"You are a bad, bad boy. Get over my knee now so I can give you a proper punishment."

He pulled his shirt off and I couldn't help admiring his perfectly chiseled physique. I sort of wanted to run my tongue over his washboard abs. And then I caught sight of the damn sunglasses again, and it killed my buzz.

When he stood up, I tugged his pants down to his knees but left his boxer briefs in place in case he got too carried away. I turned him over my knee and started spanking him. And it was immediately awkward. It clearly wasn't what he was looking for since he wasn't reacting in the least, but if he was only looking for sex, I couldn't help him. The silence in the room was excruciating. I had him stand back up and went to put some music on, hoping to set some kind of mood. I regained some confidence with Puscifer thumping through the speakers. It reminded me of the night I had done fire play with Liam.

I turned back to Oliver, and found that he had taken the opportunity to strip completely naked. Two things struck me at once: His dick, even semi-erect, was magnificent. And it had a massively gauged Prince Albert piercing, a thick rod that started on the underside of the head of his dick, and curved upward to emerge through his urethra. It was thick and bold and beautiful. I practically melted when I saw it.

Now that *I can work with.*

The jewelry he was wearing was designed to be attached to a leash or a carabiner. I needed no further instruction. I took him by the throat and pushed him backward until he was standing against the cross. Then, I took some rope and did a quick and easy tie to secure him to it. I went back to the bag to put latex gloves on and to find a small bondage clip and a thin piece of rope, which would be my homemade leash.

He smiled his million-dollar smile when I turned back to him and he saw what I was holding. And then he smacked his fucking gum again. I held a gloved palm open in front of his mouth and said, "Spit or swallow."

He spat the gum neatly into my hand. I pulled his stupid sunglasses off and stuck the gum on the outside of the frame before tossing them back on the bench. He didn't protest, but looked amusingly stunned. His sunglasses probably cost more than my car. Scarlett didn't give a fuck.

I clipped my makeshift dog leash onto his piercing, and his cock started to lengthen and swell in anticipation. I gently lifted it, but stopped short of the tension I thought he was craving. I ran my riding crop slowly along the underside of his now fully erect member and then back along the side. His whole body shivered. I rapidly flicked the crop against him, working my way up and down, covering the entire surface with little taps. They were just hard enough to make him nervous, but not hard enough to cause any pain. He was arching his back as much as his bonds would allow and thrusting at the air. His face was contorted with the agony that belongs to those who crave pain and are instead receiving the gentle ministrations of an experienced tease.

I laughed at him humping the air like a bitch in heat. He gave me a pleading laugh as well.

"Please, Mistress . . . please. You're driving me crazy."

I lunged at him, releasing the tension in the leash so that his dick once again hung between his spread legs. I grabbed him by the throat, pressed my body against his naked length and leaned in until my lips were nearly touching his ear. He went completely still, but I could feel his heart racing under my fingertips.

"I know exactly what you want. And I'm going to give it to you," I whispered menacingly, "but I don't want to hear a sound out of your mouth. Not so much as a moan or a whimper is allowed to escape these lips," I said, running the tip of my crop across his mouth for emphasis. He nodded, and I released his throat. I'm still not sure why I wanted him silent. I usually love to hear the sounds that come out of people's mouths in the throes of ecstasy. But this time, I was making concessions to please him. I was going to be gentle, even though I wanted to be rough. I was going to treat him like one of my play partners rather than a client, and I wanted him to make a concession as well. I know how hard it is to stay silent. I needed proof that he wanted this badly enough to obey me even when he had lost the capacity to think.

He silently nodded in agreement, and gave me a wink that turned my knees to Jell-O. No wonder he was so successful. He was charming without saying a word.

I picked his leash back up, and with no more teasing, stretched his dick to its length and pulled it taut. He arched his back once more and panted, but didn't make a sound. He flinched as he felt the crop touch his piercing, the source of all of that tension. I began pulling the leash back and releasing it, tiny motions that mimicked the thrusts of sex, but in this case each one stretched him a little farther and forced me to pull harder. In time with these waves of movement, I started tapping the tip of his dick harder and harder with the crop. He was now pressing his lips into a thin line and panting through his nose, as though keeping his mouth closed might stop any sound from escaping if he lost control. I switched and started tapping the underside of the head, even harder than before. I got so caught up in the moment, that for the briefest instant, I thought he had started moaning. Those guttural sounds were coming from my own throat. His every muscle was straining with the tension, and his breathing had become erratic.

I started to tap faster and faster, as only my right hand is able to do. That kind of muscle speed is built only through years of masturbating. The energy he was throwing off as sweat poured down his body drove me into a greater frenzy. I stood to one side as his balls tightened and he threw his head back with a silent cry, expelling a stream of semen past his piercing and onto the towel I had laid on the floor. He sagged in his bonds, trying to catch his breath. He still hadn't uttered a sound.

I untied him and we both laughed from the pure, simple joy of it all.

"Fuck, that was intense!" he said with a thoroughly contented sigh.

Sometimes the experience with clients was removed and clinical. There was no connection there whatsoever beyond an exchange of payment for pleasure or pain. Other times, we connected in an intense way that I can only compare to the intimacy that sometimes follows a one-night stand. Strangers can become lovers. Play partners can become something more. I had started that session in awe of Oliver's fame, but not particularly liking him, and ended up forging an electric bond.

"God, I thought you were such a stereotypical Hollywood douche bag when you came in! But, fuck, that was hot!"

"And I thought you had a stick up your cute little ass."

I chucked a towel in his face and he jokingly said, "Hey, hey! Watch the money-maker!"

As we cleaned up, he asked, "So now you know one of my secrets. Tell me one of yours. What turns you on?"

I nearly gave him a bullshit answer, but decided to be truthful.

"Penetration. I like to penetrate people."

His eyes lit up as he said, "We're going to have to play again sometime. My schedule is about to get a little nuts, but I'll work something out eventually."

"I can't wait," I said. And I actually meant it.

33. ERIN

"Scarlett, Yoshi is here to see you."

"Okay, thanks, Viv. I'll be right up."

I hadn't seen Yoshi in months and wasn't excited to play with him, but I didn't have anything else booked that night, so it would at least make the drive up there worthwhile. Besides, I had changed a lot in a few months, learned to manage my clients better. This would be a good test of that even if I found him repugnant.

We laid my usual ground rules for him in the interview. Breasts were off-limits. Some spanking was fine, but if he got too gropey I was going to call him out for it. Smelling was fine, but no licking.

We picked the lounge to play in since most of the other rooms were occupied. It was an incredibly busy night, so I could hear a diverse array of noises coming from each room that we passed as we made our way to the back. It was fun to try to guess what was happening in each room. I could only smile as I heard "bigger and thicker" coming from behind one of the doors. No question about what was happening in there.

We reached the lounge and I started our session and then took my time getting situated. I usually didn't mess with a client's time like that, but I was really wishing I wasn't about to have to put up with twenty-eight minutes and forty-six more seconds of Yoshi, so whatever little amount I could spare myself seemed fair.

"Scar-rett, I miss you so much, baby. Where you been hiding?"

"I've been right here, Yoshi. You always know where you can find me when you want me," I teased, proud of myself for not being a bitch. Yoshi was a person too, and I wanted to try to see past how gross he could be and remember that.

The session continued the way his usually did, with smelling and lewd comments, but then it took a turn in a direction it hadn't before. As his full body-smelling assessment reached my breasts, he lingered longer than usual, sniffing and then sucking in breaths through his mouth as though tasting the air. I stared at the ceiling and tried to think about my meetings on-site the next day so I wouldn't recoil from him.

"Oh yeah, baby. Suckle me! Feed me all your milk! Don't give none of it to your baby!"

Well, that's a new and charming addition to this little party. . . .

He put his mouth on my bra and sucked hard.

"Yoshi! No licking or sucking and no breast play. We talked about this in the interview."

"It's just your bra, baby. Just let me try. I'll suckle all your milk right through it."

I supposed he was technically correct, but added that to my list of things to ban if we ever played again.

He climbed onto the chaise, pressing his naked length against me. With a few clients, I might have been perfectly comfortable with this. I can admit to the double standard, but it is one of the unavoidable parts of being a sex worker. Attraction plays a part and the flip side of that is revulsion. A client I am attracted to will get away with more than one who repulses me. Is it fair? Nope.

I shuddered with revulsion as I saw precum smear from his tiny penis onto my skirt.

"Get off!" I shouted and scrambled to get up.

"Suckle me, baby. Just suckle me!" he replied and lunged for my bra, tugging it down and freeing my right breast. He latched onto my nipple with his teeth and sucked hard. It felt like he had broken the skin.

I screamed and smacked him in the mouth with a loose fist to get him to let go. I thought that would be enough to get him to stop, but he looked up at me defiantly and yanked the bra down on the other side, tearing the strap. I backhanded him without a second thought and turned to cover myself and reach the intercom. My bitch-slap didn't exactly have the desired effect. Instead of stunning him, it made him lunge at me in a rage. He bent me over the chair and pawed at my panties, trying to pull them down with one hand while holding me down with the other.

Things had gone from fine to completely out of control in an instant. I could hear someone playing in the next room, but without knowing who it was, I couldn't think what I could shout that would get their attention. Almost anything could be part of a normal session, so nothing was going to raise any alarm and get them to check.

He managed to get my panties down to my knees. I was frantically clawing his wrist, but he twisted my arm up behind my back, making me cry out with pain.

I was suddenly terrified and horribly exposed. I didn't know for sure what he was trying to do, but I knew I didn't want it. I looked down, saw his bare feet, and reacted instinctively. I stepped back and drove a five-inch stiletto down onto the top of his foot as hard as I could. He squealed and dropped to the ground to nurse his wound. The instant I could stand, I ran for the door and didn't stop until I reached the reception desk.

I quickly relayed to Viv what had happened and watched on the surveillance camera as he limped out to his car.

"Should we call the cops or something?"

She looked at me as if I were insane and I realized that probably wasn't the wisest suggestion.

"You really want to explain that to the cops? It would be his word against yours and we don't need to draw that kind of attention here. It's not like he really did anything."

"No, but he tried! I think at the very least he should be banned from playing here again. What if I hadn't stopped him?"

"Don't be fuckin' dramatic. Nothing happened and he's a good regular."

"I'm never playing with him again and I don't think new subs should either."

"Miss High-and-Mighty might not need to make money, but in my day we didn't turn down sessions and we put up with a helluva lot worse than you whiney bitches do!"

I was floored.

Erin intervened before I could reply. I didn't know how much she had heard, but she forcefully took me by the arm and dragged me outside.

"Whatever just happened, don't blame Viv for it. She can be hard, but she comes from a different generation. She's seen some shit."

I was shaken. I didn't know how I was going to be able to trust clients anymore after seeing how quickly things could get out of hand. The what-ifs crashed in my mind as I thought through the dozens of times I had put myself in vulnerable situations with other clients. Was I an idiot to be doing this?

"Don't go there," Erin said, reading my mind.

I looked up at her, but could only shake my head.

"C'mon," she said, grabbing her bag, "you're coming home with me. I know how to take your mind off things."

Home for Erin turned out to be the lavish Beverly Hills residence of a music producer/cross-dresser who I suspected had at one time been a client and now allowed Erin to live rent-free in exchange for private sessions.

As she unlocked the front door, I was trying to hide the fact that I was shaking nervously, wondering if this was a bad idea. We hadn't hooked up since AVN when I had been out of my mind on ecstasy. Amusingly, I was most worried about my skills in the bedroom. What if I didn't know how to please a woman? You would think it would be easier since we had the same parts, but I was intimidated because of my lack of lesbian experience.

My concerns were obliterated when we walked in the front door and I met Erin's roommate, Geoffrey. He was adjusting what appeared to be a robotic spanking machine while wearing a full set of women's lingerie in the middle of a sumptuously furnished living room. No matter how open-minded I thought I had become, I apparently still wasn't as enlightened as Erin.

"Scarlett, this is my roommate, Geoffrey. Geoff, this is Scarlett from work."

"Scarlett! Erin has told me all about you. It's so nice to finally meet you!"

"Likewise. Your home is gorgeous!"

"Oh, thanks! Would you girls like to play with the Spank-o-Matic? I was just about to get her going."

"We're good, thanks. I'm going to take Scarlett upstairs and have my way with her."

Her dimples deepened at my blush.

"Have fun!" Geoff waved as we ran up the stairs hand in hand.

Instead of giving me time to get awkward, she was already stripping my shirt off as she closed the bedroom door. She pressed me back against the bed, but it was too much of a reminder of Yoshi and she must have seen it on my face. I rolled above her and pressed her arms above her head. Even though I knew she was letting me, it felt good to be in control.

I took my time touching and kissing my way down her body, amazed that a human being could be that soft. Each time I did something that made her gasp or moan, I made a mental note, learning what drove her wild. It was thrilling.

By the time I teased my way to her clit, she was panting and flexing her hands in a silent plea.

"Please, Scarlett . . ." she begged.

I licked her clit, and she moaned deeply.

"Mistress Scarlett . . ." I teased, reminding her of the shit she'd pulled with me on my first day.

"Please, *Mistress* Scarlett!"

I gave her what she wanted, thrusting two fingers inside her and finding a rhythm with my tongue on her clit.

From downstairs began a steady thumping followed by Geoffrey screaming, "No—*thump*—please! Let me—*thump*—out! Let me *out*! —*thump*—Someone help me! I'm trapped in this—*thump*—machine!"

I hesitated, and Erin groaned, "Don't you dare stop! He's fine. He usually sets it for twenty minutes and he's locked in it for that long. Safe word is 'petunia,' so unless you hear that, get your fucking tongue back down there."

I slapped her on the thigh playfully and said, "Hey, *Mistress*, who's in charge here?"

She just laughed her delicious laugh and I went back to the task at hand.

At first, I found it hard to block out all the screaming coming from downstairs, but as Erin's moans got louder I took it as a challenge to drown him out. She bucked wildly, and I felt her pulsing around my fingers as she came hard. Causing a female orgasm was a heady feeling.

The thumping downstairs had stopped.

34. ALEX II

I took some time off work at the Dungeon to determine whether I would be comfortable continuing to work there after what had happened. Within a week, I knew that I wasn't ready to give it up. I already missed so much: the girls, the thrill of a new session, my regulars, but above all, I missed who I was when I was there. A compromise formed in my mind. I wasn't going to take any more submissive sessions, instead sticking to scenarios in which I was theoretically in control. It wasn't foolproof, but it was a trade-off that I could live with. I considered taking the test to become a full-fledged Mistress, but decided I was better off remaining a Switch. I had noticed that newer clients were more comfortable taking a Domme session with a Switch than a Mistress since they seemed less scary. This way I could also still sub for the occasional favorite client if I felt like it.

Alex was my first client when I started picking my shifts back up, which was perfect because he was familiar, but it was also daunting because a week off hadn't given me any new ideas for his regular visits.

"I'm going to lose my mind in this session. I have Alex for three hours and I have no idea what I'm going to do with him. I've done every gross thing I can think of . . . and some I would never have thought I would do . . . and I'm out of ideas!"

"Have you done the human ashtray with him?" asked Erin without looking up from her book. "Smoke a cigarette and ash in his mouth. Make him swallow it," she suggested.

"I've done it, but can definitely do it again. Good idea. That only leaves me about two hours and fifty minutes to fill. Any other thoughts?"

Erin wrapped her arms around me from behind. Her lips on my neck were feather light.

"I have lots of filthy suggestions," she said, "but they all involve you naked in my bed. And Alex sure as fuck isn't in them."

"Not helpful," I breathed as her hand slid down my stomach.

"Not my job to be helpful."

Raven screamed, "Lesbians!" as she arrived back from her session and dumped piles of rope on the couch to sort and recoil.

"Why does she always do that?" Erin asked with exaggerated annoyance.

"Jealous," I said with a straight face and kissed her on the cheek.

"You lezzies want to help me put this shit away?"

"Not particularly," Erin said over her shoulder as she walked out to the patio with a cigarette and her book in her hand.

"I'll help you with that if you help me come up with some stuff to do with Alex. I have him for three hours and need suggestions."

"Lick your boots clean? Human ashtray? Play out a medical fantasy where you cut off his man parts and then serve them to him for dinner? Lick the broom as you sweep the floor? Lick the toilet seat clean?"

"Ew, you've made him do that?"

"Don't ask for suggestions and then judge me for them, Judgey-McJudgerpants! You want my ideas or not?"

She tossed me a tangled pile of rope that I started working through.

"I do—I do! Sorry. Not judging. I just don't know how the man doesn't end up in the hospital regularly."

"I bet his immune system is crazy. Like he'll survive whatever wipes the rest of us out when antibiotics stop working. It'll just be Alex and the cockroaches left."

"Funny. What else you got?"

"*Oh!* Make him some tampon tea, but don't actually let him drink the real one. Blindfold him and substitute it for normal tea at the last minute. You can threaten him with it the whole session and let the anticipation build! God, I'm good!"

I wanted to say, "Time out. What the *fuck*? Please tell me you're joking."

But what came out of my mouth was, "But I'm not on my period."

"No worries. I am. Hang on!"

She ran to the kitchen and came back with a large mug and a plate. I stared in dumbfounded silence as she ran into the bathroom and then reappeared holding the mug triumphantly in front of her. She had covered it with the plate, so I didn't have to see its contents, but I could imagine.

"Don't look at me like that or I'll take my gift back! It's genius and you know it!"

"You're a sick fuck," I responded, but I couldn't keep a straight face.

"I can't believe I'm doing this," I muttered as I left the dressing room, mug in hand.

"You're welcome!" she shouted after me.

I was hoping to make it past the desk without Caterina seeing what I was carrying and was relieved that she was in the middle of what sounded like a thoroughly uncomfortable phone call.

". . . Ma'am, as I've already said, I can't give you any details about that particular credit card charge. You will need to discuss it with your husband, who is the cardholder. . . . I understand your frustration, but there's really nothing I can tell you."

Sounded like we may not be seeing one of our clients again. Or would be seeing him much more often.

I hustled Alex out of a reception chair and straight up the stairs to the cave. I stashed the coffee cup behind the stereo and turned on some Nine Inch Nails. Maybe with loud enough music, I wouldn't be able to hear my thoughts.

It took me two and a half hours to work up the courage to produce Alex's special tea. Even then, I couldn't bring myself to look at it. The way his face lit up when he saw it told me everything I needed to know. Raven had nailed it.

I hadn't planned ahead enough to have mixed up a different tea concoction, so my decoy cup just contained hot water. It didn't matter. He was so wound up with anticipation by then that he came as soon as I raised the liquid to his lips. In Alex's mind, his tampon tea fantasy had been fulfilled.

35. BRIAN

By the time a client named Brian came in to see me, I was getting relaxed about some of my interviews. If the session involved territory that I thought needed guidelines, then I still found myself hammering out almost every detail beforehand. But if the session was something simpler—feet, humiliation, sissification, etc—then I was starting to find it easier to be more flexible and work through what the client wanted during the session. I had seen enough crazy shit that very little surprised me anymore. Until Brian.

When we interviewed, he indicated that he wanted me to be his small-penis therapist, a sexy but bitchy doctor who emotionally tortured him with my icy glares and cold, judgmental silence. I tried to size him up and decide whether he actually had a teeny dick or whether it was a monster that he wanted me to pretend was tiny. He was a moderately tall white dude, so I couldn't rely on stereotypes and couldn't tell from what he was wearing. I was just going to have to wait and see.

"Small-penis therapy sounds good to me. Do you want me to interact with you in any specific way? Do anything corporal to you?"

"You just need to be cold, bitchy, and judgmental. And when I hit on you, just glare and ignore me."

Well, that was going to be tough. . . .

"Okay," I said, "I think I can manage that."

"I'll basically do everything. You just have to glare, and be mean to me, and talk as little as possible. I'll ask if I can do my exercises, and you don't have to direct me because this is supposed to be my regular therapy, so I'll know what to do."

"So to be clear, you want no impact play, no physical interaction, and as little verbal interaction from me as possible. You just want to be ignored, spoken down to, and mocked when I do speak?" I asked, already thinking how easy and cathartic this was going to be.

"Yes. It should be straightforward. You'll see."

"Lovely. Shall we see what rooms are available?"

We chose the medical room as it had the right vibe and a perfect couch for me to sit on. The doctor's comfort was important after all. I put on a Die Antwoord CD quietly in the background when we went in. I didn't want it to feel any less like therapy, but I really hated silence in sessions. I sat down on the couch demurely with my notepad in hand and glared at him with utter disdain.

"Uh . . . Hi, Doc. How's it goin'?" he asked with just a hint of a stutter.

"Could we get on with this, please? I'm really not here to socialize," I replied, sighing dramatically.

"Um, all right. Yeah, of course. So, should I just go ahead and strip down then?"

"Indeed."

He took his clothes off and carefully folded them, laying them on the surgical table in the corner. He walked toward me, rubbing his hands together awkwardly, and that was the first time I saw the teeny tiny organ that he called his dick. When I got home and tried to describe it to Amelia, the best I could come up with was the "Cave Dick." It literally receded into a pouch of skin when it wasn't erect and barely protruded when it was hard. There was absolutely no chance he could get it into a vagina. Brian would die a virgin.

I had a fleeting pang of guilt, but there was no place for those feelings here. He had found a way to deal with his tiny prick, and it was my job to be a heartless bitch to help him fulfill that fantasy, not to pity him.

Thankfully, I didn't need to try to hide the fact I was staring at his lack of manhood. Instead, I cocked an eyebrow pointedly to hammer the thought home.

"Shall I begin my small-penis exercises, Doctor?"

"Indeed," I said with a little extra emphasis directed toward his genitals.

He awkwardly started doing a sort of leaping lunge sequence around the room. A naked man with the tiniest penis I had ever seen was squatting and lunging and jumping around the room and I was expected to sit there with a look of derision on my face. What a strange life I was leading.

"So, uh, nice weather we've been having, huh, Doc?"

I gave him my "Are you seriously talking to me right now" glare and looked back down at my notepad.

"Okay then . . . Would you maybe, um, wanna go get a coffee or something sometime?"

"No. Not in the least. Now focus on your tiny-penis exercises."

I got up and walked over to the CD player as though it was suddenly very important. I bent all the way over to fiddle with the buttons, which was totally unnecessary, but given that the slit on my leather dress went all the way up to the middle of my ass, I gave him quite a glimpse of my drawers. I stayed bent over and slid one foot up and down my calf absently.

When I finally turned around and walked back to sit on the couch, he had that desperate look in his eyes. It reminded me of my dog when he rolls over expecting a treat, but I'm eating my own meal with no intention of giving him anything. I watched Brian's Adam's apple bob up and down as I resumed my icy stare, rotating between scathing eye contact and looking at his Cave Dick with disgust.

He spent the next forty-five minutes or so hopping and flopping and rolling and lunging his way around the room. He did some combination of a lunge and a push-up at one point, and I watched in fascination as his erect penis slid in and out of its cave like an eel. Could he fuck himself? Was this a being that could have sex with itself, in which case I should be jealous rather than pitying him? I never asked. Brian wasn't really the talkative, bonding type, but I still wonder sometimes.

By the time he was finished with his exercises, he was covered in sweat and panting. And I had just barely managed to hold it together without breaking character once.

"So, uh, is mine the smallest penis you've seen today?"

I assumed the answer to this was supposed to be an affirmative, so I nodded absently just in case it wasn't the answer he was after. Besides, it was the truth.

He sighed deeply.

"So that means I have to do the special treatment . . . again?"

"Yes. Do we really need to go over this every time?" I asked to distract from the fact that I had no idea what special treatment meant.

He walked over to where he had folded his clothes and returned with a water bottle that he had cut the top off of. He knelt in front of me and placed the bottle directly in front of his knees. Now I was intrigued.

"May I commence the chant, Doctor?" he asked gravely.

"You may," I responded, sliding to the edge of the couch in anticipation.

He pulled his penis out of its cave with one hand and started to jack off with the other. From what I could see, he was only managing to get two fingers on there.

"I drink cum, therefore I am. I drink cum, therefore I am," he chanted, keeping intense eye contact.

I laughed menacingly without really meaning to as I realized his intention. Suddenly the water bottle made more sense. I had come to adore watching a man consume his own spend. Most do it to be emasculated, but there's something primitive about a man who takes it without complaint that gives me lady-wood. I managed to regain my composure in spite of my excitement.

"I drink cum, therefore I am. I drink cum, therefore I am!" he shouted.

He kept chanting over and over, continuing to get louder until I was quite sure he could be heard in every part of the Dungeon. He was screaming the phrase by the time he shuddered and ejaculated into the bottle. He shivered and looked up at me expectantly.

"Do I really need to drink it, Doctor?"

"Yes. Why do I need to repeat myself? If you aren't going to take your treatment seriously and take your medicine as directed, I'm simply going to have to stop seeing you."

He picked the bottle up and held it to the light, gazing at its contents with total disgust. He then lowered it to his face, making the mistake of inhaling deeply to smell it. He recoiled with revulsion, and looked at me with pleading eyes. When I simply glared and looked at the bottle pointedly, he sighed, and I knew he was going to do it.

He slowly tipped the bottle up and opened his mouth in preparation for its contents to slide onto his tongue. It had become more viscous with his stalling, so he had to shake the bottle to get it to flow in the direction he needed it to. Just as it was about to flop out into his mouth, he panicked and flipped it back up. Now I was irritated.

"You're wasting my time here. I have patients waiting who are actually interested in following my treatment and aren't just here to muck about. Take your medicine. Or get out."

He whimpered, but lifted the bottle back to his mouth and started shaking it again. The semen, which was now tepid and goopy, slid back toward his mouth, and he moaned as it poured out onto his tongue.

"Swallow it," I said, when I noticed that he was just holding it in his mouth.

He looked desperate for another option, but did as he was told and took his medicine.

One of the more awkward parts of Brian's session was the flip that happened after the fantasy had played out. This was fairly common with clients, but none were quite as pronounced. He avoided eye contact, rudely rejected all conversation, and seemed to be genuinely ashamed of what he had done. The first time, I was bothered by it, but I also felt sorry for him. As time went on, I just shrugged it off. He treated me with an absolute lack of respect, but he was the one who had just paid to wiggle around naked on the floor with his tiny penis and perform some kind of ritual in which he drinks his own semen, while I got paid to sit fully clothed and judge him. I hardly felt like I was the one who should feel uncomfortable in that situation.

I arrived back in the dressing room at the same time as Raven and found Erin and Storm on the couch watching a Pablo Picasso documentary. I sat on the floor between Erin's legs, and she started to rub my neck in slow, sensual strokes.

"You seem tense. Tough session?" she asked.

"Nah, it wasn't too—Raven, what the fuck is on your underwear?"

She was in the middle of getting changed from her scene, and there was an unmistakeable large brown streak across the back of her white granny panties. She turned to look at it in the mirror, shrieking as she ripped them off and threw them across the room.

"Oh, my God, oh, *my God!*" she squealed, dancing in place naked and shaking her hands with revulsion. I had never seen Raven act like such a pansy. "I played with Dan and he wanted to ride me around like a pony. He was naked, but I thought I had a towel covering me. Oh, my God. Fucking skid mark. Fucking fucking fuck! Skid mark! *Ew!*" she yelled, running into the bathroom and turning the shower on.

The rest of us were laughing so hard we could barely breathe. Apparently, Raven could handle doing things to people the rest of us deemed unacceptably revolting, but when the tables were turned, she had a meltdown.

Storm managed to stop laughing long enough to ask, "Why can't men wipe properly? Like what is the problem there?"

"And you guys wonder why I only do bitches?" Erin replied.

Storm continued, "I have this one really old client who always has tiny little chunks of poo clinging to his butt hairs. I make it a game to see if I can knock them off with the paddle."

I choked and Erin pounded me on the back.

"That—is—disgusting!" I coughed out.

"Humans are disgusting," concluded Storm with stereotypically Russian nonchalance.

"Amen," said Erin, "but not you, my love," she mumbled against my ear. "You're perfect."

I tried to ignore how she had addressed me, but I was a little concerned. Erin came across as tough, but she was a sensitive soul and she loved to be in love. She had moved in with the last girl she had been with after two weeks, and the rumor was that she had been engaged on three separate occasions. I wasn't judging. I wished I could throw my cynicism to the wind more easily and believe in love like that. But it seemed like a really good way to get hurt.

She knew perfectly well that I had a boyfriend whom I was committed to, but she had gradually started dropping more hints about us, as though she was pretending he didn't exist. I had attempted to get her to come home with me and play with him in the hopes that it would make me feel less like I was breaking the rules of my open relationship, but she was offended at the very suggestion.

"I'm not interested in him. I only want you," was her answer.

I sighed. "What if we only come as a package deal? He's been relaxed about what's going on between us, but if we don't start including him, I'm not going to be able to keep doing this."

She ignored what I was saying.

"If you were my girl, I wouldn't let anyone else be with you."

"Maybe that's why I'm not your girl. . . ." I teased.

"Yet."

36. BOY

We "latex bombed" the local burger joint after work one night. For no real reason at all, a group of us converged upon this mundane establishment dressed in our finest latex outfits. Raven's latest useless meathead boyfriend was there along with Boy. I wondered how she managed to get her man of the hour to be okay with her having a slave. Or five. Last I checked, she also had two slaves who came in and cleaned her house, a regular foot guy, and some guy who liked to be forced to spend money on her in ridiculous designer shopping sprees. He called it "financial domination." This was all in addition to the clients she saw at the Dungeon. I didn't see how a vanilla guy could possibly fit into that picture, which, I supposed, was why the BDSM scene was so incestuous. Raven's new date was a personal trainer, which was a change from the string of struggling musicians she had just gone through.

We were gathered around a huge, picnic-style table enjoying our burgers when the talk inevitably turned to one of our clients.

I choked down a laugh as Erin blatantly rolled her eyes at Meathead's latest ignorant remark.

"So you're telling me a dude can be into cross-dressing and not be a faggot?" he yelled across the table.

"Keep it down, baby," Raven said, taking his arm.

"What, like you're trying not to draw attention to yourselves dressed like *that*?" he responded.

His tone was disrespectful and I saw Boy bristling. I can only imagine how difficult it was to sit there and listen to someone disrespect your Mistress, who you treat as a goddess, and not be able to say anything without sounding jealous. He focused determinedly on his fries.

"Not that kind of attention, *bro*," said Erin, unable to remain quiet. He didn't seem to catch that her use of "bro" was mocking him.

I could see where this conversation was heading and it wasn't going to end well. I sought a quick subject change by asking, "Raven, would you be okay with it if I took Boy as my date to a formal at the hospital on Friday? Wes can't go, so I need a date."

I wanted to go with someone since I would already be completely outnumbered by drunk men, and thought Boy was the perfect solution to give me a buffer.

"What's mine is yours, love. Boy"—she looked at him intently—"if Scarlett isn't completely pleased with your behavior, there will be hell to pay. Don't embarrass me."

"Yes, Goddess," he replied obediently. I could tell he was excited.

Erin, on the other hand, looked appalled.

"If you're going to keep acting like I'm not even here, maybe I should just leave," she snapped.

"Wait, what the fuck did I do?" I asked with genuine confusion. I couldn't see the landmine I was heading for.

"We haven't exactly put a title on what's going on here," she said, gesturing between us, "but I would've expected a little more consideration for my feelings."

"I can't take you to a work event," I said flippantly, still hoping she was kidding. She wasn't.

"Why the fuck not?"

"Because I'm trying not to draw attention to myself and if I show up with you, people will talk."

"You're such a hypocrite. So you're totally fine with fucking me, you just don't want anyone to know about it? You think I would embarrass you?"

"It's just a stupid work event. These people have sticks up their asses. I don't want them thinking I'm a lesbian."

As the words tumbled from my mouth, I could hear how awful they sounded. The hurt and anger in her eyes were justified. I wanted to step out of my body and slap myself.

"Well, since we wouldn't want there to be any confusion about your sexual preferences, we won't do this anymore. Fuck. You."

She got up and left.

Everyone else around the table except Raven awkwardly avoided eye contact.

"Want a hand up out of that hole you just dug for yourself?" she offered, but I could hear the reprimand in her voice.

"You know I didn't mean it like that. I just . . . I can't show up with her without causing a shitstorm that I don't need right now."

"It's not that you can't, but you won't. If you really felt something for her, you wouldn't give a fuck what it caused. You'd be willing to deal with it. She just realized that's probably never going to happen."

All I could do was sigh and shake my head. As much fun as I was having with Erin, I didn't see it as anything more than that. And it wasn't really anything to do with being a lesbian or not. I knew that was a cop-out. Outside of the bedroom, we had almost nothing in common.

Except stubbornness and pride. We both had that in spades.

After I initially tried to apologize and she shut me down, I refused to try again. And she carried on like there had never been anything between us. It would be months before we dropped the bullshit.

In the end, taking Boy as my date nearly caused more talk than taking Erin would have.

The formal was being held in the lobby of the new hospital. It was packed with wealthy donors, doctors, hospital administrators, and some of the construction team. Everyone was dressed to the nines and mingling in small groups around the elaborately decorated room, clustered more heavily near the bar stations. Boy looked dapper in a tux and was much better at making small talk than I was. He could certainly turn on the charm. What he couldn't seem to turn off was the programming that said I was his Dominant.

We were midconversation with a group of department heads I recognized from my validation meetings. They were all much more relaxed and pleasant with a few drinks in them than I remembered them being. I was enjoying the conversation, but needed to excuse myself.

I turned to Boy and asked, "Will you hold my drink while I go to the ladies' room, please?"

"Yes, Mistress," he replied automatically, taking my wineglass.

I should have just played it off and walked away, but I glanced up in alarm to see whether any of them had heard it. They definitely had. And they definitely picked up on my distress. I forced a smile and headed for the bathroom.

Fuck.

When I returned, Boy looked close to tears. He handed my drink back to me, and I noticed he'd had it refilled.

"I'm so sorry, Goddess. It just slipped out!"

I looked around to make sure no one had caught this one and then said, "It's fine. Just no more Goddesses or Mistresses. Stick to my name if you need to call me anything."

He nodded.

"Which, to be clear, is Jenny, not Scarlett."

How had I not anticipated this happening? It was my fault we hadn't gone over the ground rules ahead of time. Boy was a nervous wreck the rest of the night and overcompensated by trying to make it up to me.

We were chatting with Ellen, one of the nurse managers, when he asked pleadingly, "May I get you anything, *Jenny?* Something else to drink?"

He said my name as a benediction. Poor guy couldn't help himself. He was too well trained.

"Sure, I'll take another glass of wine."

He practically ran to the bar.

"Would you like anything?" I asked Ellen.

"Probably shouldn't, but why the hell not . . . I'll take another gin and tonic."

I turned to tell him, but he was already in line. I had to shout to get his attention.

"Boy! Will you grab a gin and tonic for Ellen too, please?"

One look at Ellen's face, and I started to laugh. I didn't know what else to do. My worlds were bleeding together whether I wanted them to or not.

37. ALEX III

It had only been the beginning. A few months later, I was supposed to be getting ready for a meeting, but instead I was stressing about the session I knew I had booked with Alex that evening. I was once again out of ideas of things to make him do and felt like I had repeated the same sessions over and over. Maybe this wouldn't bother some girls, but it seemed unacceptable to me. How hard could it be to come up with something new and perversely revolting to make another human being do? Preferably something that took a really long time given that I had four hours to kill. I always came up against the same barriers though. The first was that I wasn't willing to violate the rules of the Dungeon, so that took a number of options off the table. The second obstacle was my own comfort level. I really didn't want to make him do something that would potentially make him ill or permanently hurt him in some way. We had already crossed well beyond anything I would have imagined myself being comfortable with, so I was getting more flexible out of desperation. There was, however, still a line in my mind that I wasn't willing to cross.

I had spent most of my morning on the jobsite musing upon this when I had a flash of inspiration. Thinking back to the tampon tea, I realized I hadn't crossed a line, but had managed to introduce novelty simply with the *threat* that I was going to. I knew Alex's ultimate fantasy was to be forced to eat shit. Several times, I had mixed up disgusting food concoctions to resemble feces, but he had to have been able to tell the difference. What if I took real shit into the session and threatened him with it only to have him eat a fake poo concoction? If I played it the right way, his mind would be blown. In that moment, it seemed like a perfectly reasonable, if not ingenious, solution. I just needed some feces.

I thought about using dog poo, but a walk at lunch didn't yield anything. When it reached late afternoon and I felt the urge to go, it seemed as though the gods of fetish were smiling upon my idea and had provided. I dug through the kitchen drawer by the coffeemaker and grabbed a few sandwich bags to take with me to the bathroom. I tucked them in my laptop bag and walked over to the bathroom trailer. As I squatted over a sandwich bag at my serious job, at a children's hospital of all places, I came to recognize that something within me had shifted. Thankfully, I had the bathroom to myself because I couldn't help laughing at the absurdity of it. At one time, doing this would have been inconceivable to me, but then it just seemed like the best solution to a problem. No big deal. All I could do was shrug and embrace the madwoman I had become.

I tucked my disgusting contraband carefully into the inner pocket of my laptop bag after double-bagging it. I couldn't hide the wicked grin on my face as I sat back down at my desk and started to count down the hours. This was going to be good.

My appointment with Alex was scheduled at 5 p.m., so when 5:20 rolled around and he still wasn't there, I was worried that he wasn't going to show. By six, I was pretty convinced that he wasn't coming, but he did have a four-hour window blocked out, so there was still a chance he would come late and just do a shorter session. I was thrilled when a fantasy wrestling guy came in and wanted to do a scene with me. Since I was pissed that Alex looked like he was going to stand me up, going Ronda Rousey on some guy's ass was exactly what I needed to work out my frustration. It helped that he was a good-looking firefighter. After an hour of sweaty, nearly naked wrestling with a hot, muscled dude, I had completely forgotten about the poo that was still stashed in my bag. My mind was occupied with far more appealing thoughts of taking said fireman home with me and continuing our wrestling where there weren't any rules.

For the sake of my dignity, I would like to say that I remembered shortly after that and promptly threw the baggie of shit away. Unfortunately, if I tell the truth, it was a full two days later that I remembered it was in my laptop bag . . . or, more accurately, was reminded.

If it had been discovered at the Dungeon, I could simply have explained the truth to whomever had found it and had a good laugh at my expense. Instead, it happened at the jobsite. And it was my mother who pulled it out after reaching into my bag to find my car keys.

As soon as the words, "Sure, they're in my laptop bag. You can grab them," left my mouth, I instantly remembered my stowaway. I jumped up from my desk, but it was too late, she was lifting the sandwich bag out and the recognition of its contents was written all over her face. She promptly dropped it and looked up at me dismayed.

"Sorry! Totally forgot that was in there!"

In hindsight, I had a few options that made a decent amount of sense to explain it away. I could've said I was having stomach issues and needed to take a stool sample to the doctor. I could've denied that it was human poo and claimed it was dog shit, and I hadn't been able to find a trash can, so I had stashed it and then forgotten about it. Did either of these pop into my head? Nope. The best I could come up with was, "I was in traffic and had to go really bad. I didn't have time to pull over, so I went in a sandwich bag."

"Should you maybe get rid of it?"

"Uh . . . yeah. I just forgot about it when I got here. This morning. It hasn't been in there long. I'll take it to the bathroom now."

"Okay. Would you mind getting your car keys out for me as well?"

"No problem."

I pooped in a sandwich bag because I was in traffic?

I shook my head. It would take years before the mortification faded enough for me to be able to share that story with someone. The silver lining, I mused, was that no matter what my mom was think-ing in that moment, there was no way she had concluded that I had pooped in a bag to convince a client at the Dungeon where I worked as a Dominatrix that he was eating real shit. The ludicrousness of my secret would keep it safe. For now.

38. CALLS

It's easy to portray working in a dungeon as nonstop action, but in reality, there were shifts that were so slow the minutes seemed to drag by, and we all begged the desk Mistress to leave early. Sometimes we handled this by turning one of the rooms into a slumber party and curling up to binge-watch a TV show together. Other days, we invented raucous games or practiced the skills of our trade on one another. Occasionally, we went looking for trouble and devised elaborate pranks. Because I was new, Erin's first-day ruse convincing me that the delivery guy was my client had felt like she was bullying me, but I had quickly learned that it really just meant I was part of the gang.

During a slow shift, Raven and I switched all of the CDs in one of the rooms to play the *Barney & Friends* soundtrack. We barely repressed our giggles when we realized Erin would be the next one to use that room. She picked a CD out of the stack that was labeled Nine Inch Nails, but it was really one of our decoys. We left the first song alone, but after that it changed to absurdly annoying kiddie songs. I wish I could have seen her face when it started to play. In typical Erin fashion, she was unfazed and blamed her sub for the error. She made him listen to it while she caned him to tears. We tried to act innocent when she got back from her scene, but we cracked under her gaze and laughed hysterically.

"You fuckers!" she jokingly shouted as we ran away and hid.

She retaliated by planting fake dead mice for Raven and I to find. I swear I didn't squeal like a little girl. At least I didn't freak out as bad as Raven did.

The three of us eventually turned our devious minds on Lady Caterina. We sat on the patio out back and took turns prank calling the desk. Cat was unflappable: always calm, polite, and firm no matter what the call was about, and she almost never hung up on anyone. She would end the call when she felt they were just trying to get a free phone session and weren't actually moving toward booking anything, but even then she was patient. We passed the phone around, doing different voices with each call and asking for everything from sperm cupcakes to poo finger paintings. When that didn't work, Raven tried being as offensive as she could manage, using racial slurs that had me blushing. Cat didn't sound amused, but she handled it gracefully. When Erin used a baby voice to describe exactly how she wanted her diaper to be changed, it was too much. I don't know who broke first, but we started to giggle before Erin hung up the phone. From inside we heard Cat squeal with sudden realization. She charged outside with a crop in her hand, sending us fleeing through the Dungeon. She pursued us as we scattered, swinging the crop and yelling, "You little monsters! I thought it was a full moon or something and all the crazies were calling! Were all of those calls you three?"

Raven and I did the only sensible thing. We both shook our heads and pointed to Erin.

I was scrambling to get ready to go to a Rammstein concert with the girls, and was running terribly late, so when my phone rang with an unknown number, I answered it without thinking. I rarely answer numbers I don't have saved, but in the back of my mind I thought maybe it was one of the girls I was about to meet calling me. They were always changing numbers and phones.

"Hello?" I answered distractedly, while trying to zip up a thigh-high boot.

"Hi. Jenny?"

I froze and my heart started to race. I knew that voice. It was probably the first voice I heard when I was born. But I hadn't heard it in nearly eight years. It took me a long moment to say, "Yes. This is Jenny."

"Jenny, it's your dad."

The flood of emotions that happened then is hard to describe. At first I was angry that he felt he could still use that title. But to hear how unsure he sounded, the vulnerability in his tone, I wanted to hug him and tell him it was all going to be okay. I knew how hard it must have been to call me. But I hadn't told him it was okay to call me. What made him think he could just call out of the blue and disrupt my life like this? And somehow more dominant than all of those warring thoughts was a memory. His voice, that deep voice with his perfect British accent, reminded me of him reading *The Lord of the Rings* to me when I was little. It all came racing back in an instant: being curled up next to him in bed listening to the story unfold and feeling so safe and so very loved. I could still hear him in my mind doing each of the characters' voices. And it hurt. Fuck, it hurt. He didn't deserve what had happened to him, but I didn't deserve what he had done to me either. I had missed him desperately and knew I still loved him, but it was all clouded by rage so potent I could taste it.

"Hi. How are you?" I managed to get out after a long pause.

What a stupid question to ask, dumb-ass. Eight years of thinking about what you would say to him and that's *the first thing out of your mouth?*

"I'm doing okay. I lost a few months there, but I'm starting to piece it back together."

"I'm sorry. I thought about calling you, but I didn't have your number."

"It's okay. Look, I don't want to keep you long, but I wanted to make contact and thought maybe we could talk again sometime . . . maybe start to rebuild."

"That sounds . . . good. Can I call you sometime next week and we can chat some more?"

"I would like that. It's good to hear your voice."

"You too. I'll talk to you soon."

"Okay. Bye for now."

I pushed the End button and just stared at my phone. I was keeping my mind blank lest the floodgates open. I was not going to cry. Fuck him. He wasn't getting any more of my tears. And fuck her for all of it. It didn't seem real that I had just spoken to my father. I had accepted that I was never going to talk to him again, had mourned him as though he was dead. I desperately wanted to just stay home and cry. I took a shuddering deep breath and decided that wasn't happening. I was going to the show and I was going to feel good . . . even if it took some drugs to get me there.

39. TILL

Rammstein, one of my favorite bands, are a German rock group who practically burn the venue down with their incredible pyrotechnics. Do I speak German? Nope. But I don't need to. Till Lindemann, the lead singer, speaks my language fluently . . . the universal tongue of devilment and sex. Their show helped me not to think about my phone call, but even through the sparkly haze of the MDMA I was on, I could feel sadness and loss burning in the periphery of my mind. If I stopped focusing on other things, it burned more fiercely, consuming the joy of the moment, and I felt myself losing control. That simply wasn't acceptable. I refused to give in to it, forcing myself to be present with the grinding beat of the music and Till's gloriously rolled German *r*'s. I wanted to cauterize the part of my brain where memories of my dad lived. Since I couldn't burn away the pain, I would just have to ignore it and savor the fire on stage. I suspect I have a bit of a fetish for fire, so once I managed to be present, my Molly-addled brain struggled to process the magnificence of their show.

My high was cresting just as the performance came to an end. All of the band members took a knee on the edge of the stage in a humble display of love for their fans. I was convinced they were kneeling for me and me alone. I wanted to be their Mistress. Since I couldn't be theirs, I needed to blow off some steam.

A foolish young man catcalled me on the way out of the venue . . . and it was on.

"Hey, sexy! Sexy, it's my birthday! Don't I get a birthday present?" I could hear him yelling in our general direction.

"Just leave it," said Raven.

"You of all people are saying to leave it? Fuck that."

"Here we go," Raven whooped to the rest of our crew.

I whipped around and slowly made my way to the bench he was sitting on, appraising him as my platform thigh-high boots clicked across the pavement. He was a slightly pudgy, but cute guy in his early thirties. I didn't think he had much luck with the ladies . . . shocking, given his finesse in addressing me.

"Did you have something to say to me?" I asked quietly.

His friends backed away a few feet, and he looked a little less sure of himself. Clearly, he hadn't been expecting me to engage. *Sorry, sweetheart. You chose the wrong bitch to fuck with.*

He swallowed and looked me in the eye. "It's my birthday. You should give me a present."

I could hear my girls cracking up behind me and I struggled to maintain a straight face.

"Okay," I responded simply, and I could see the surprise on his face.

I placed a knee on either side of him on the bench, straddling him like I was about to give him a lap dance. I ground forward, pressing the swell of my breasts toward his face, whispering seductively in his ear, "So you're the birthday boy, are you?"

He nodded, smiling with anticipation.

"You know what we do with birthday boys where I work?"

He shook his head.

"We punish them."

I bit his ear lobe and pressed my knee hard against his balls. He choked with shock.

"Aw, birthday boy thought he was getting a stripper and really picked a Dominatrix."

I kept my knee pressed firmly against his balls, wrapped a hand around his throat, and leaned back to look him in the eye. He was a little afraid, a bit insecure, and a whole lot turned on.

Perfect.

"Do you have something to say to me?"

"I'm sorry," he stuttered.

I slapped him hard across the cheek. From his stunned reaction, I didn't think he had ever been slapped before, and it turned me on. As high as I was, even my stinging hand felt amazing.

"Mistress . . ." I suggested.

"I'm sorry, Mistress," he quickly corrected.

"Good boy."

I twisted to sit on the bench next to him.

"Over you go," I said mildly, patting my knee as though it was a foregone conclusion.

He laughed awkwardly, looking at his friends, not sure whether I was serious. I glanced at Raven.

"It's only going to get worse if you make her wait. Mistress Scarlett *hates* waiting."

He shuffled his weight across my legs and I could feel insecurity and tension in every line of his body. I was pushing him completely out of his comfort zone and he didn't know if he liked it. I brought my hand down hard on his ass, making him jump, but I knew that his jeans would absorb most of the blow.

"So how old is the birthday boy?" I asked his friends playfully.

"Eighty-seven!" one of the guys answered, seeing where I was heading with it.

"Eighty-seven?" I asked over my victim's protests. "I don't think your friends like you very much! Oh, well . . . eighty-seven it is."

I spanked him five times on each cheek, counting aloud. I was being gentle, lulling him into thinking it was all just for show. I cocked an eyebrow at Raven and nodded toward him. She came over and ran her fingernails down his back, making him shiver.

"I think these pants are getting in the way, Mistress," she said, reaching under him to unfasten them. She yanked and pulled them down around his knees, exposing his black boxer briefs.

He jerked to get up, but she held him down for a moment to say, "You can pull them back up if you want, birthday boy, but that would be the end of your birthday spanking!"

I felt him reluctantly relax back down on top of me. It was all the consent I needed to continue. Now I could give him a real spanking. I didn't waste any more time, quickly spanking in sets of ten as I counted quietly. Most of them were gentle, but I gradually got heavier, throwing in the occasional good one just to let him know that I could at any time. My last ten were heavy enough to make my hands throb, and by then, the people who had crowded around to watch were counting along with me.

"Eighty-five . . . Eighty-six . . . Eighty-*seven*!"

He was panting heavily, but I could feel his boner pressed against me. I considered taking him home with me, but dismissed the idea. He had served his purpose. I felt like Scarlett again, powerful and in control . . . not like Jenny, the hurt little girl who was struggling to hold it together. Besides, I wanted to fuck someone, and no matter how far I had just pushed this vanilla boy, he was a long way from being kinky enough for that. Wes got quite the surprise when I got home, riled up and ready to go.

40. URETHRAL SOUNDS

Once I embraced the fact that I had a penetration fetish, I got to push the boundaries and explore outside of work, but I didn't think that particular fixation would get much fulfillment at the Dungeon. No penetration was one of the golden rules. We all broke the rules for someone at some point. Most did it for extra cash, but I did it for the thrill. I did it to answer the call of the raging pervert inside of me, who wanted to be inside of someone else. Perhaps that's what it's like to be a fifteen-year-old boy.

It had been months since I had seen my celebrity client, who we are calling Oliver, so I had begun to assume that I wouldn't be seeing him again. According to TMZ, he had been a busy guy since I had seen him last. I wasn't taking it personally. So I was surprised and delighted when he appeared one random night without an appointment.

When I met him in the interview room, he was once again wearing his sunglasses and smacking his stupid gum, but the smile on his face told me he was doing it on purpose in acknowledgment of how much it had irritated me last time. I hugged him and we chatted for a moment about nothing before I got down to what kind of session he wanted to do.

"I have a surprise for you, Mistress Penetration," was his response.

I leaned back to peer out the door and see whether Caterina was paying attention, but she was battling someone on the phone.

I put a finger to my lips to get Oliver not to say any more. I didn't know what he had up his sleeve, but I was guessing it was against the rules, so better if he showed me when we got to the room and I could decide how to handle it. I had to think through where we could play so Margaret, the house slave, couldn't possibly be lurking and see what we were up to. As far as I knew, she didn't have any hidden holes in the cave.

"Do you want to play for an hour again in the cave?" I asked.

"Let's do it."

I was admittedly nervous as we climbed the stairs. If he had brought a strap-on or a butt plug or something of the like, I didn't really want to play with it here and risk getting caught. I tried to think through whether it would be appropriate to suggest meeting up outside the Dungeon instead, but I wasn't sure that was something I was willing to do either. He was gorgeous, rich, and famous, but I had boundaries for a reason. I could also imagine, in this day and age of celebrity stalking, someone seeing us, finding out where I worked, and spreading it across the Internet. Waking up to a phone call from my mother to find out why I was being splashed across tabloids as a Dominatrix did not sound like my idea of a good time. That would go over really well on the jobsite too.

We passed Raven on our way up to the room and the baddest bitch I know was momentarily flummoxed by Oliver's presence. To him, I'm sure she looked indifferent, but I knew her well enough to know that she was barely keeping her jaw off the floor. She mouthed, "Cameo!" to me as I passed her, but I just rolled my eyes and shook my head. This one was all mine.

The urge to know what his surprise was as soon as I closed and locked the door was overwhelming, but I controlled myself. To admit to that level of curiosity was to relinquish power to him, and it was hard enough to contend with his presence.

He took his sunglasses off and put them on me, and I wanted to melt to the floor at the casual contact. Instead, I held out my palm in front of his mouth until he spat his gum out. I chucked it in the trash bin in the corner and turned back to find him already almost naked.

Mmm, yes please.

When he was finished undressing, he pulled a small leather bag out of his jacket pocket and set it on the side table next to the spanking horse. I straddled the spanking horse and faced him with anticipation written all over my face. His eyes followed the line of my open legs to the thin strip of fabric that covered the goods, and I couldn't help smirking. All (straight) men really are created equal in that regard.

He opened the bag and pulled out lube, cleaning wipes, and a smaller bag. This one unzipped and then unrolled like it was designed for makeup brushes. Inside was a kit of urethral sounds. My heart started to thump wildly in anticipation. I had never tried sounding before, but always kept it in a special place in my mind.

Urethral sounds are metal rods that are about the length of my hand and vary in thickness. They look like medical tools, which makes sense given their original function. They were first used before antibiotics had been discovered and syphilis caused scar tissue to block the urethra in a man's penis. The doctor would stick a metal rod down into the penis, and force entry until the blockage was cleared. To most men, this is a cringeworthy description, but like all kinks, there are many who profess it is an incredible sensation. I had taken a workshop about sounding at a convention in Denver, but had never been able to apply what I had learned. I had been waiting to meet someone with a little more experience who could teach me and let me play with the different techniques. What better experience is there for a penetration freak with penis envy than fucking a guy's dick?

Now this gorgeous man was giving me my chance. I instantly forgave him for surprising me.

I put on gloves and went to stand over him. He talked me through the various shapes and thicknesses, but said that since he had been doing it for so long, there was no need to work our way up. He pulled out the thickest sound that twisted gently toward the top. I lubed it up while he removed his piercing from the head of his cock. I was grinning like a small child and could barely stop myself from jumping up and down with excitement.

"With this shape," he explained, "you insert it slowly and have to twist past the 'stops' in the urethra."

"Ready?" I asked, glancing at his erect cock like it was my new toy.

"Ready," he said, holding it up for me and pinching the head to open the entrance. I didn't need any more invitation than that.

I grasped the base with my left hand, taking control from him, and with my right hand placed the tip of the sound inside of his urethra. I barely had to work it in since his piercing had already stretched the opening at the tip, but the tissue tightened as I slid the rod deeper. The technique had been described to me in the past as dropping the sound in rather than pushing it, and I now understood the description. It slides easily until it meets an area of resistance from the urethra, and then a twist is needed to work it through and keep it sliding down again. It was the most erotic sensation, sliding that sinuous metal rod inside his flesh rod as he lay back and groaned. If I let go, it started to slowly work its way back out, so I played with this, letting it slide up and then pushing it back down.

"Can you come with something in there?"

"Absolutely," he said without hesitation. "Wanna see?"

I nodded vigorously, not wanting to be deprived of any of this experience.

"Do you want to try it with your finger in there instead?"

I lost my grip on the sound and barely caught it before it came all the way out.

"Are you kidding me? I can actually put my fucking finger in there?"

"Hell yeah. Lube it up and give it a shot."

I surrendered control of the sound back to Oliver, and grabbed the lube bottle to pour it all over the glove of my right ring finger. Oliver had found a rhythm now, thrusting the sound up and down, clearly as excited by this as I was. He let it slide all the way out and I laid it back on the table on a waiting paper towel. I thought I was going to orgasm as I worked the tip of my finger into his dick, stretching it slightly. Once I had the first knuckle in, I got to feel the sliding sensation from the inside. I hadn't gotten far when I felt an impediment and had to work past it, twisting and gently moving through the squeezing muscles. After that, my finger slid all the way down until my hand prevented it from going any deeper. I could feel his flesh squeezing around it. This was probably the closest I would ever get to feeling what it is like to penetrate a woman with a cock, and I was practically vibrating with arousal.

Without a word, he took hold of the base of his dick, replacing my left hand, and began stroking upward. He could feel my finger both inside and out, and I could feel every stroke of his hand from the inside. He started with slow erotic strokes, letting me savor the bizarre sensation. Before I knew it, we were moving in concert, my finger being pushed up and down slightly by his movements, which were becoming faster and faster. I wanted full control, so I knocked his hand away and took over his stroking motion. Now I could feel everything. I experienced a rush of power, that thrill that comes from being a Domme in her element. My movements became frenzied, and Oliver's breathing turned erratic. He bellowed a groan, and I felt him start to ejaculate around my finger and out of the tip in long spurts. I slowly withdrew my finger. Oliver lay there, still thrusting a little and letting the tremors work their way through his body.

"That was fucking incredible." He sighed and let his head fall back.

"Tell me about it. You just blew my mind!"

When he laughed, his abs flexed showing his perfect six-pack. It must be exhausting to look that good. He sat up and leaned forward to kiss me, but I turned at the last second and gave him my cheek. I felt the intimacy too, but not like that. We weren't lovers, but sexual pioneers who had just gone on an adventure. No need to spoil it by making it into something it wasn't.

"We're definitely going to have to do that again," he said as he started to put his clothes back on.

I never saw him again as a client, but when I see him on the screen, I get electric butterflies in my stomach remembering that day. I had fucked a man's dick with my finger and made him come. I was powerful. I may not have a cock, but I could still penetrate one if I felt so inclined. Oliver had created a monster.

41. VICTOR

Rich burst into the trailer as I was just packing up to head to the Dungeon. I could tell he was agitated, but I initially avoided eye contact in the hopes that I could escape without having to engage. When I eventually glanced up, he was chalk white and shaking.

"What the fuck happened?"

"Victor just died."

I closed my mouth before saying something stupid just to fill the stunned silence.

"Was there an accident on-site?"

"No. He just had a heart attack and dropped dead as he was trying to leave the parking lot."

I didn't know what to say, so I gave him a hug. Victor was Vance's right-hand guy on-site. I didn't think Rich knew him very well, but it was tragic nonetheless. It had to have also made him consider his own mortality. They were a similar age, and Rich wasn't exactly taking care of himself.

I arrived at the funeral alone, but quickly found a group from the jobsite to sit with. I didn't know Victor well, but a number of us had come to show our support. His wife spoke first, and she was lovely and incredibly composed. She was charming and funny and painted a picture of Victor that most of us hadn't gotten to see, having only known him at work. After a photo slideshow of his life, the preacher assumed the podium to speak. And the tone in the room shifted palpably.

For twenty-five minutes, the man hurled fire and fucking brimstone at us.

"*Burn!* You will all *burn* in the fiery torture of hell if you do not change your ways and walk the path of righteousness. I know that"—he glanced down at the podium—"Victor wanted me to speak here today to warn you all that your souls are in danger if you do not accept Jesus as your Lord and Savior."

Did he now, you angry little man? Since you don't seem to remember his name, I'm not sure you knew him very well.

"I know that in this room there are fornicators, loose women, and blasphemers!"

All of the above.

I contemplated raising my hand, but out of respect for Victor's family decided to behave.

"Victor's loved ones can rest easy, secure in the knowledge that his soul is in Heaven, awaiting the day when they will be reunited. Will your family be able to say the same thing?"

Probably not. But if it's fuckers like you populating Heaven, then I'll take my chances in Hell. Sounds like that's where all the fun people will be.

He continued in that vein until most of the room was shifting uncomfortably. I played a game looking through the room trying to decide who would actually fit this nutjob's standards.

Muslim, divorced, blasphemer, atheist, definite fornicator . . . nope, nope, nope, nope, nope. I came up with a few possibilities and decided that they were probably the real perverts. Like my client, Hal the accountant, who fantasized about African tribes gang-raping and mutilating white women. He looked like Dilbert and would have fit in at this guy's Christmas party. I wondered what Angry Little Man's deal was that had him feeling so guilty he was compelled to spend his life screaming at the rest of us to atone.

I could hear Dominic in my head saying, "Religions are like penises. It's fine to have one, and I don't give a shit what you do with it in private . . . but please don't whip it out in public or try to ram it down my throat."

When he was finally finished, we all trooped out into the reception area. I saw Rich making his way up the other aisle and was pleased to see that his wife was with him. They looked happy. He saw me looking and winked. Maybe he was going to get his life back on track, whatever that meant.

Angry Little Man had taken up his post at the door to the reception area, so we all had to file past him and shake his hand. It seemed most people felt the need to thank him or compliment him on his sermon. I was just going to smile and keep moving, but he took my hand and stopped me.

"You look like a lost soul, young lady. Would you like to talk about anything?"

I wanted to laugh, but it wasn't really funny. He had managed to pick the Dominatrix out of the room. What had given me away? Could it have been the look of disdain on my face the entire time he had been speaking? Or did he just have a thing about "saving" pretty young women?

"No, thanks. Doing just fine. Have a nice day."

I couldn't get away from him quickly enough. I *was* a lost soul. My religion was love, acceptance, and forgiveness. And this narrow-minded Angry Little Man had none of those things to offer me. I could, however, find them in abundance at the Dungeon, and I was suddenly eager to get to work.

As I drove up there, I called my mom just to tell her that I loved her.

Then I took a deep breath and called my dad as well.

When he picked up, I said, "Hey. Just wanted to tell you I was thinking of you and to see how you were doing."

I wasn't ready yet to drop the L-bomb again with him, but wanted him to know that I cared about him. There had been more than enough hate and pain in our lives. Now we just needed love.

———

Death has a funny way of lurking in the wings long enough that you can almost forget that he rules your life. And then he chooses to emerge and seems like he's making up for lost time. We all knew that Liam was probably going to die before us. He had made it past the average life expectancy for someone with cystic fibrosis and he had limited access to health care so was at a considerable disadvantage. We all knew it was going to happen, but that didn't mean I was prepared to see it on Facebook when I was scrolling through my feed before bed. Dozens of people had already posted messages of grief and love to his wall. There was no denying it. He was gone.

I absently ran my fingertips over the tiny spot on my rib cage that had blistered and scarred after our fire play. I wanted to carve it deeper to make sure it never faded away, as though that would help me to hold on to the precious few memories I had of Liam.

I knew he had been in and out of the hospital for a few months, but was so caught up in my own life that it hadn't crossed my mind that I would never see him again. I thought they would get him tuned up and I would lock eyes with him the next time I went to a play party.

His memorial for people in the scene was being hosted on the following Monday evening by the other dungeon that had reopened after the fire. I glanced at my calendar and saw that I would need to get someone to cover for me on-site so that I could go. I had an MRI being delivered that day and was scheduled to oversee the transport and after-hours calibration. My mom was not amused when she found out.

"I have a memorial to go to," I attempted to explain. "Someone I knew in college passed away."

"Jenny, I don't want to be harsh, but flaking on something this big at work for a college acquaintance's memorial isn't the responsible thing to do. You've been the one coordinating it for months, so it wouldn't work to have someone else take over last minute. We would need to reschedule, which is a big deal and would potentially have massive cost and schedule implications. Remind me who the memorial is for again . . . ?"

I couldn't remind her because I hadn't told her, and I was sure she knew that. Her bullshit detector had gone off and she clearly thought I was either lying about the memorial to get out of work (which would be super fucked up) or hiding something about it from her.

How could I explain that it was someone who meant a lot to me even though I had never mentioned him? She was right about work, but I desperately wanted to be there to grieve with the people who had become like a family to me. I sighed, accepting that this was going to inevitably end with me going to work, so arguing with her further would only raise more questions.

Instead, I said, "You're right. I'm sorry. I wasn't thinking. I just got caught up in the shock of losing someone. I'll be there for the MRI."

"Okay. I'm sorry about your friend. It's not that I don't care. . . ."

"I know. You're just looking out for me."

My friends in the scene couldn't understand how work could prevail over the need to be at the memorial, but almost none of them had jobs in the real world. A few gave me the impression that they felt it was a slight to Liam that I wouldn't just tell work to fuck off. Funerals aren't really for the deceased, though, they're for the people who are left behind to come together and feel a little less alone and maybe a little less mortal. I was surprised to hear that the person who had been most vocal in my defense was Erin. The next time we worked together, I cut the passive-aggressive bullshit and gave her a hug. She was rigid at first and then melted against me, as relieved as I was to let go of the nonsense. We didn't rekindle our relationship and were never close again, but I was glad that it ended with love and not anger.

I knew it was going to happen eventually. In a city like L.A., the odds of running into a specific person randomly are minuscule. The odds of running into a client outside of the Dungeon have to be exponentially greater for the simple reason that the universe has a sense of humor. The other girls had told stories of encountering clients at a gas station, at a bar, or (in one particularly funny instance) at a baby shower. The consensus was that these accidental meetings were always more uncomfortable for the client than the woman in question. I had imagined what it would be like stumbling upon Alex in a bookstore or Sissy Harry in a restaurant and smiled to myself at the absurdity of it. I was therefore totally unprepared for the seriousness of my own real-world client run-in.

I walked into the conference room at the hospital followed by my mom on an innocent Tuesday morning. It was my meeting, but she was there to lend me some weight with her presence and observe. It was a meeting to familiarize a newly hired department head with their space and equipment in the new building. I looked up to acknowledge the participants who were already present and froze as I locked eyes with none other than Yoshi. Adrenaline pounded through my veins, sending me into fight-or-flight so quickly I nearly dropped the paperwork I was carrying. At first, he looked as stunned as me. And then he smiled. The fucker smiled.

It sent a chill of dread creeping up my spine.

Whatever. Fuck him. I wasn't some timid little girl that he could mess with anymore.

He had as much to lose as I did if he said something stupid. He could out me, but he would need to explain how he even knew about it. Mutually assured destruction.

I gritted my teeth and made it a point to be as polite and professional as possible, forcing myself to make eye contact with him throughout the meeting. My intention was to regain power by making it abundantly clear that he had no effect on me whatsoever. It worked. By the end of the meeting, I had stopped faking it, and truly felt like I had the upper hand with him again.

Then he flashed me his phone, and my heart sunk. He had pulled up my page on the Dungeon's Web site. I could only watch in horror as he pulled my mom into the hallway. I didn't know what to do. I could run out and try to stop him, but that might make it worse. The asshole didn't even know she was my mom. He just thought she was my boss. I was shaking so badly I thought I was going to be sick.

I sat back down in my chair and resigned myself to whatever was happening. If she found out, I would just have to deal with it.

She popped her head back in and said, "You coming?"

I searched her expression for some indication that he had outed me, but she looked totally normal.

"What did the doc want?"

"Nothing. He was just getting my contact info."

I didn't know whether it was a threat or I was just being paranoid. Had that even really been what was on his screen? I thought I had been given a reprieve, but he could change his mind at any time.

42. LORNA

I had, as usual, waited until the week before taxes were due to start working on filing mine. As employees of the Dungeon, we were considered independent contractors, which meant we got butt-fucked on our taxes unless we were smart about claiming business expenses. What, you didn't think Dominatrices got away with not paying taxes, did you? Even as a Mistress, I couldn't avoid that the Man is Master to us all.

The previous year I hadn't known what I was allowed to deduct, so I was completely unprepared and just filed the additional income without including any expenses. Raven had since let me borrow her accountant slave for an afternoon and he gave me a crash course in what receipts to keep and how I could file them. After this year, I wanted to get audited just so I could watch the IRS guy's reaction as I explained why a single tail whip, floggers, nipple clamps, rope, and the wild assortment of other items I had purchased for my work at the Dungeon qualified as business expenses. It would be a little different from the postage stamps and printer paper that he was used to seeing.

I was down to the wire, but I was ready. I had my receipts organized in neat piles around the table and a spreadsheet with the correct deduction codes for each item.

My mom came over to have lunch with me in the middle of my process and, with a frustrated sigh, I went to sweep all of my piles off the table, but I just couldn't do it. I was emotionally exhausted and sick of telling her lies. When I had been sure that Yoshi was going to blow it, I had been ready to vomit with panic. But if I was honest with myself, I was also relieved. I hated the idea of her thinking differently of me, but by hiding what had become such a huge part of my life, I was pretending to be someone that I wasn't anymore. At the very least, I was hiding a part of myself that I wasn't ashamed of. Scarlett was one of the best parts of me, and I felt that my mom deserved a little more faith than I was giving her. I needed to trust that she would love me no matter what. If she was going to find out, I wanted it to be on my terms with me controlling the message. In an instant, I decided to tell her.

"What's all this?" she asked as I cleared a big enough space for her to set the food down.

"Ugh, taxes." I sighed.

"Leaving it to the last minute, are we?"

"Always."

I watched her take in the receipts and the extra paperwork beyond a W-2.

"Why all the receipts? You know you can just take the standard deduction and not keep all of these, right?"

"Yeah . . . about that."

My hands were trembling under the table.

"I've been working a second job for a while now and I've been keeping it a secret because I didn't think you would approve."

She didn't bother asking what it was. She just looked worried and waited for me to continue. I wasn't sure I had my thoughts in order, so I just started babbling and hoped it would come out okay. If I hesitated I was going to chicken out.

"I've been working as a Dominatrix. Before you jump to any conclusions about what that means, I'm not having sex with anyone. And I'm not technically a prostitute."

Her eyes were huge.

"I work at this place called the Dungeon with a bunch of other girls who do the same thing. It's all really safe and clean . . . and we have these clients who come in with fascinating fetishes and we play them out. But there's no penetration or exchange of bodily fluids or anything like that. I was curious, and it has opened my eyes to this whole other side of people."

She hesitated another moment to see whether I was finished and then broke into a smile.

"Good for you."

"Excuse me?" This was not the reaction I had anticipated.

"I'm proud of you for having the balls to do what you want. I wish I had experimented more when I was younger."

"Good God! That's your reaction? I've been terrified for almost two years that you would find out and my life would be over!"

"Jenny, you're an adult. It's your life. I want you to be safe and wouldn't want you to do anything you would regret, but ultimately they're your mistakes to make."

"Well, fuck me," I said as I slumped back into my chair trying to process it.

"So are you going to tell me more about it now?"

"Uh . . . sure . . . I'm just really stunned."

"Oh, come on. Your old mother isn't that much of a fuddy-duddy."

Turns out, she really wasn't. I won't embarrass her by getting too specific, but let's just say the apple doesn't fall far from the tree.

Wes was surprised that I had revealed my secret to my mom, but quickly embraced the idea of sharing, taking it to mean that he could tell whomever he pleased. We were at his friend's apartment with a group of his buddies from law school one evening when he took things too far.

Joints had been passed around and numerous beers consumed, but I stayed sober since I was driving and had to work both jobs the following day. I had struggled through a hangover one too many times. Sitting at my desk and keeping my head down to make it through the workday is one thing. Having to follow that up with clients at the Dungeon was another entirely. Being a Dominatrix is physically and mentally taxing work. It takes focus or you can hurt someone . . . well, unintentionally hurt them that is. You wouldn't want your hairdresser to be sleep-deprived and out of it from the night before . . . you sure as shit don't want someone who's hitting you in that state.

I had mostly checked out of the conversation and was scrolling through a hilarious client request e-mail about me being a giantess and devouring teeny little men when I was snapped back to reality by Wes's voice.

"Did you guys know that Jenny works two jobs?"

He was buzzed, I could tell, but I cocked my head at him in surprise. What the hell was he playing at?

"She's Jenny by day and Scarlett the Dominatrix by night."

I didn't react to the curious faces that turned my way. There was still an opportunity to play it off as a joke if I didn't get upset.

"Oh yeah, you know me . . ." I said with dismissive sarcasm.

"No, c'mon, it's fine. You can tell the guys. She works at this place called the Dungeon and her customers are into all kinds of weird shit. Look—she's on the Web site if you don't believe me!"

That cocksucking Web site is nothing but trouble.

"I don't think you need to show them that." I tried calmly glaring daggers at Wes.

"Give them a little demo then. Show Matt what you do!" Wes said, patting his friend Matt on the shoulder.

As I look back on it now and try to remember the combination of words and actions that followed, I can't come up with anything that would explain what happened next: I fucking gave in and did it.

I remember hating myself as I straddled Matt and whispered scary things in his ear, in the confusing mix of seduction and intimidation that I had mastered over the years. Deep down, I think I felt like I owed Wes something. Like he allowed me to do what I wanted with my clients, so I should be willing to do what he wanted with his friends.

I emotionally detached as I would with a client, and tried to tell myself that it wasn't a big deal, but in the back of my mind a voice was screaming that this was wrong. How dare he treat me like a toy to be passed around to amuse his friends? I had never felt so worthless. I was supposed to be a Goddess in his eyes and instead I felt like trash. No client had ever made me feel so objectified.

Matt's fingertips brushed my bare thigh as he said dreamily, "She has really soft skin for a white girl."

Matt was Indian. *Is he saying Indian girls have softer skin? Wait, did he just talk about me like I'm not here?*

I shrugged and thrust my knee hard against his balls, knocking whatever he was about to say next out of him in a rush of breath. Then I turned on my mental autopilot, putting on a show for this group of drunken fools. It wasn't really their fault, though.

I was appalled at the way Wes was treating me, but what was even worse is that I didn't stand up for myself. I performed like his fucking dancing monkey. I went through the motions of dominating Matt, blowing his mind, but my own mind was reeling. How had things become so topsy-turvy? I was supposed to be the Domme, and here I was doing my sub's bidding. We were supposed to be in a loving, open relationship in which we encouraged each other to explore and enjoy ourselves, but somehow any tie between us had been lost. He didn't give a fuck what I was doing or whether I enjoyed it. Had he ever? Thinking back, our sex life had always been about me dominating him for his pleasure. Certainly, I enjoyed it most of the time or at the very least was amused by it, but that wasn't what it was about for him. Words from my breakup with Henry echoed in my mind.

I have never had an orgasm in your presence, and you don't even care!

Was I really here again? I had grown and changed and fucking *lived* in the years since Henry, but I was still in a relationship in which my partner, the person who was supposed to put my needs first, put them somewhere between "irrelevant" and "if it amuses my friends."

I felt sick as we got in the car to drive home. Wes babbled away excitedly in the seat next to me about how epic the night had been and how he was going to be a legend at school. I glanced over at him and couldn't find the man I had feelings for. Through his actions, he had become a stranger. I opened my mouth to explain how deeply he had just hurt me. I closed it again without uttering a syllable. If he didn't understand that it was wrong in the first place, I would be wasting my breath trying to explain it to him.

I tuned him out and stared out of the windshield. I caught sight of the moon and noticed that only the tiniest sliver was showing. It struck me how well it suited my bleak feelings of worthlessness. And then I gave myself a swift kick up the ass and changed gears. I chose instead to see it as an offering of a new beginning, a chance to take everything I had learned and experienced and use it to grow.

I always assumed that being in an open relationship was what would ultimately break us up if anything did, but in the end, that wasn't really the problem. The real problem was a lack of respect.

43. ANDREW

I was a flurry of nerves as I got ready to have dinner with my dad for the first time. I didn't know what to wear. In the grand scheme of things, it didn't matter, but it seemed singularly important in my edgy state. The last time I had seen him I was still a child, and now I was a grown woman. I wanted to look like one, but didn't want to look like I was trying too hard or taking it too seriously. In other words, I didn't want to dress like a librarian just to impress him. But I also didn't want him to be disappointed in how I had turned out. I kept berating myself that I shouldn't care what he thought, but there was no way to make myself believe it.

After trying on what felt like 912 possible outfits and leaving my room strewn with clothes, I departed on time in a suitably demure, business-casual dress with patent leather platform stiletto heels . . . my favorite trampling shoes. Just standing in them gave me confidence. If I got too nervous, I planned to look down at them and imagine all of the men I had crushed beneath them. Visualization is a powerful tool.

We were meeting at a restaurant down in La Jolla, so I had over an hour of drive time to gather my thoughts. I felt vulnerable in a way I had never experienced, and I didn't like it. I wanted so badly to have him back in my life, but was terrified that I would get hurt again.

I didn't want to need him. My whole body was shivering with nerves by the time I pulled up to the valet. I got out of the car, and as I found my balance on my heels, I also found my center mentally. Scarlett didn't get nervous. Scarlett made people nervous. I squared my shoulders, gave the valet a flirty smile beneath my lashes, and sauntered into the restaurant like I was going to meet a client in the interview room.

My dad was already seated at a table, so the hostess led me there. I had the silly thought that he might not recognize me, but decided that surely I hadn't changed that much. I saw him an instant before he saw me, and then our eyes met. I compelled myself not to look away. On the inside, my emotions were a roiling maelstrom that threatened to overwhelm me. I produced a calm smile and hugged him without letting it show.

"Good to see you!" I grinned with obviously forced levity.

He smiled back. For a fraction of a second, I thought he was going to cry and knew I would have no chance of holding it together. Thankfully, he swallowed, and the moment passed.

Now what the fuck do we talk about?

"How was your drive?" he asked.

"Not too bad. Not much traffic, so I made good time getting down here. How about your flight?"

"Not too bad either. Unremarkable really."

"I've missed you," I blurted, meeting his eyes and lowering my guard a bit. We could chatter superficially all night, but that wasn't why I had come here. I decided to be brave and take the first step to meeting him halfway.

"Me too." He sighed.

It was uncomfortable and I could feel the lure of small talk tapping on my brain. We could take the easy way out, deal with the hard stuff later, but deep down, I knew I wasn't programmed that way anymore.

"Well, this is a little weird, right? We know so much about each other, but are practically strangers," I admitted.

"We'll just have to rebuild."

With that, we talked through dinner, filling in the gaps from the past seven years. It was deeper than small talk, but still superficial enough that we weren't touching any land mines. We didn't mention Eleanor or Danny, just skirted around it when the conversation got too close. I thought I was fine, but then I started to get frustrated with the way we were avoiding it like it was going to go away.

I lost control, blurting, "What the hell happened?"

He shifted uncomfortably, physically backing away from addressing the issue. It made me angry. Why were we here if we weren't going to talk about it? How could we possibly go forward without confronting what was lurking behind us? I needed answers, damn it. I sighed deeply, in an instant accepting that I was never going to get them. He didn't have most of them to give and the few he did would be too painful to put out in the open. The man had experienced enough pain for one lifetime. Asking him to rehash any of it to make me feel better would be cruel. If we moved forward, those would be the terms: we could start something new, but I would have to find a way to lay the past to rest without his help. I didn't know if I could do it. I wanted to be a big enough person to rise above it and shower the situation with love, but thinking that is easy. Doing it when you've been hurt that deeply is fucking hard.

Did I really need him to acknowledge that I hadn't been the crazy one? That one had been proven with brutal finality. None of us were ever going to understand why she did it, least of all him. So what was I hoping for?

I thought I wanted an apology, but now that I was here, I mostly just wanted to hug him and tell him that I was sorry.

We grow up thinking that our parents are "grown-ups," which means they shouldn't make mistakes. And then one day, you wake up and you're supposed to be a grown-up and a parent, and you realize that age and offspring don't really leave you any better equipped to handle the madness that life throws at you.

We parted that night with hugs and an understanding that we would look forward instead of back, and find a way to be a family again.

Something strange and unexpected began to happen in my mind after we started to heal our relationship. I felt whole again in a place that I didn't know had been broken, and I saw my future differently. I wanted to be the kind of woman that he had always encouraged me to be. Not to say that I wasn't, but there was a glaring problem. I didn't want to introduce him to Wes. I tried to reason through why that would be, but I just kept arriving at the conclusion that I knew he wasn't right for me. My dad would see through him in a heartbeat, and I didn't want him to know that I had become the kind of woman who allowed herself to be treated the way I was by Wes. My dad made me feel like I deserved better. Even with the gap in our relationship, seeing him had reminded me that he had always understood me in a way that almost no one else did. He didn't just see who I was, but who I wanted to be.

44. TREASURE TROLLS

I was burdened by an inability to flip the switch back on in my relationship to see Wes the way I used to. But a weight had also been lifted. I didn't have to live in perpetual fear of my mom finding out about my other life now that she knew just what I had been up to. That should have been more of a boon, but I felt restless and jaded at the Dungeon in the weeks that followed. I was grumpy and knew I was taking it out on my clients, but couldn't seem to shake the feeling that I was just over all of it. I was ready to move on, but transitioning away from the world that had become my new family seemed unthinkable.

The night my frustration came to a head, the Dungeon was painfully slow. I watched the hours tick by until I was finally resigned that I wouldn't have a client that night and just wanted to go home. Naturally, a couple came in just under an hour before we closed. Whoever took them was going to have to stay late, and I was determined it wouldn't be me. They asked to meet all the Switches and Dommes. I didn't even make eye contact when it was my turn in the hopes that they would take a hint.

I saw enough to note that they looked remarkably like treasure trolls. They were both about five feet tall, and that's being generous. The man looked about fifteen years older than the woman, probably in his late fifties. He had graying black hair, and an unfortunately large, odd-shaped nose dominated his features. It was hard to see what she looked like because her lank, mousy hair hung in front of her face, and she didn't bother raising her head when I stepped into the interview room. I walked back out after simply saying, "I'm Scarlett," confident that they wouldn't pick me. So of course they did. Evidently, a sneering, disinterested Domme with a shitty attitude was exactly what they were looking for. I sighed deeply when Viv told me they wanted to interview with me, but didn't complain any further lest I compound my headache by having her chew me out.

Let's get this shit over with.

The man indicated that their names were John and Lena. I took a moment to look them over properly before continuing with the interview. John was not an attractive man, but he had a warm smile and was polite. Lena, on the other hand, was the most terrified, timid-looking person I had ever met. Something about this really bothered me. I was used to being around subs who were subservient and respectful, but there was an air of pride to their submission. They were empowered through their relationship with their Dominant. Lena just seemed cowed. The waves of emotion that were rolling off her were intense and definitely not in a good way. She was oozing misery and discomfort. There were three scenarios I could envision that would be causing this. One: She's just painfully shy and that's how she acted in a situation in which she was uncomfortable. Two: Elements of their relationship were either physically or emotionally abusive. Or three: She had no desire to be there and was being forced to do something she wasn't happy with. None of those were scenarios that I wanted to deal with, so it was with extreme reluctance that I agreed to do an hour-long session with them.

As John and I had begun discussing the terms of the scene, I was surprised to learn that they were both submissive and wanted me to top them together. I had seen many couples in which both were tops or Switches, but this was the first time I could think of in which both were subs. I still had a lousy attitude about the situation as a whole, but they had piqued my curiosity. John's eyes were alight with excitement as he told me, "I've been here a few times before, but not with Lena. I usually play with Erin, but Lena liked you best, so we came in when you were working."

I guess that explained why I hadn't deterred them. I thought he was possibly just flattering me, though. Lena didn't look like she'd ever had an opinion in her life. I kept trying to engage her in the discussion, but gave up when she still wouldn't talk or make eye contact. She looked like she was trying to curl her body in on itself to make it disappear. I was worried.

"Lena, are you sure you want to do this? We don't have to do anything you aren't comfortable with."

"She's fine," John assured me. "She just shuts down when she gets nervous, but she'll be okay. She's been excited about this for weeks."

I had never seen a less excited-looking treasure troll.

When we got to the chamber, I ordered both of them to strip down to their underwear while I arranged the rope and toys that I had grabbed at random. We were going to do some simple bondage, light impact play, and end with hot wax. There was nothing complex or interesting about it, so I went through the motions without being present. On autopilot, I tied them up facing each other and made them hold hands.

They looked adorably awkward and I was struck again by how unfortunate looking they both were. I wasn't deliberately being mean. There just wasn't any getting around it. I alternated spanking them for a few minutes. John was responding, but Lena continued to be a black hole in the room. Concern for her was pulling me from my apathetic state. I lifted her chin and made her look me in the eye. I stroked her cheek gently without saying anything, then allowed her to drop her gaze once more. I was trying to reassure her without forcing her to talk, but I was also just trying to get a baseline read on her before we started doing anything heavier.

As I took John by the wrists and bent him over the spanking bench, I was fighting to engage myself in the scene. I still really didn't want to be here, but I swallowed it and kept going through the motions. I told myself that some days that's the best you can manage, but I knew it was a lie. When another human being is laying their trust at your feet, it is a privilege, something that should be honored with your full attention, regardless of whether you are being paid for it or not.

I tied John by his wrists and ankles so that he was lying on the bench. I positioned Lena on the other side of the bench, and began using a crop on them both. Watching Lena silently flinch was too much for me. I untied John, and said, "Slave, your job is to serve my female slave as I tease her with hot wax."

I smiled at Lena reassuringly as I laid her on her back and retied her ankles and wrists. I nodded to John, and he obediently began massaging her feet. I thought maybe putting someone under her on the totem pole might make her feel more confident. It didn't work. She lay there rigid as a board as I got the candles and a lighter. I decided to try one more thing, and if it didn't work, then I was calling the scene. I wasn't comfortable continuing with her like this, no matter what John said.

I rummaged through a drawer and found a simple black blindfold and put it on her. The transformation was the most dramatic I had ever seen. She almost instantly relaxed. I lit a handful of candles and let them start to melt, while I teased Lena with my fingertips. She positively melted beneath my touch. Her lips parted, and her breath began to come in soft pants. When her hips arched off the table, I took the first candle and poured just a drop of the hot wax on her thigh. She tensed in surprise, but immediately followed it with a moan, her hips begging for more. I alternately stroked and poured small amounts of wax, getting so into it that I forgot I was supposed to be giving John instructions too. I glanced up to find him just standing to one side grinning. He waved his hands in negation and stepped back, indicating that I should continue with Lena and he would observe. With that simple gesture, I understood that there was real love between them. Most men I had seen in a pay-for-play situation would take their pleasure, sometimes even at the expense of their partners, but John was willing to forgo his own experience to allow the focus to be on Lena. I suspected she didn't let go often. I could relate.

She blossomed before me from treasure troll to siren. I had found her repugnant and now I fucking wanted her. I wanted her bad. Beneath that blindfold, she was liberated and wildly feminine. To this day, she is one of the sexiest women I have encountered.

Our time was just about up, so I poured the last of the pooled wax over her, and started to bring the intensity of the scene back down. As I blew the candles out, I smiled, remembering the first time I had tried wax play with Wes. I fucked it up so badly, but he had been nothing but forgiving and supportive. He had been willing to trust whatever I asked him to, always game for the next adventure. We had been on such a journey together, but I wanted something more. I wanted what I had just seen from John. I needed to know what it was like to be with a partner who would put my needs first so that I could do the same for him without getting lost in the relationship. It made me sad to think about ending things with Wes, but it made me sadder to watch John help Lena clean up and know that I was never going to have what they had if I stayed with Wes.

The universe had slapped me in the face with my bad attitude. I felt so guilty for the way I had judged both Lena and John before really knowing anything about them. I had spent years learning not to judge and to honor my clients' trust, and had begun to forget those lessons. I suddenly understood that the anger and bitterness that Lady Viv carried around was what happened if you spent too long in this world. I needed to get out before I lost sight of the good that came from the Dungeon in all of the bullshit.

John and Lena chatted excitedly as I finished cleaning up. They said they would come to see me again one day, but I knew that I wouldn't be working the next time they came in. This would be my last scene at the Dungeon. It was the reminder I needed and the note I wanted to end my career as a professional Switch on. I could still maintain the friendships I had formed when I was retired, and I would always have Scarlett with me when I needed her.

45. BURNING MAN

We had celebrated my retirement from the Dungeon, and even though I wasn't working anymore, I still attended play parties and made time to hang out with the gang. I hadn't ended things with Wes yet. In some ways, the Dungeon was a harder Mistress to end things with, and part of me was still mourning the loss of the routine I had grown used to. To get me out of my funk, Dom and Vanessa had persuaded Wes and I to take a week off work and go to Burning Man for the first time with them. Burning Man is a festival in the desert in Nevada where fifty thousand people build a city out of nothing for a week and party their asses off. There are all kinds of spiritual and social aspects to it, but for the group I was going with, it was mostly about having a good time.

The lines to get in to the event were insanely long, so by the time we made it to our camp and set up our tents, I had been awake for well over twenty-four hours. It was too hot to sleep and we were all on some kind of upper—from Adderall to speed—so it seemed like a good idea to start our Burn by stirring up some trouble in the giant tented bar in the center of our camp. Armed with a bag full of toys, we set up in the center of the bar and played with one another until we managed to lure some more adventurous people to experiment with us. Popping people's kink cherries is always exciting and we were busting them left and right. Guys were offering up their wives just so they could watch us spank them, which we generally turned on the husband by instead teaching the wife how to punish him. I got caught up in the atmosphere of revelry and was flogging an adorable young frat boy when I felt a tap on my shoulder. Interrupting a Domme when she is in the middle of a scene is totally unacceptable, so I turned, ready to eviscerate someone. In front of me stood a stunning young woman scantily clad in a bikini and lace, wearing a dream-catcher necklace. Being attractive is not an excuse for bad manners, though, so I gave her my scariest bitch face and asked, "Is there some kind of emergency that made you feel it was okay to interrupt me?"

She smiled prettily, nodded, and replied without a hint of hesitation, "I need you to fuck me . . . please, Mistress."

The people around us had been watching the exchange to see how it would play out. They whooped and clapped at her response.

The young man I had been flogging said, "Sounds like a legit emergency to me!"

I couldn't help cracking up and agreeing. "Who are you here with?" I asked, looking around.

She indicated three guys standing to one side with massive grins on their faces.

"You guys cool with this? Is she in a relationship with any of you? I don't want to start any drama."

"She's all yours!"

I looked for Wes to at least make eye contact and let him know what I was up to, but he was perfectly happy having his balls kicked by two older women. I shrugged and took her by the hand, leading her back to my tent.

Why the hell not?

She was dainty and gorgeous, but for some reason I wasn't really attracted to her. She was an entertaining novelty, but there was no spark there for me. I had reached a point that fulfilling someone's sexual fantasy wasn't that big a deal. I think it was partly that I was just that jaded and partly that while I was performing acts that should be deemed intimate, there was no actual intimacy in it for me. I was unaware of it, but I had a wall up with everyone. I could have fun and exchange pleasure, but I wasn't connecting.

Conveniently, this pretty little thing wasn't looking for a connection. She was looking to get fucked. And I was happy to oblige.

I led her to my tent and was appalled to discover that it was swelteringly hot inside, but I wasn't going to fuck her on the sand and it was the only place I could think of, so we were just going to have to make it work. I took her by the back of the neck and kissed her hard, making it absolutely clear who was in control. She melted against me and I deepened the kiss, exalting in the feel of her supple surrender. When she started to grind her hips against mine, I commanded that she strip and lie back on the air mattress while I grabbed my strapon. My toy bag was outside the tent, so I stepped out and rummaged until I found the harness and a suitable-looking big black cock to attach to it. I stripped naked and stepped into the harness, grinning with anticipation. Gods, it felt good to have a dick on and be about to use it!

When I walked back into the tent, I found her wearing nothing but the dream-catcher necklace, playing with herself on my bed.

"Good girl," I encouraged her, and stood back to watch as she continued. It was too fucking hot for foreplay, so if she got things started, then it was less work for me.

"Please, Mistress. *Please* fuck me now," she begged.

"Get on all fours."

She did as she was told, arching her back and spreading herself with her hands. I knelt between her legs, positioned my cock, and just barely rocked forward. I paused before thrusting the rest of the way in to enjoy the spectacular view. She cried out as I filled her, so I maintained a slow rhythm at first to let her get accustomed to its girth and then I stopped being gentle and pounded her hard. She wanted to get fucked after all. I found her clit with my thumb and rubbed it the same way I had seen her do herself, with quick side-to-side movements. She was moaning incoherently and thrashing her head from side to side. And I was fucking melting. Like actually melting. Dripping with sweat from every pore in my body. I thought she was probably close to orgasm, but I couldn't keep going without a break. I flipped under her and brought her down on top of me, feeling our breasts mold together in the slick heat. I kissed her and took her by the hips, getting her to grind hard. As her movements became more rapid, I rubbed her clit again hoping she would come quickly.

She started to chant, "Yes, yes, yes, yes!" and I waited for her imminent climax.

And with no further warning, she lost consciousness and collapsed on top of me. I frantically flipped her onto the mattress and knelt over her trying to figure out what the fuck was going on.

Did I just fucking kill her? What is this bitch on? Why didn't I think to check? Fuck. Fuck. Fuck!

A deep breath and Occam's razor would have led me to the conclusion that she had simply fainted from the heat and likely dehydration, but I was in a full-blown panic until I had established that she still had a pulse. The one other time I had knocked a partner out accidentally, he had come to almost immediately, but she was showing no signs of waking up. I shook her gently. And then a little less gently. I grabbed a bottle of water and dumped it over her head.

Her eyelids fluttered open and she smiled blissfully and said, "That was incredible."

"It was fucking scary. You passed out. Come out here and sit on a lawn chair and get some air while I figure out what to do with you."

Once I had her seated in the shade, I ran back to the bar area to consult with my group. The bar went nuts with cheers and applause when I entered. I was totally oblivious to the fact that I was wearing nothing but a pair of boots and a strap-on and I must've been bright red and dripping sweat.

I looked around for the girl's friends, but they appeared to have left. Raven, Dom, and Vanessa offered me high fives, but I dismissed their congratulations, still worried and feeling responsible for the girl.

"The chick passed out. While I was fucking her. Like unconscious. One minute she was about to come, the next I thought I'd killed her!"

I couldn't get them to stop laughing long enough to focus. Dom turned to the crowd and shouted, "Scarlett fucked a chick unconscious!"

I had to laugh a little myself at that one.

"But seriously, what do I do with her now? Should I find a ranger and get her medical help or something? She seemed sober, but now I'm thinking she might be on something and I just didn't catch it since I don't know her."

"Here . . . have her drink some water and some Gatorade and when she's feeling better we'll walk her back to her camp. I don't think there's any need to involve the authorities. Though, it might be worth it just to see their faces as you explain what happened!"

I was relieved to find her where I left her, still conscious. I threw some clothes on and kept an eye on her while I got her to hydrate. We sat in silence until she eventually said, "Can we do that again?"

"I think you need to just rest and hydrate for now."

"Well, what if I come back another time? Like tonight?"

I was flattered but not interested. She had scared the piss out of me and I mostly just wanted to not be responsible for her anymore.

"I don't think that's a good idea. We had a good time. Let's just leave it at that."

She looked like she wanted to argue and I didn't want to hurt her feelings, so I stood up and suggested we get the others and walk her back to her camp. When we dropped her off, my friends hung back and I gave her a hug. She kissed me and put her dream-catcher necklace over my head.

"This is so you never forget me."

Fat fucking chance of that.

I have no idea what her name was, but I will never forget the chick I fucked unconscious at Burning Man.

I was something of a legend in our camp after that. On the Playa, the hallowed ground where Burning Man is held, there is a much despised phenomenon known as "shirt cocking" in which a (usually older) man wears nothing but his shoes and a dress shirt. This means that their man parts dangle about in full view. Some camps find this so unappealing that they have banned shirt cockers from their areas. I felt I had earned the right to shirt cock, so for most of the week, I wore nothing but my boots and a white linen dress shirt . . . and my big black cock of course. People fucking loved it. I can just about guarantee that my cock got more attention than any other on the Playa that year. We didn't have to go looking for trouble. Trouble found us.

We were invited by one of my cock's many adoring fans to attend an orgy in the Roman Orgy Camp, and we were intrigued. We had all been to many play parties that could probably be deemed orgies, but none of us had ever been to a more classical vanilla orgy.

I walked over with Wes, Vanessa, Dominic, Raven, Minx, and our camp leader, Captain Killjoy. We didn't know what to expect as we all stripped naked in the entryway where all clothing was required to be left. I was used to knowing exactly what protocol to follow, but I was a little in the dark on this one. Were we supposed to interact with other people or just observe? If we wanted to interact, what was the proper way to engage another party?

It ended up being irrelevant. Apparently, the vanilla interpretation of an orgy was simply to be in a large room in which other people are having sex while you are having sex with your partner. All around the tent, everyone was coupled off, and not doing any more interacting than stealing the occasional surreptitious glance at other couples. It was just a little innocent exhibitionism by our standards.

We were disappointed that there was nothing new here for us, but decided to make the best of it by at least playing as a group and seeing if maybe we could instigate something. Vanessa and Minx started to alternately deep throat Dominic, which left Raven and me to top Captain Killjoy. CKJ was into small-penis humiliation, so we made him sit against the wall and play with himself while we hurled insults at him.

"You call that a dick?" I snapped at him. "That looks more like a pussy to me. I've seen clits bigger than that pathetic excuse for man-hood!"

"Aw, is the little sissy man going to cry because he doesn't have a real penis?" Raven prodded.

The tone of the orgy had shifted. The rest of the couples could definitely hear us, and with the exception of Dominic, every guy in the room seemed to be struggling to block out what we were saying. A few of them seemed to suddenly be having performance issues.

I lowered my voice a little, but it was so quiet in there that I'm sure they could still hear me.

We hissed insults until Killjoy came with a grunt. I looked around and noticed a few couples had left. I wondered whether they had fin-ished or we had scared them off.

Raven jumped in on Dom's scene and spanked both of the subs while they continued to service Dominic. I mounted Wes in reverse cowgirl, fucking him and punching him in the balls at the same time. I punched him harder the closer he got to coming, until he threw his head back and yelled in a mix of agony and bliss.

The remaining couples weren't even pretending not to stare any-more. I was pretty sure they had never seen a guy get punched in the balls before. Seeing a guy get off while it was happening must have been melting their minds.

I pulled on my big black cock. Raven bent Minx over for me, and I thrust into her hard. I would normally have been driven wild by the experience but I couldn't seem to get out of my own head. I had suddenly realized that I had become what I set out on this journey to be: a woman who knew exactly what she wanted and was comfort-able getting it. We were too fucking wild for the Burning Man orgy, and it felt good. But something still felt hollow. I couldn't shake the sense that something was still missing. I had what I thought I wanted . . . and it wasn't enough.

I met Dominic's eyes, and I think he may have guessed how I was feeling. He and Vanessa had something different from what Wes and I had, and I think they had gotten there by being their authentic selves. I had come a long way, but I wasn't quite there yet.

46. THE TEMPLE

So far, my Burn had only been filled with the wilder elements of the festival: drugs, partying, and nudity. I had been overlooking the spiritual side, a side that I was skeptical about going in. Every year there is a temple constructed on the Playa that is burned the day after the Man burns. It had been described to me before I went, and it sounded like it fell somewhere between hippie-dippie and hipster.

The temple had primarily become the space where Burners grieved those they had lost. Small shrines filled every shelf and nook of the place. The wooden walls, beams, and decorations were covered with deeply meaningful messages. The quiet at the temple stood in stark contrast to the continuous cacophony on the rest of the Playa. Sometimes people were playing strange instruments that sounded as if they belonged in a Buddhist temple, but the rest of the time only whispers and quiet sobs could be heard. It was nearly the end of the week before I decided to check it out. I expected to be an observer, a tourist witnessing something that didn't touch me.

I parked my bike just outside the grounds and walked through the entrance. I was immediately uncomfortable around the people who were leaving. They all looked like they were coming from a funeral. It was obvious most had been crying and many were holding one another. I wasn't comfortable displaying extreme emotion in front of others and didn't really know how to handle it when others displayed theirs around me. I avoided eye contact and kept walking.

Once my eyes adjusted to the dim light of the main room of the temple, I began to take in the messages and shrines all around me. The power of the place was like a punch to the gut. I was unprepared for the impact it had on me and almost immediately felt tears stinging my eyes that I couldn't rationalize.

I came across a shrine to someone's young son who had died of cancer and couldn't help thinking of my half brother, Danny. I had only seen a few pictures of him, but I held his face in my mind and did the closest thing to praying I had ever done. I sent him the love I had never been allowed to give him and acknowledged that even though his life had been short, he mattered.

Then I thought of Eleanor and couldn't find the rage that I had been burying for so long. I did, however, find the tears I had been repressing. I didn't even try to prevent the inevitable.

There, on my knees in the hot sand, I released the flood of tears that I had been holding back for months. The silent sobs shook my whole body and I surrendered to the power of the grief. I don't know how long I knelt there before the crying stopped and I felt empty of everything. I was empty of the grief, but also of the anger and resentment that I had been clinging to for years. An old man in a cloak handed me a Sharpie without saying a word, simply bowing his head and leaving me to my grief. I took a moment to consider how to translate what I was feeling into something that could be written. On the wall of the temple I scrawled the words that would release me from the pain:

Danny, I love you.

Eleanor, I forgive you.

There was so much I would never understand about what had happened and a thousand whys that would never be answered, but my epiphany that day was that it didn't matter. The tragedy was unspeakable. But in the depths of my soul, I understood that it wasn't really her fault either. The brain can be beautiful, but it can also be terrible when something goes wrong. If everyone we encounter is fighting a battle we know nothing about, then hers was a far scarier conflict than most of us can even imagine. Medication can help with some things but it can also make the person a shell of who they once were, a prospect almost as terrifying as the alternative. My years of exposure to people who truly can't help who they are and what they are into had given me new perspective into her ordeal. When she was telling stories about the things I was doing—breaking into their house, trying to poison her, playing mind games with her—she truly believed I was doing those things. To have to live in a world like that must have been frightening and isolating.

I don't know what happened in the intervening years, whether she started behaving more erratically or exhibiting clear symptoms of her disease. I suspect those closest to her knew that something wasn't right but never in their wildest imaginings thought that she would end her own life and take her child with her. Dwelling on it wouldn't help anyone, but acknowledging it might. After it happened, absolutely everyone who was connected to my family remained silent when it came to the media. There was the initial story and then no more information, so the story died long before it might have in other situations. I was so grateful for that at the time that I've had to think seriously about whether to open up about all of this publicly. My conclusion has been that there are more people out there struggling with mental illness than anyone realizes and I want them and the people who love them to know that they're not alone. I don't know what the answer is, but it is clear that what we're doing now isn't working. Perhaps in speaking up, I can help someone find the strength to get help or to support a loved one who is in a dark place. Maybe next time when the old man on the corner is raving, someone will see him as the man he is and not the disease that now possesses him.

I felt curiously light as I walked my bike back to camp to buy some more time to get my thoughts in order. I had made my peace with the dead. Now I just needed to find a way to do the same with the man they had left behind. As I watched the temple burn, I decided that I had been given a gift: another chance with my dad, and I wasn't going to squander it. I considered that he could have been taken too, but he was still here, and we still had a chance to heal together.

Just before I had left the temple, I caught sight of a line that someone had written over the doorway: "The deeper that sorrow carves into your being, the more joy you can contain." I was determined to find such joy to fill what the tears had seared away that I would overflow with it, bathing everyone I cared about with love. I didn't have any anger left, but love I had in abundance.

I had come to Burning Man expecting to be fulfilled by the sex and partying, and instead it had made me feel jaded and hollow. I *never* expected to be moved by the place, but had experienced the spiritual release that would allow me to lay to rest the ghosts that haunted me. One of those ghosts was the specter of the woman I had once been: the woman who didn't demand respect from her partners or value herself.

I had plans to spend a weekend with my dad, and there was something I needed to do first to be able to build the kind of future that I now knew I deserved. It was time to end my relationship with Wes. He was still a dear friend, and we had been through so much together, but this was not the partner I wanted to walk through life with.

As far as breakups go, it was the most polite and civilized I had ever heard of. We parted with words of love and support in acknowledgment of all that we had experienced together.

47. KRIS

In one of my favorite ancient Greek works, Plato attempts to explain how love came about. He tells us that long ago, people were not the beings we know today, but were two people fused together into creatures with four arms, four legs, and two heads who moved in a spinning cartwheel of blissful happiness. These beings made the mistake of siding with the Titans in a failed uprising against the gods of Olympus, so Zeus was forced to punish them. He was faced with a conundrum: if he destroyed mankind, there would be no one to pay homage to the gods, so that punishment would backfire . . . but he couldn't very well have the humans getting off easy and thinking they could revolt ever again. He decided to punish them by splitting them all from their mates and scattering them about the Earth, left forever searching for their other halves.

I found mine.

Kris had been right in front of me for a long time, but I was too busy looking in a hundred other directions to notice. He ran the job for the general contractor, which meant he was the man in charge on the site where I worked. We had spoken a few times, generally when I had to go to his office and explain something that our team had fucked up. He usually didn't say much, preferring to listen, but when he did it was always worth hearing. I got nervous when I had to go and talk to him. The guy intimidated me. After everything I had been through, I didn't think it was possible, but he just seemed so impossibly centered. After years of navigating people's insecurities, I could tell that he was a man who knew who he was and was completely comfortable with it.

He was six foot five with dark hair and brilliant blue eyes.

It wasn't love at first sight. But once we opened our eyes to the possibility, we fell fast and hard.

At the end of the job celebration, we finally took notice of each other.

Free drinks meant that almost everyone in our corner of the restaurant where the celebration was taking place was hammered within about an hour. Our company had paid for our team to have hotel rooms a few blocks away so that we could enjoy ourselves and no one would drive home drunk. I had driven my teammates over to the restaurant in a coworker named Ron's SUV since it could fit more people than my truck. I was confident that I would be sober enough to give them a ride back to the hotel at the end of the night.

As usual, I was one of only a few women, and as the night went on, the others slowly left until it was just me and the boys. Calls to move the party to a strip club had me musing over who would be working nearby that night and whether I should send the drunken boys in their direction. As they threw back another round of tequila, I decided Minx was more than capable of handling them, and pulled out my phone to give her a heads-up.

Cliff, one of the architects, knocked it from my hand as he wrapped his arm around me and pressed me against his sweaty flesh. His hot breath on my face smelled like he had already puked and was now replacing the lost booze. Cliff spent too much time at the gym and clearly felt that his bulk made him irresistible.

"I have a hotel room across the street," he yelled over the noise with awkward emphasis and a look in his eyes that made it clear he thought I was a sure thing.

"That's good, Cliff! You definitely don't need to be driving home," I replied, being deliberately obtuse.

"You should go with me," he slurred as his hand slid its way down to my ass.

I slithered from his grasp, and laughed it off, deciding to be merciful instead of shredding his ego with my sharp tongue.

"You're not going to get anywhere behaving like that with me, but maybe you should join the strip-club group and give that a shot there!" Minx wouldn't be as gentle, but she didn't have to work with him the next day.

Cliff took the hint and moved on to talk to someone else. Kris appeared and stood next to me, his proximity making me suddenly very conscious of his broad shoulders and towering height. I was aware of his closeness, and it felt electric. Kris was manly in a way that Cliff, with his overblown muscles and swagger, would never achieve.

I noticed that his beer looked as warm as mine, and he didn't seem at all drunk. I found a man who stayed in control of himself intriguing.

"I was just about to come over here and save you," he said, "but it looks like you handled it yourself."

Within me, Scarlett bristled.

"I'm not really the damsel-in-distress type. But thanks anyway," I said brusquely.

He ignored my dismissal and asked, "How long do you think before Bruce gets himself kicked out?"

He gestured to behind the bar. Bruce, who was from the hospital's purchasing department, was in the process of hoisting his considerable weight over the bar, where he proceeded to pour his own beer.

"Good Lord! Should we intercede?" I asked, already moving toward him.

"Let it play out," he said with mischief in his eyes, lightly putting his hand on my arm to stop me.

He had broken the barrier of touch, and instead of being pissed about it, I was surprised to find I wanted more.

It didn't take long for security to appear, and kick our entire group out instead of just Bruce. For some unfathomable reason, two of the guys I was supposed to be driving back to the hotel were insistent that we also give wasted Bruce, who was still trying to persuade a hospital executive to take him to a strip club, a ride back to his house instead of just putting him in a taxi. As Bruce lived about half an hour away, this was a nonsensical idea, but there is no reasoning with drunks. Ron insisted that if I wasn't going to drive Bruce as well, then I needed to give him his keys back so he could do it. He swore he was sober enough to drive, and despite my doubts, I couldn't prove otherwise since he wasn't acting as inebriated as the others. I kept arguing until Ron compromised and said they would wait a little while at the bar next door until he sobered up enough to drive. I gave him his keys feeling irresponsible, but accepting that he was an adult. I wasn't going to wait and drive all the way to Bruce's house with them, though, so I stepped away and started looking up the number of a cab in my phone.

"Why don't you let me give you a ride?" Kris asked, appearing at my side once again.

I eyed him skeptically, wondering if this counted as him "saving" me, but swallowed my pride and said, "Thanks, that would be great. I'm just at the DoubleTree down the street."

"Cool, I'm parked over here," Kris said, steering me with a gentle touch on my bare shoulder.

What the fuck is it about this guy?

I was irritated because I wanted him, and it didn't make sense. He seemed as vanilla and straightlaced as they came, and yet all he had to do was touch me and I wanted to drop my panties in the middle of the parking lot. It was an enigma, and I didn't like it.

"This is me," he said, indicating his company car.

"I always wonder who 'that guy' who backs his car into the parking spot is, and now I have my answer: you're *that* guy! Always struck me as pretentious," I said it teasingly, but I was baiting him, trying to see how he would react.

He didn't. He just smiled and ignored my asshole remark, which I found even more confusing. I pulled the door handle, but it was still locked. I looked up expectantly, but he had already walked to my side of the car. He leaned over me, waiting to unlock the door so that he could open it for me. I rolled my eyes, but got in.

Not that kind of girl, buddy.

We made small talk for the five minutes it took to get to the hotel. He stopped at the lobby entrance, and I found myself asking, "It's still early. Why don't you park and let me buy you a drink to say thanks?"

A drink is rarely ever just a drink, is it? I had to know whether the electricity between us was real.

Vanilla he may have been, but straightlaced he was not. We had a drink and then tumbled into bed and had the kind of sex that stripped away all the bullshit and left me wondering how I could have existed without him to complete me. It made me feel like I was on MDMA, but I wasn't even drunk. I haven't touched a mind-altering substance stronger than scotch since that night. I don't need drugs to surrender control with Kris.

Because it wasn't kinky, there were no gimmicks or toys or titles to hide behind. There was a power struggle, but it was unspoken and deeply intense, and I will freely admit that in the end, he had the upper hand. I didn't need to call him "Sir" for him to know it either. And I fucking liked it.

I know at this point, darling reader, you're accustomed to me forking over the juicy details in generous portions, but I may need to leave you unsatisfied on this one lest our grandchildren be forced to read the gory details of our sex life. It should be enough to know that it was good enough to make me believe in marriage. I don't even mean some variation of a poly or open marriage. The man blows my mind so much that I felt comfortable, excited even, that I wouldn't have sex with anyone else again. I would imagine most people wonder "what if" when they get married . . . what would it be like to sample the other sex or have a threesome or an orgy or . . . or . . . or . . . ? I've done it all. I don't need to wonder. I know that he's better than all of it combined.

I ended up coming to a conclusion that never would have crossed my mind at the beginning of my journey. To truly connect with one partner on a deeply intimate level, be it vanilla or kinky, is the holy grail of sexual experiences. Once you get past the initial awkwardness of sexual encounters with multiple people, there's nothing really hard about it. It's relaxed and all about everyone getting off or at the very least enjoying themselves. But to open yourself completely to another person is a transformational experience. Before anyone freaks out, let me clarify that I'm not saying it's only possible to achieve this with one person ever, but I do think it can only be achieved with one person at a time. And maybe you and that one person let other people fill holes in your relationship, or act as guest stars to spice things up, but they are still your person . . . your match, your partner, at your side ready to face down the world.

I am by no means implying that finding a man is the goal of the journey, but for me, finally becoming part of a healthy relationship was the most obvious sign that I had grown to love and accept myself. You will never find your match until you first embrace your authentic self.

As our relationship blossomed, I tried to shock him with stories of my days at the Dungeon. I think I was trying to show him my worst, convinced that it was going to push him away. I refused to be ashamed of anything I had done, but that didn't mean I wasn't terrified that he would reject me for it. If he was going to, I wanted to get it over with quickly instead of getting hurt when there was more at stake. There was no need to have worried. He took it all in stride. I had been constructing a bulletproof persona for so long that I struggled to let my guard down with him. But he was patient and eventually broke through. At the end of every day I spent with him, my cheeks hurt from smiling. He made me feel like I could do anything.

He challenged me in ways that I wasn't prepared for, and eventually forced me to see myself differently. In his eyes, my value wasn't tied to my sexuality, something that had become muddled for me along the way.

It all became clear in the most mundane of moments.

We were walking down a sidewalk on our way to lunch when I

felt his fingers on my hips and instantly wanted him. I melted beneath his strong hands, but the gesture wasn't intended as a caress. All he did was shift me over a few feet toward the building and continue walking where I had been.

"What the hell was that?" I asked him.

"I'm supposed to be on the outside. I walk between you and the cars."

"Why?" I was utterly confused.

"Because I'm the man."

At my raised eyebrow he smiled and elaborated, "Don't get your hackles up. I'm supposed to protect you. You're worth protecting."

I was about to sarcastically question how exactly he planned to protect me from the impact of three thousand pounds of steel. But something stopped me. I was worth protecting. I could tell he meant it and it shut up my smart mouth. No one had ever made me feel like that before. He wasn't being a caveman, but a gentleman. And he thought I was a lady.

Over the last few years, dozens of men had worshipped me with reverence or served me with absolute obedience, but ultimately it was all about their pleasure. They were doing it because it turned them on to do it. Not because they knew me well enough to think that's how I deserved to be treated. I didn't need to be on a throne with Kris at my feet to feel worshipped. He had made me feel like a goddess by shifting me two feet over on a sidewalk.

We eloped in October of 2013.

Getting married felt right, but a traditional wedding just wasn't us. We wanted to stay focused on the marriage and not get lost in the wedding. We didn't tell anyone we were getting married, but needed at least one witness to be there. It didn't feel right to have a stranger as a witness, though, so we solved this by each having a grandmother present. We told them to dress up because we were going to high tea on the *Queen Mary*. As the dessert arrived, Kris mentioned that we would need to hurry a bit because we were late for an appointment. They were surprised and apologetic that they hadn't realized we had somewhere to be.

Kris explained, "Actually, we were hoping you would come with us. You see we're getting married and need someone there to witness it."

The grandmas were delighted. We met a photographer and an officiant on the steps of the newly built courthouse. I looked into the eyes of the man who still gives me butterflies and vowed:

Kris, I promise to love you for all of my days.

I adore and accept you exactly as you are, and for everything you have yet to become.

My love for you is unconditional and without hesitation.

I will always support you and be on your team . . . us against the world, my love.

I promise to listen to you and learn from you, even when it means admitting I'm wrong.

I promise that we will challenge each other to grow and adventure.

I will celebrate your triumphs and mourn your losses as though they were my own.

I will spend my days by your side and my nights in your arms.

I take you as my husband 'til death do us part.

Above all, I promise to love you best.

So . . . am I still kinky? That's a tale for another book.

I will tell you this much: These days I serve an extraordinarily demanding Master. He's ten weeks old and mostly seems to be into sleep deprivation and nipple torture.

With motherhood begins a new journey. Isn't that the real lesson, though? We talk about finding yourself or learning who you are as though each of us has some finite and fixed meaning to be gleaned from observing our actions. But it doesn't work like that. We are ever evolving and changing. I think the wonderful psychologist Daniel Gilbert put it best when he explained, "Human beings are works in progress that mistakenly think they're finished."

Motherhood, it seems, will be the biggest test of my newfound sense of self. It is challenging not to get lost in the overwhelming needs of the tiny human that we have created. It's easy to forget that I still matter too.

Being a mother has softened my hard edges. There is no need to pretend I'm a hard-ass or put on a tough-guy act. Or rather, there is no point because no one is going to buy it when I'm singing the Winnie the Pooh song in public just to keep my son smiling. Besides, I pushed a fucking human out of my lady bits without any drugs, so I don't feel like I have anything left to prove in the tough-guy department.

I feel so lucky to have brought a life into the world who is already surrounded by so much love. As I have introduced him to each of the people who will continue to keep me grounded, I have imagined the role they will take in his life. His aunt Amelia will be an emotional rock should ever he need one. Crazy Auntie Raven will probably try to take him to a strip club as soon as he hits puberty. Aunt Vanessa and Uncle Dom will show him that marriage can come in many forms. His grandma will give him the same unconditional love that she has always given me.

There were tears in my eyes when I laid him in my dad's arms for the first time. His grandpa will be a central part of his life because we overcame tragedy and found a way to be a family again. They will teach each other that love can heal even the deepest of wounds.

My husband, my love, my match will show him what it means to be a man and how to treat a lady.

I hope that I can teach him to love freely and without fear of judgment.

ACKNOWLEDGMENTS

Thank you to my family for your unwavering support, most especially my parents for encouraging me to tell the story exactly the way I needed to, and Nanny for not batting an eyelid when I finally shared what my book was about. You are the most badass grandma in all the land.

There are a number of people I would love to recognize by name, but can't because I've gone to great lengths to protect their identities. You know who you are. Thanks for being part of the journey.

I am grateful for the remarkable women who mentored and guided me along the way as a Switch, but also as a human being. They know far more than I ever will about BDSM, but were always supportive and generous with their knowledge. Again, you know who you are. I adore you for all that you taught me, most of all for teaching me how strongly women can support one another.

Leopoldo Gout saw the potential in this tale, believed in me from the beginning, and offered his wisdom along the way. He also introduced me to my agent, Lisa Gallagher, who is as lovely as she is brilliant. I would have been lost without her sharp insight.

Thank you to my phenomenal editor, Elizabeth Beier, and the

entire team at St. Martin's Press for patiently guiding me through the publishing process for the first time.

Finally, I want to acknowledge my husband for being my fucking everything—and also for taking the baby for endless walks to give me time to write—and my son for teaching me the point of it all.